Conversations About Illness

Family Preoccupations With Bulimia

Everyday Communication: Case Studies of Behavior in Context
Wendy Leeds-Hurwitz & Stuart J. Sigman, Series Editors

Smooth Talkers: The Linguistic Performance of Auctioneers and Sportscasters
  Koenraad Kuiper

In Search of a Voice: Karaoke and the Construction of Identity in Chinese America
  Casey Man Kong Lum

Confrontation Talk: Arguments, Asymmetries, and Power on Talk Radio
  Ian Hutchby

Conversations About Illness: Family Preoccupations With Bulimia
  Wayne A. Beach

The Fragile Community: Living Together With AIDS
  Mara B. Adelman & Lawrence R. Frey

Conversations About Illness

Family Preoccupations With Bulimia

Wayne A. Beach
San Diego State University

LEA   LAWRENCE ERLBAUM ASSOCIATES, PUBLISHERS
1996   Mahwah, New Jersey

Lawrence Erlbaum Associates, Inc., Publishers
10 Industrial Avenue
Mahwah, New Jersey 07430

Cover design by Mairav Salomon-Dekel

Library of Congress Cataloging-in-Publication Data

Beach, Wayne A.
    Conversations about illness : family preoccupations with bulimia /
Wayne A. Beach.
        p.   cm. — (Everyday communication)
    Includes bibliographical references and index.
    ISBN 0-8058-1756-5 (alk. paper). — ISBN 0-8058-1757-3 (pbk. :
alk. paper).
    1. Bulimia—Patients—Family relationships. 2. Communication in
the family—case studies. 3. Grandparent and child—Case studies.
4. Conversation analysis. 5. Denial (Psychology)—Case studies.
I. Title. II. Series.
RC552.B84B43   1996
616.85′263—dc20   96-8103
                                                                   CIP

Books published by Lawrence Erlbaum Associates are printed on acid-free paper,
and their bindings are chosen for strength and durability.

Printed in the United States of America
10 9 8 7 6 5 4 3 2 1

To *Di,*
for thoughtful chats and loving support;
and to *Brandon,*
who entered our lives in the midst of this project:
though just learning the language, already our best teacher.

Contents

Series Editors' Preface   ix

Introduction   xi

1   Finding Bulimia   **1**

    Overview of Research on Bulimia   *3*
        Sociocultural Influences   *5*
        Interactions With Family and Friends   *6*
        Overreliance on Self-Report Data   *7*
    Grandparent Caregiving   *9*
        Overreliance on Self-Report Data   *10*
    Conversation Analytic Alternatives   *11*
        Toward the Identification of Institutionally Relevant
          "Constraint Systems" in Casual (Family) Talk   *15*
    Summary and Implications for Study   *18*

2   From Troubles to Problems   **20**

    Occasioning the "Problem"   *24*
        Troubles and Problems   *27*
        Situating the G–S Interaction   *30*
    Problems With Unsolicited Assistance   *32*
    Establishing a Pattern of Pursuit and Avoidance   *35*
    Summary   *37*

3   Overcoming Resistance   **39**

    Variations of "Pursuing a Response"   *42*
        Common Knowledge? Getting Another to Acknowledge
          and "Own" the "Problem"   *44*

Pursuit: Laying Grounds for Reasonable Assertion   46
        Claiming and Imputing Knowledge   47
        Laying Out Consequences   50
        Citing Sources and Offering Evidence   53
    Summary   59

4   Avoiding Ownership   61

    Approximating Denial   64
        Discounting   64
        Accounting   67
        Withholding Response: No-Talk (Silence)   70
        Topic Closure   73
        Humor: Downgrading Seriousness of Attributions   76
    Summary   78

5   Preoccupations   80

    The Delicacy of Preoccupations: An Overview   83
    Disaffiliations and Their Consequences   85
        Unwitting and Tailored Descriptions   87
        Topical Puns   90
        A Sarcastic Withholding   92
    The Poetic Construction of an Idiomatic Expression   93
        Poetic Aftershocks   96
    Summary   98

6   Interaction and Social Problems   101

    Toward Interactional Understandings of Social Problems   102
        Social Contexts?   103
    Conversations About Illness   104
        Routine Predicaments   107
        Beginnings   108

Appendix   Transcription Notation Symbols and G–S Transcript   113

References   126

Author Index   139

Subject Index   143

Series Editors' Preface

Little is known about the ways in which family members express concern about one another's medical problems. Equally underexplored are the ways in which medical problems themselves are defined, constituted, and contextualized by family members' interactions with each other, and by their access to and invocation of various professional institutions and resources. Wayne Beach's *Conversations About Illness: Family Preoccupations With Bulimia*, the fourth volume in the "Everyday Communication" series, provides useful perspective on these issues.

Conversations About Illness examines a single conversation between a grandmother and her granddaughter using the techniques of conversation analysis. In this case study, the grandmother, who is also a registered nurse, repeatedly expresses concern for the granddaughter's health and well-being. The grandmother alleges that the granddaughter displays unwise and unhealthy actions indicative of bulimia, and questions the granddaughter's motives. In turn, the granddaughter denies and otherwise rejects ownership of the allegations, and attempts to divert the topic. The grandmother's concern is unsolicited, and the granddaughter rejects it as unnecessary and inappropriate.

Beach studies the continuous and negotiated character of a conversation about bulimia. The interaction is characterized by a sequence of initiation/pursuit/avoidance of alleged wrongdoings involving health behavior. The analysis reveals the grandmother's and granddaughter's contrasting orientations to health behaviors. In the process, readers are given a glimpse into how even expressions of concern and caring may result in conflict between family members. Moreover, the analysis reveals details of the tension between the "essential problematics of caregiving" on the one hand, and on the other the "avoidance of wrongdoing" by those denying that problematic health behaviors exist and merit the attention being given to them.

Although bulimia is the central focus of this monograph, the implications extend beyond this particular problem. In his conclusion, Beach considers how family members confront and address a variety of personal and social problems displayed by loved ones and, in turn, how those confronted routinely deny and discount alleged wrongdoings. The case study thus provides a foundation for understanding the interactional organization of previously unexamined social/family problems—bulimia and grandparent-caregiving—and for comparing such talk with related institutional discourse, such as psychiatric interviews, family therapy, and counseling related to various diseases and family predicaments.

Conversations About Illness moves beyond situating illness in physical bodies or individual perceptions; rather, it proposes as a topic of investigation the experience and discussion of illness clearly framed within existing social relationships.

Wendy Leeds-Hurwitz
Stuart J. Sigman

Introduction

The grandmother–granddaughter conversation examined in this book offers only a glimpse of interactions revealing the altogether pervasive and often troubled coexistence of family medical predicaments. Special attention is given to eating disorders in the ways these family members get caught up and thus preoccupied with an illness "problem": the solicitation and avoidance of admitting to, and seeking professional help for, bulimia. However routine such interactional involvements may be, the constituent practices and interactional consequences of initiating, confronting, avoiding, and seeking to remedy bulimic problems remain largely unspecified. Little is known, therefore, about real-time contingencies of choice and action, coauthored by individuals displaying ordinary yet contradictory concerns about health and illness. There is clearly much to learn about families as primordial institutional systems whose members must somehow deal with unanticipated yet ongoing medical problems, and the present analysis hopes to make clear that far too little is known regarding the distinctive character of how family members routinely talk through real or idealized medical concerns.

This case study involves a single audiorecorded and transcribed conversation, nearly 13 minutes in length, as a point of departure for coming to grips with a limited but revealing set of interactional moments between a grandmother (G) and her granddaughter (S/Sissy). Understanding the nature and problematic consequences of family medical talk necessitates repeated inspection of the interactional organization of such occasions, involvements best preserved by naturally occurring recordings and carefully produced transcriptions. The availability of such materials affords researchers and clinicians alike the opportunity to describe and explain family members' orientations to bulimia, and by doing so to access what members themselves come to treat as meaningful throughout illness processes. By drawing attention to G and S's moment-by-moment, occasioned solutions to evolving courses of action, it becomes possible to reveal how these solutions reflect here-and-now relevancies of what these participants, for reasons often (but not always) explicitly provided in their conversation, acted upon as meaningful and thus in meaningful ways.

In most general terms, the focus of this book addresses why and how the study of social problems such as bulimia and "grandparent caregiving," often described in terms of the "social context" of health and illness, might be practically understood through an examination of language and social interaction. Attending to how family members rely on interaction to routinely order, produce, justify, and manage their daily affairs and understandings, engaging in subtle and deceptively complex actions such as imposing and disregarding constraints regarding health behavior, reveals how families socially construct and in these ways make available their institutional orientations and priorities. More specifically, the focus rests predominantly with how G and S display contradictory preoccupations with bulimia: Just as G is persistent in her conviction that soon-to-be married S is consistently vomiting her food and therefore bulimic (e.g., as one means of losing weight to appear thinner and become more attractive), so does S consistently fail to directly admit, take ownership for, and agree to seek professional help in order to remedy alleged health problems put forth by G. It is the continuous and negotiated character of this interaction that the following analysis seeks to make clear, especially the curiously disaffiliative and at times conflicting resources G and S rely on throughout their conversation. However, certain actions can also be shown to display cooperative and even playful moments in the midst of otherwise serious matters involving an eating disorder.

Because understandings about family interactions of this sort are minimal, a detailed examination of a single case seems particularly merited.

Through an examination of how G and S socially construct their concerns with bulimia and its consequences, it will become apparent that a shift is made from inherently individualized conceptualizations of bodily disease or psychosocial illness toward an understanding of the kinds of embodied interactional activities family members bring to one another's attention as practical and significant reasons for informing actions. Here we can see, for example, just how it is that methods for expressing concern and caring by individuals may nevertheless eventuate in interactional troubles and problems between family members. With G and S, there is evidence of what might in general terms be described as the "essential problematics of caregiving": Although displays of basic concerns for others' health and well-being are routine occurrences between family members in home environments (and, of course, across friendship and various support networks), even the delicate and well-intended management of such occasions guarantees neither agreement on the nature of the alleged problems nor, consequently, a commitment to seek professional help as a predominant means of remedying a medical condition. In such cases, the very existence of an illness is itself a matter of some contention to be interactionally worked out. And it is perhaps both predictable and symptomatic that those explicitly denying (or as with S, indirectly failing to admit) that problematic health behaviors exist, also somehow let it be made known that far too much attention is being given to possibilities and consequences of illness in the first instance.

The issues raised here give rise to basic questions:

- What interactional activities are involved in getting a family member to acknowledge that he or she has a serious problem, and to seek assistance from health professionals as one means of remedying the described illness?
- How do those alleged to be ill fail to directly agree with and/or offer resistance to a family member's diagnosis, and how is such resistance responded to and possibly overcome?
- Regarding bulimia, how are preoccupations with eating, food, thinness, shape, appearance, and weight deeply embedded yet recognizable throughout the talk-interaction?

At the outset, however, it is important to clarify that these and related questions emerged gradually throughout the course of this project. It is both the allure and defining characteristic of *unmotivated*, data-driven observations that eventual recognition of the broader significance of materials examined are more retrospective than prospective in nature.

From the title of this book, *Conversations About Illness: Family Preoccupations With Bulimia*, readers might understandably assume that this investigation was conceived from a set of a priori, longstanding, even systematically explored concerns with how families deal with the illness "bulimia." But any such notions need to be dispelled in favor of far less grandiose beginnings.

The work presented herein is not a reflection of self-proclaimed expertise on eating disorders in general nor bulimia in particular, either as a researcher or resulting from direct personal or family experience with such an illness. In fact, the conversation between G and S was one of many volunteered recordings within the San Diego Conversation Library (SDCL) that, for some time, had remained unnoticed and thus gone unattended. For reasons long forgotten, several short segments of the recording were utilized in classes as evidence of what I then put forth as instances of "blaming," and a full transcription was only gradually produced and refined. It was at this point that a set of local, at times befuddling, observational problems arose: in the first few moments of the conversation, trying to figure out the rather curious fashion in which G appeared to reject S's seemingly innocent invitation to go for a walk, first by questioning S's underlying motive for walking and eventually concluding "That's stupid." Through analysis, it did become increasingly clear that G's apparent attribution of motive, and possible wrongdoing toward S's walking, was designed in consideration of S's vomiting and generally poor eating habits. However, such eventual understandings in no way minimized or dismissed the analytic, here-and-now tasks of coming to grips with a range of complex actions inherent to the moment-by-moment contingencies of this (and every) conversation. The methods or techniques recruited by G and S to coauthor this occasion, and what if anything such activities might reveal about the displayed character of family preoccupations with an eating disorder such as bulimia—not to mention the interactional organization of conversations about illness most generally—remained not only unarticulated but for a considerable period of time were simply not primary explanatory resources throughout a host of repeated listening sessions of the G–S audiorecording and inspections of the transcription.

By not bringing social problems such as bulimia to the G–S interaction a priori, but instead working first toward explicating how and just what it is that these participants are contingently orienting to in meaningful ways (i.e., in real-time situations of local choice and action), it has hopefully become possible to avoid the inherent seduction of prespecifying patterns of interaction by reference to what is known, and thus far too often taken for granted, about ways in which large-scale "macro/societal" problems are evidenced in ordinary conversation. I would like to think that discovery per se has at least been given a fair chance regarding some of the ways family members work through medical problems most generally, although especially how they deal with an eating disorder such as bulimia. Had the initial and explicit task focused on understanding bulimia as a form of illness, especially as a means of redressing and resolving bulimic problems, it is doubtful the set of findings put forth in this book would have been generated. Of course, it remains to be seen just how these findings regarding the interactionally organized nature of talk about bulimia might be informative and of value for families, practitioners, and analysts alike.

The unmotivated character of this research does have its limitations, however, and it is perhaps far too often that discussion of these potential problems get raised only as tagged-on implications within the conclusion of a book or article. By raising them at this juncture, however briefly, they can be utilized by readers as a partial lens for framing both what the analysis has become and its unmotivated inception. It also encourages readers to consistently seek grounding within the interaction that might be put forth as evidence representing "larger" claims, a task very much at the heart of what this and other inquiries must constantly be concerned with regardless of the nature and implications of the interactions being examined.

The first such limitation involves the G–S conversation not being part of a larger corpus of systematically collected materials, driven by a host of focused research questions resulting from theoretical and empirical concerns with family medical/bulimic interactions. There is, no doubt, a price to pay for this. Although diverse interactional materials are brought to contrastive bearing in order to reveal both idiosyncratic and generalizable features of the G–S conversation across numerous speakers, topics, and occasions, it remains only a single conversation. Any such snapshot of everyday affairs imposes constraints for understanding ongoing "problems" with bulimia and other forms of illness. Second, no demographic or other background data exist for G–S. It is not known, for example, whether G has been a primary caregiver for S, if S lives with G, the relationships among G, S, and S's parents (e.g., their marital status), and any social or medical history whatsoever regarding this family. And finally, the interaction was not videorecorded, which is, and increasingly so in studies of language and social interaction, useful for understanding how setting-specific features as well as non- vocal phenomena such as gaze and gesture are used, relied on, and at times actively recruited by participants in ways contributing to the ongoing development and organization of this conversation and relationship.

Many readers may conclude that these limitations cast doubt on the worthwhileness and ultimate importance of the study, and suffice it to say I have reflected on and share several of these concerns. But there are alternative considerations that aid in balancing such critical assessments. First, the single case allows for more attention to be given directly to the interaction as a practical achievement, one meaningfully produced by and for G and S and in these ways made available for subsequent analysis. This results in examinations and observations where there is minimal confounding (and potentially, clouding) with extrasituational information, and subsequently with what might be described as the inevitable "transportability problem" of constantly attempting to link up demographic and background information as explanatory devices for understanding locally organized moments in conversation. Second, audiorecordings are often sufficient data sources, even in face-to-face (rather than telephone) conversations, for discovering how participants make available their understandings of the real-time, moment-by-moment contingencies of the interaction at hand. And finally, as noted, in time it has become increasingly apparent that the emergent findings may nevertheless offer something significant by speaking to more encompassing issues of family medical talk and bulimic problems in particular. This is the case even though findings emerged, by and large, void of being driven by the need to address particular kinds of questions germane to a social problem such as bulimia, including what prior research had identified as relevant and indicative of recurrent difficulties.

Over the past few years I have, however, informally asked students, family members, and friends if they had participated in conversations about the illness bulimia. (Reportings being just that, the synopsis provided here may provoke curiosity but is less a finding than reconstructions of field notes about possible social events.) A slim majority of these individuals reported they had not; they were generally unaware of the increasingly problematic nature of eating disorders especially, although not exclusively, on college campuses. Others described such experiences as routine. The most commonly reported set of interactions involved telling stories and otherwise gossiping about people they knew, and/or experiences they had observed, involving other students', friends', and family members' abnormal methods for losing weight (i.e., vomiting, laxatives, diuretics, excessive exercise). Fewer still reported having interacted directly with others about their problems, and most often, as attempts to inform others that they were aware of, curious about, and perhaps concerned with yet bothered by their "odd" behaviors. Several individuals, however, reported that they pushed further by attempting to solicit from the alleged bulimic both admittance and commitment to seek professional help; such efforts, when they occurred, were reported as reserved almost exclusively for family members and close friends (for reasons such as "you have to really care," or "otherwise I figure it's none of my business"). In all cases, those alleged to be bulimic were described as "being secretive" or "in denial" about the "problem."

It is this latter set of actions, reported by only several individuals, that nevertheless best typifies the activities comprising the G–S conversation.

In chapter 1, "Finding Bulimia," an attempt is made to situate this study within prior research on bulimia and, relatedly, grandparent caregiving. The proposed causes, consequences, and approaches utilized to study these inherently social problems are overviewed. A necessary and considerable interest in family interactions is evident, but owing in part to overreliance on self-report methods and findings, studies focusing directly on recorded and transcribed conversational materials were not revealed. The chapter concludes with an overview of conversation analytic alternatives as suitable methods for examining interactions addressing, at least in part, concerns with and orientations to illness.

The data analysis offered in chapter 2, "From Troubles to Problems," begins at the beginning: How G (also a registered nurse) initiates and brings her "case" to S, occasioning and indirectly raising the problem of bulimia by not only refusing S's invitation to go for a walk but also questioning S's motive for walking. Attention is given to how troubles are topically generative in the ways G constructs problems out of S's stated troubles, displaying concerns with S's health and well-being by alleging S's lack of responsibility in coming to grips with her illness.

Relying on multiple resources for ensuring that S treats G as informed and takes her allegations seriously, thus laying grounds for reasonable assertion, chapter 3 addresses the interactional work of overcoming resistance:

attempts to solicit from S direct admittance via affirmation of responsibility, and commitment to seeking professional assistance for the "problems" S repeatedly fails to "own" (e.g., consistently vomiting her food as a means of becoming thinner for her upcoming wedding). In the ways G engages in a variety of actions—establishing, claiming, and imputing "knowledge," laying out consequences, citing sources, and offering evidence—the interactionally achieved character of "confrontation/insistence" is made apparent, as are routine and emergent difficulties in offering and receipting unasked for "advice."

In chapter 4, similar attention is drawn to how references to "denial" fail to adequately capture S's alternative methods for avoiding ownership of the problems G has constructed. By discounting the legitimacy of G as a viable source, accounting for the reasonableness of her actions, withholding responses through silence, seeking topic closure, and humorously downgrading (e.g., laughing-off) the seriousness of G's attributions, S can be shown to enact a series of actions amounting not only to a lack of affiliation and alignment with G's stated problems, but also the very possibility that problems exist mirroring the attention being given to such illness behaviors.

Just as conceptualizations of "confrontation" and "denial" have been shown in earlier chapters to underspecify the family medical predicaments G and S noticeably work through, so is it the case that the very circumstances they have coproduced and are caught up in are evident as preoccupations in chapter 5. Understood herein as detailed, interactionally organized phenomena rather than an upshot of individuals' mentalistic processes, S's conjoined preoccupations with bulimia and her wedding are interactionally apparent despite her failing to directly admit bulimic problems: first, as unwittingly tailored to and implicated within the very circumstances she is attempting to describe, and second, how these actions may also emerge through an easily unnoticed "speech error" produced in response to having been found in error—one version of double trouble apparent in S's attempts to characterize and thus remedy the situation she is caught up in. By examining environments of potential conflict between G and S, such as G's consistent withholding of commiseration and sympathy from S's expressed anxieties and concerns—it becomes possible to systematically address whether and how "poetics" emerge spontaneously in everyday talk, and the relevance of these understandings for unmasking such delicate involvements revealed throughout problems with bulimia.

Conclusions and implications for examining interaction and social problems are laid out in chapter 6. Discussion begins with making explicit what the study of interaction might offer toward basic understandings of bulimia and grandparent caregiving as practical, conversationally organized achievements. It is suggested that the indigenous activities of "social contexts" have not been systematically examined, resulting in "theories of social action" in their infant stages. Studies such as the one discussed here offer substantive alternatives by focusing on problems inherent in the social construction of illness (e.g., with contradictory and disaffiliative orientations such as withholdings of "commiseration" from persons struggling with an illness). The implications of this investigation extend well beyond bulimia to a vast array of inherently interconnected, casual and institutional involvements between family members, friends, and bureaucratic representatives (e.g., in long-term caregiving, dealing with cancer and Alzheimer's disease, during psychiatric interviews, and HIV/AIDS counseling sessions).

ACKNOWLEDGMENTS

From the inception of this project, I have benefited greatly from the comments of students, too numerous to mention here, and participants in unmotivated data sessions during Conversation Play Groups at San Diego State University and elsewhere. Several colleagues have offered generous insights and support as these materials were being developed—Greg Desilet, Rich Frankel, Phil Glenn, Chuck Goodwin, Char Jones, John Heritage, Robert Hopper, Michael Hyde, Jenny Mandelbaum, Doug Maynard, Mike Motley, Anita Pomerantz, Robert Sanders, and Manny Schegloff—at times incognito under the guise of anonymous reviewers, the upshots of which are hopefully conveyed throughout this analysis. Particular thanks to coeditors Stu Sigman and Wendy Leeds-Hurwitz, not just for careful readings and detailed comments but also for the inception of an "everyday communication" series.

Earlier versions of chapters 4 and 5 were published as "Avoiding ownership for alleged wrongdoings," *Research on Language and Social Interaction*, 24, 1990/1991, 1–36, and "The delicacy of preoccupation," *Text and Performance Quarterly*, 13, 299–312. Appreciation is extended to Boreal Scholarly Publishers and Distributors, Ltd. and the Speech Communication Association for permission to incorporate this work. The inclusion of the painting "Patterns of Behaviour," by Barry Kamen, is also made possible through his permission and Virgin Records Ltd. and UB40.

Patterns Of Behaviour
(Artist: Barry Kamen)

1
▼▼▼▼▼▼▼

Finding Bulimia

Those who are sated loathe honey; but to the hungry soul every bitter thing is sweet.

—Proverbs 27:7

Bulimia is an exceedingly common eating disorder approaching "social epidemic" (Gordon, 1990) proportions. The American Psychiatric Association (1987, 1993) offers both manuals and practice guidelines suggesting that bulimia is diagnosed across a predominantly female population (approximately 90%) involving 1% to 10% of middle to upper class adolescent and college-age women (see also Bemporad et al., 1992; Drenowski, Yee, & Krahn, 1988; Haller, 1992; Strober & Yager, 1988–1989; Yager, 1988);[1] approximately 1 out of every 200 teenage women suffer from starvation and binge disorders (Marx, 1991).[2]

Considerable attention has been given to biological, developmental, family dynamic, and related psychosocial causes and consequences of eating disorders—to symptoms, diagnosis, clinical treatment, and intervention methods

---

[1]A proportionate minority (5%–10%) of eating disorders exist across diverse male populations, especially those preoccupied with obesity, sexual identity, and sports/exercise (see Farrow, 1992). There is, therefore, some irony in the original Proverb appearing at the outset of this chapter: the "He who is" in original text was purposefully altered to "Those who are" with these concerns in mind.

[2]There are notable similarities and distinctions between anorexia nervosa and bulimia that occupy a good portion of the research and therapeutic literature on eating disorders. Haller (1992), for example, reported that patients may alternate between illnesses; estimates suggest that 30% to 80% of bulimics have anorexic histories.

1

for anorexia and bulimia, on the one hand, and relatedly to cognitive, social, and cultural influences promoting bulimia that have been forwarded as negatively impacting not just health, but communication and relationships over time. Whether understood as an experienced illness, an explicit focus of clinical intervention, or a set of activities generating considerable biomedical and psychosocial research interest, bulimia in the very least reveals a complex interplay of mind, body, and social action.

But just how such an interplay gets worked out in social interaction is the focal concern of this and remaining chapters:

- What is known about the kinds of interactions bulimics routinely get involved in with family members or friends as a set of distinctive, interactionally organized practices?
- In what social activities is bulimia embedded, therefore readily apparent, and what evidence warrants such a claim?
- In short: Where is bulimia, what is the nature of its occurrence, and what activities and occasions comprise the social existence of this eating disorder?

These questions reveal a partial reconstruction of the issues guiding the latter course of this investigation: finding what is known about and put forth as "theories" seeking to explain bulimia, especially the social and thus communicative dimensions of this illness; and determining how such explanations might serve as grounds for attempting to show the relevance of prior research to subsequent analysis of the conversation between the grandmother (G) and her granddaughter (S/Sissy). It is shown to be a predominant feature of these diverse research efforts that, first, although priority is given to causes and consequences of illnesses such as bulimia, proportionately little is said about the details of social interaction constituting and encompassing actual processes of bulimic actions and relationships. And second, when interaction and social relationships do comprise the focus of empirical investigation, findings are almost exclusively rooted in perceptual data derived from self-report measurement techniques, questionnaires, and interviews.

This chapter begins with a necessarily brief overview of research on bulimia as a backdrop for understanding inherent problems in discovering how family and friendship interactions are put forth as a cause and consequence of eating disorders. And as G and S comprise a grandparent–grandchild relationship, an overview is also provided of empirical investigations focusing on relatively recent concerns with *grandparent caregiving*. Overreliance on self-report methods and findings reveals the unequivocal need for direct examinations of family conversations about illness; individually based limitations of prior research give rise to the utility of conversation-analytic (CA) alternatives for coming to grips with real-time interactional involvements such as G and S, and ways prior research on both casual and institutional talk-in-interaction can itself be shown to have bearing on the ensuing analysis.

OVERVIEW OF RESEARCH ON BULIMIA

Individuals displaying bulimic tendencies are routinely described by medical professionals and social scientists as preoccupied, even obsessed with food and thinness. Nearly universal agreement on diagnostic symptoms seems to exist:

> A diagnosis of bulimia nervosa is made when a person has recurrent episodes of binge eating, a feeling of lack of control over behavior during binges, regular use of self-induced vomiting, laxatives, diuretics, strict dieting, or vigorous exercise to prevent weight gain, a minimum of 2 binge episodes a week for at least 3 months, and persistent overconcern with body shape and weight. (Haller, 1992, p. 658)

This description stresses the utilization of abnormal, episodic methods for weight loss but also the feelings and concerns of bulimics (see also Halmi, 1985). In addition to a lack of control over binge eating and obsessive preoccupation with body shape and weight, specific additional personality attributes, mood states, and eating patterns (Davis, Freeman, & Solyom, 1985; Lambley & Scott, 1988; Rebert, Stanton, & Schwarz, 1991; Steiger, Puentes-Neuman, & Leung, 1991; Steiner-Adair, 1991; Vitousek & Manke, 1994) have been identified as constituent features of the interpretive and consumptive world of bulimic persons: predictably low self-esteem; self-worth tied to low weight; extreme self-criticism; overwhelming and conforming need for others' approval; social isolation and distancing; affective instability due to overly anxious, depressed, tired, apathetic, embarrassed, irritable, hostile, and moody predispositions; individuals who not uncommonly eat alone, but are secretive about diet and self-indulgent eating habits as well as reliance on vomiting, laxatives, and diuretics for weight loss and general appearance management (see Herzog, 1982).

Taken together, such personality attributes reflect often serious psychiatric disorders, what Bemporad et al. (1992, p. 509) described as "profound underlying personality pathology" and thus "comorbidity" with bulimia (Yanovski, Nelson, Dubbert, & Spitzer, 1993), especially affective, substance, and obsessive–compulsive use disorders (Farrow, 1992; Woodside, 1993). And there are a host of additional problems, not the least of which are irrational and thus dysfunctional beliefs (Lohr & Parkinson, 1989), alcohol abuse (Goldbloom, Naranjo, Bremner, & Hicks, 1992), fear of psychosexual maturity with a general inability to develop age-appropriate sexual identities (Meades, 1993), and overall sexual dysfunction (Simpson & Ramberg, 1992).

Despite what appears to be overwhelming agreement on personality and eating-habit symptoms leading to diagnosis, alternative characterizations of bulimia are offered depending on the unit of analysis put forth. Rather than looking to personality profiles of the individual, consider a second depiction by Haller (1992) regarding "medical complications":

> potential medical complications include electrolyte and fluid imbalances, hyperamylasemia, hypomagnesemia, gastric and esophageal irritation and bleeding, gastric dilation, large bowel abnormalities (due to laxative abuse), edema, and fatigue. Swelling of the parotid gland bilaterally, dental erosion, gingivitis, and knuckle calluses (from inducing vomiting using the fingers) are common physical symptoms of bulimic behavior. (p. 659)

Here, physical symptoms and thus bodily consequences are described, often in technical medical terminology, revealing quite clearly that bulimia typifies not just a potentially debilitating psychosocial illness, but also multisymptom organ abnormalities resulting in diseases across "the skeletal, gastrointestinal, pulmonary, endocrine, and cardiovascular systems" (Cerami, 1993, p. 165).[3]

Bulimic tendencies and complications are both diverse and complex (e.g., see Bulich, 1988–1989): Food imbalances and generally unhealthy dieting can affect thoughts, feelings, and actions in dramatic ways; numerous "biopsychiatric" interrelationships have been posited (see Marx, 1991) linking the role of neurotransmitters and the brain to biological and psychological explanations for behavior; chemical deficiencies and imbalances have been forwarded as explanatory factors causing and influencing the progression of bulimia, and can be treated by means of "psychopharmaceuticals" in addition to therapeutic, behavioral, and "psychopathological" interventions involving the individual, group, and family (see Haller, 1992; Igoin-Apfelbaum, 1992; Labov & Fanshel, 1977; Leon, 1990).

Developmentally, as transitions from adolescence to adulthood occur and problems arise between children and parents (see Yates, 1990), the female child may identify primarily with the mother, resulting in traditional feminine qualities (Wurman, 1988–1989) but also a perception that the mother is frustrated and unhappy; this promotes a sacrifice of more autonomous capabilities, evident in a need for validation from yet general fear of men, and thus the corollary obsession with body type and overall appearance (Boskind-Lodhal, 1976).

---

[3]The well-known distinction between illness and disease—for example, individuals' meaningful history, experience of, social interactions and stories about illness, on the one hand, and the evidence of disease via physical and thus bodily manifestations and consequences, on the other—can be recognized throughout literature on bulimia, is a microcosm of ongoing concerns with humane versus technical medicine (see Byrne & Long, 1976; Chenail, 1991; Engel, 1977; Frankel, 1984; Heath, 1986; Mishler, 1984; Silverman, 1987), and in general, the argument against biological reductionism (e.g., see Benoist & Cathebras, 1993) or what Cassell (1985) summarized succinctly in observing that "doctors treat patients, not diseases" (p. 1).

Sociocultural Influences

Sociocultural pressures on women to be thin, popularized and diffused through press and media, are perhaps the most commonly understood social causes of bulimia (Schwartz, Thompson, & Johnson, 1982). When considering epidemic proportions of eating disorders among women on college campuses (Carter & Eason, 1983; Drenowski et al., 1988), individuals rely on bulimic behaviors to manage stresses arising from what Gordon (1988–1989) described as historical shifts in both expectations and demands for thinness among females.[4] Binge eating and vomiting become imitated, learned, and are often normalized practices, at times having ritualized status for women attempting to maintain some control over their body image across an increasing variety of social groups. Given cultural overemphasis and socially critical evaluations of feminine beauty, ideally and predominantly by reliance on criteria of thinness and exercise (Nasser, 1988), bulimic-prone persons eventually treat themselves as constantly inspected and visually objectified (McLorg & Taub, 1987). Obtaining slenderness is therefore not just prerequisite for, but tantamount to social acceptance and the avoidance of stigma due to excessive weight.

As Yager (1992) observed, it is paradoxical that increasing preoccupations with "healthy lifestyles" may contribute signficantly to unhealthy and dysfunctional eating disorders. In reference to earlier surveys of female populations at UCLA, Yager reported that "surveys repeatedly show that about three quarters of women whose weights are fully in the normal range feel too fat and wish to lose weight: indeed, some studies have shown that they desire on average to weigh only slightly more than the weights in the anorexia nervosa range" (p. 679; see also Kurtzman, Yager, Landsverk, Wiesmeier, Bodurka, 1989). In compulsive cases of this sort, the body becomes the locus of conflict: "Bulimia is viewed as an effort to make up for the lack of inner sources of self-esteem by living up to external ideals of perfection" (Wurman, 1988–1989, p. 167; see also Benoist & Cathebras, 1993).[5]

---

[4]In late 1995, news headlines reported studies indicating that cigarette companies were directing their media campaigns to young women as the highest percentage category of new smokers: Increased smoking ensures the maintenance and/or loss of weight (e.g., Virginia Slims). Questions remain, however, about the proportion of young women who smoke cigarettes and engage in bulimic behaviors. Similarly, if young women break the smoking habit, what proportion become bulimic to ward off weight gain?

[5]The inherent conflict between internal and external priorities is omnipresent in the literature on bulimia, and uniquely though coincidentally summarized as follows: "They saw the glory of the world displayed; they saw the bitter of it, and the sweet" (Dawson, 1867–1900); "From the heart of this fountain of delight wells up some bitter taste to choke them even amid the flowers" (Lucretius, 99–55 BC). And regarding assumed relationships among family interactions and eating disorders, "Bitterness attracts bitterness and then multiplies by feeding on itself" (Brownlow, 1972).

Histories of disturbance in early and ongoing relationships promote what Bemporad et al. (1992) summarized as "a lack of security and pronounced difficulties in trusting others, and in simply being an authentic individual in the presence of others" (p. 509). This observation provides a foundation for raising more direct questions regarding the patterns and assumed problems bulimics have when interacting with family members and, more generally, social networks involving individuals concerned with and suspecting of their possible illness.

Interactions With Family and Friends

Rather than treating such factors as poor self-image, the overwhelming desire to please others, and excessive need for external approval as randomly occurring or self-imposed symptoms of bulimia, the research literature puts forth dysfunctional family environments as major causal forces, perhaps even the "root causes," of eating disorders (Bemporad et al., 1992).

Bulimic individuals are more likely to emerge from suburban family environments that are competitive, achievement-oriented, and appearance-centered (Harper & Shillito, 1991). A typical sketch involves middle to upper class, "high pressure" families (Siegel, Brisman, & Weinshel, 1988; Yager, 1992; Yager, Gwirtsman, & Edelstein, 1991) in which both parents work; owing to workaholic, passive, and/or frequently absent fathers, it is the mothers who are primary, often overly protective and involved caregivers. Parents tend to critically impose idealized models of weight and appearance on their children, just as parents and siblings may engage in such activities as teasing others about eating, exercise, and habits consequential for achieving fat-free bodies. In terms of birth order, at least for small families, bulimics are highly likely to be the eldest or only daughter (Lacey, Gowers, & Bhat, 1991).

Studies relying on self-report measurement techniques have consistently evidenced a strong relationship between eating disorders and abnormal patterns of family interaction, although little or no self-reported differences across subject populations have been reported (e.g., see Kent & Clopton, 1992; Strober & Humphrey, 1987; Thienemann & Steiner, 1993). As with literature on social support and family functioning generally, the vast majority of findings have been generated from diverse self-report measures (Franks, Campbell, & Shields, 1992). Compared with repeat or nondieters, bulimics perceive their families to be dysfunctional due to such factors as low affective involvement and responsiveness, poor family communication, problem-solving skills, and behavior control (McNamara & Loveman, 1990). Binge eating activities have also been found to be more frequent when bulimic women perceive family members to have poor problem-solving skills rather than cohesive styles of interaction (Waller, 1994): Bulimics perceive their families as considerably more dysfunctional on dimensions of "cohesion, ex-

pressiveness, conflict, recreational orientation, emotional support, communication, and need for counseling" (Schisslak, McKeon, & Crago, 1990, p.
185; see also Kog & Vandereycken, 1989). It thus appears "that eating-disordered behavior may be a symptom response and/or coping strategy for
women in dysfunctional families" (Lundholm & Waters, 1991, p. 97). For
example, through analysis of relationships among personality, family traits,
and symptomatic behaviors it was revealed that high school girls' self-reports
suggest symptomatic eaters are more likely to be moody, have obsessive concerns with the body, and be self-critical (Steiger et al., 1991). And among
family members, bulimics display the most realistic perceptions and thus valid
descriptions of interactional styles and overall problems with sufferer's family
(Waller, Slade, & Calam, 1990).

Extending beyond the family, a recurrent and significant fear of intimate
relationships has been confirmed across bulimics and control subjects responding to the Fear of Intimacy Scale (Descutner & Thelan, 1991; Pruitt,
Kappius, & Gorman, 1992). Grissett and Norvell (1992) evidenced how bulimics perceive less social support from family and friends, enhanced negative
interactions and conflict, and reduced social competence. Attention has also
been drawn to bulimics' overall stress and their perceived changes over time
in levels of satisfaction across other relationships (Meades, 1993; Thelan,
Kanakis, Farmer, & Pruitt, 1990); ratings of female college students have
been shown to be negatively correlated with satisfaction in relationships with
males, with no significant differences in levels of satisfaction for same-sexed
relationships (Thelan et al., 1993).

Overreliance on Self-Report Data

A substantial corpus of investigations relying on bulimics' and family members' perceptions of their family environments and social networks (see also
Blouin et al., 1994) reveal the exceedingly common utilization and labeling
of measurement scales. Findings such as "poor communication," "increased
conflict," or "low cohesiveness" are generated from the correlation of variables rather than the inspection of socially organized, interactionally achieved
activities.[6] Specific instances of just what poor communication and other
findings look like in real-time conversational involvements are noticeably

---

[6]A somewhat parallel analysis is provided in Coulter's (1973) *Approaches to Insanity*, where
an overview is provided of how "aetiologists" searching for the genesis of "schizophrenia"
identify family interactions as primary social causations. Further, as related to inherent
limitations of self-report data, there are fundamental problems in capturing "complex orders
of human activity" (p. 41) by operationalizing social theories on the basis of quantitative indices
and variables (see also Atkinson, 1978; Cicourel, 1964; Coulter, 1979; Sudnow, 1967), just as
there are limitations to phenomenological inquiries emphasizing the "context of self" (e.g., see
Zaner, 1981).

absent. These and related results, although inherently interesting and pre-dictive across diverse respondents, remain indirect assessments of social in-teraction on its own merits; they are based on individual reports about in-teraction rather than examinations of actual behavior jointly produced by and for interactants themselves. There are also inherent problems when, in addition to the construction and validation of scaling measures (see Coker & Roger, 1990) and questionnaires (Rosen, Srebnik, Saltzberg, & Wendt, 1991), expert ratings and standardized interviews are employed for diagnosis and to determine family members' attitudes toward eating, psychiatric status, and overall social functioning (Collings & King, 1994; Cooper, Clark, & Fairburn, 1993; de Zwaan et al., 1993). For example, although trained coders employed two different behavioral observational systems to differentiate and reveal differences in bulimic–anorexic from control families in a study by Humphrey, Apple, and Kirschenbaum (1986), this coding of interaction by means of predetermined categories and schemes gives priority to how each coding system contributes to the predictive power of the other, rather than to finely detailed examinations of bulimics' actual interaction practices and patterns (see W. Beach, 1990c; Garfinkel, 1967; Heritage & Roth, 1995). Similarly, when Grissett and Norvell (1992) reported that observers not aware of group membership still rated bulimics as "less socially effective" (p. 297), the constituent and interactive details of such a claim remain elusive.

Similar problems exist in field studies employing interviews. Promoting an agenda for naturalistic examinations of such activities as the "discourse of femininity," Hepworth (1993) accurately observed that just as "research on eating disorders has been dominated by a positivistic scientific model for over a century," so is it the case that "qualitative research has been marginalized by mainstream research and its dissemination" (p. 179; see also Spitzack, 1993). Nevertheless, as a means for understanding routine and ongoing problems faced by British health care workers managing anorexic patients in a state psychiatric hospital, Hepworth relied exclusively on interviews (only with workers) and a form of discourse analysis emphasizing recurring "themes" as the preferred method "to theorize relations between social processes and individual subjectivity" (p. 180). Unfortunately, although interviews can reveal rich information regarding individuals' lived experiences (e.g., see following discussion of Minkler & Roe, 1993), interview-generated reconstruc-tions of social processes offer only typified and overly generalized versions of possible connections between talk and social structure (see W. Beach & Lindstrom, 1992; Boden & Zimmerman, 1991; Drew & Heritage, 1992).

The upshot of this discussion might best be capsulized by Grissett and Norvell's (1992) prescription: "Results highlight the need for further investi-gation of the quality and type of *interactions* in bulimic women's lives" (p. 293; italics added).

GRANDPARENT CAREGIVING

The study of family caregiving has traditionally focused on the involvements of female spouses, parents, and adult children caring for chronic or terminally ill "elderly" family members (i.e., over 65 years of age), especially the normative yet stressful burdens, strains, and consequences of providing in-home, informal, long-term care (see D. Beach, 1993; Biegel & Blum, 1990; Brody, 1985; Brody, Johnsen, & Fulcomer, 1983; Cantor, 1983; Cicirelli, 1992; Clipp & George, 1990; Kane & Kane, 1981). Given an increasingly aging population, it is expected that continued research attention will be given to elder-care, although impacts of caregiving on young adults (D. Beach, 1994), including grandchildren (Creasey & Jarvis, 1994), is beginning to be recognized. But little is known about what might be described as the inverse of elder-care, namely, how older adults such as grandparents are more or less actively involved with or committed to facilitating the growth and development of their grandchildren.

Grandparent caregiving is on the rise, thus such caregiving processes are increasingly predominant as a research topic (see Bengston & Robertson, 1985; Homolova, Hoerning, & Schaeffer, 1984; Kornhaber & Woodword, 1981; Minkler & Roe, 1993). Yet, gaining direct access to grandparent caregiving remains a problem, as summarized by Hagestad and Burton (1986): "All too often we have looked at grandparenthood in isolation, not taking into account how it is embedded in a web of relationships and lives" (p. 471).

In their book entitled *Grandmothers as Caregivers*, Minkler and Roe (1993) took a significant step toward remedying this problem by seeking to understand the practical and situated consequences of grandparenting across social and cultural contexts within which African-American grandmothers care for grandchildren with drug-abusing parents (especially crack cocaine). Relying on two-part in-depth interviews with grandmother caregivers (as well as observations, field notes, and direct community involvments), priority was given to retaining the integrity of women's voices by transforming reported experiences into data. Although results offer a unique storified history and heuristic analysis of women's caregiving experiences and described incidents, family relationships were events reported about rather than directly examined (i.e., via recordings and transcriptions of actual caregiving occasions), and thus only minimal understandings of how grandmothers and grandchildren conversationally organize "caregiving" are offered. It is important to note that this is not a critique of Minkler and Roe's (1993) broad-reaching study, but an articulation of priorities and, consequently, the inevitable limitations of types of questions that can be answered by interviews and participant observation data. For example, soliciting grandparents' lived experiences about a "typical day" (p. 213) through probing interview protocols—coping styles for dealing with difficult situations, changes in marital relationship since the onset of caregiving, or how caregiving had altered relationships with adult children—reveals little about the communication activities implicated in the practical achievement of daily tasks and activities. By focusing on individuals' reconstructions of feelings, experiences, and levels of awareness (e.g., toward physical and emotional health status, work, grandchildren and their health), the relational and thus collaborative behavior contextualizing that subjectivity remains untapped and unnoticed, most notably, the conversational resources recruited and the patterns cogenerated by grandparents and grandchildren in the routine course of dealing with everyday life affairs. This by no means discounts ongoing concerns with ill persons' or caregivers' personal well-being (e.g., see George, 1979; George & Gwyther, 1986; Montgomery, Gonyea, & Hooyman, 1985; Morse & Johnson, 1991); it simply articulates the lack of cumulative knowledge regarding the omnipresence of interaction as a vehicle for accomplishing a vast amount of caregiving tasks and assumed responsibilities.

Overreliance on Self-Report Data

The overreliance on self-report data (especially measurement scales, questionnaires/surveys, and interviews) is evident throughout a limited corpus of grandparenting studies (see Bengston & Robertson, 1985; Downs, 1988; Schmidt, 1982; Troll, 1985). This is the case even though important matters such as "selective investment" (Cherlin & Furstenberg, 1985, p. 97) by grandparents toward their grandchildren are addressed, as are attempts to establish vital connections between grandparents and grandchildren by soliciting children's thoughts, for example, that grandparents are "mentors, caretakers, mediators between child and parents, same sex role models, and family historians" (p. 81). The problems and promises of self-report data have not been entirely overlooked, however, as Hagestad (1985) has observed:

> Several of us who have studied grandparents and grandchildren have been puzzled by some seeming paradoxes in our data. On one hand, interviews and questionnaires present an overall impression of grandparents as important forces in the lives of the grandchildren. On the other hand, it is hard to pinpoint what it is that grandparents *do.* . . . Our problem might be that we have concentrated too narrowly on concrete behavior and actions, and have not considered the wider family context. (pp. 37–38)

The initial conclusion regarding difficulties in determining what "grandparents *do*" appears aligned with the present discussion in two key ways: (a) what people report that they do is a different activity than doing the activities reported; and (b) there is a compelling need to move beyond exclusive reliance on self-report data and toward observation and analysis of situated (frequently social) actions. However, Hagestad's later speculation that the source of the problem may stem from an overconcentration on "concrete behavior and actions" at the expense of understanding "the wider family context" is not consistent with concerns expressed herein. In marked contrast, research efforts have, thus far, universally failed to come to grips with the social organization of grandparenting behaviors and actions; because naturally occurring interactions have not themselves been treated as contextually rich sources of information, it is actually "the wider family context"—as constructed through self-reported data—that has been given priority.

Much can be said about reported beliefs held by family members in terms of relationships between autonomy and freedom of choice of individuals being cared for, and how caregivers may paternalistically intervene:

> in the making and executing of decisions for the welfare of that person. . . . The interventionist may also use force, deception, threat, misinformation, manipulation, or other strong means in the process of intervening in the decision . . . [when] one is convinced that one knows what is best to maximize benefits and minimize harm to the individual. (Cicirelli, 1992, p. 27)

But the distinctively social features of these and related involvements—just how these activities get interactionally brought off throughout the initiation, management, and negotiation of decisions about health-related actions and their possible consequences—can only remotely be grasped through measurement scales assessing family members' beliefs toward "respect for autonomy," "paternalism," and "ethical situations" (Cicirelli, 1992, pp. 206–234).

And similar to the previously reviewed research on bulimia, researchers focusing on intergenerational relationships have noted inherent problems with generating overly global claims where "only with difficulty can the existing theoretical constructs be applied in an empirical context" (Homolova et al., 1984, pp. 8–9). Although attempts to interconnect global and ungrounded theory with empirical observation lies at the heart of the stated problem, related but unstated concerns rest with the following key questions: What limitations are imposed on the study of intergenerational relationships when self-reports are the predominant method of investigation? If the "empirical context" is perceptually rooted in reports about relationships, what then can be said about the practical organization of intergenerational interactions? In short, what counts as "social context"?

This chapter concludes by proposing CA alternatives for understanding social contexts by investigating interactions and their constituent activities.

CA ALTERNATIVES

Participants in interaction routinely make available their orientations to, and thus understandings of, the moment-by-moment contingencies of unfolding actions—circumstances that cannot be fully intuited nor anticipated in advance, the details of which are impossible to capture by means of self-reported information. Basic questions underly concerns with excavating the constituent and organizing features of collaborative actions: How do specific kinds of actions get brought off as demonstrably relevant by and for participants? What is the distinctive, methodical, and achieved character of any given spate of interaction? On what behavioral (and scenic) resources do participants rely in contributing to and providing solutions for immediate interactional circumstances? These queries begin to address how participants delicately tailor their talk-in-interaction in ways influencing the recognizable evolution of practical courses of action. By attempting to describe and explain the precise ways participants' actions make a practical difference, impacting the continuous and negotiated character of everyday conversation, the empirical focus rests with providing evidence revealing (among other features) the inherent consequentiality of communication:

> For the target of its inquiries stands where talk amounts to action, where action projects consequences in a structure and texture of interaction which the talk is itself progressively embodying and realizing, and where the particulars of the talk inform what actions are being done and what sort of social scene is being constituted. . . . How does the fact that the talk is being conducted in some setting . . . issue in any consequences for the shape, form, trajectory, content, or character of the interaction that the parties conduct? And *what is the mechanism by which the context-so-understood has determinate consequences for the talk?* (Schegloff, 1991, pp. 46, 53; italics added)

The consequentiality of communicative actions becomes important, therefore, first for participants of interaction and second for analysts of conversational organization: not as some removed, telescopic conceptualization or component of social order, but as evident in how participants differentially and embeddedly reveal and document, each for the other, "what is going on" within a given spate of talk and in consideration of its attending relevancies (see W. Beach, 1990b, 1991a, 1995b; Jefferson, 1981; Sigman, 1995; Wootton, 1988). Stated somewhat differently, exactly what gets achieved is undeniably the upshot of how speakers fashion, shape, and make available to one another their understandings of the local environment of which they are an integral part.

Although the research assumptions undergirding these concerns are varied and complex (see, e.g., Atkinson & Heritage, 1984; Boden & Zimmerman, 1991; Drew & Heritage, 1992; C. Goodwin, 1981), the following three sets of issues briefly summarize and begin to map out relevant CA commitments and priorities.

First, CA employs research methods fashioned after the social phenomenon being examined: the independent and natural existence of social order. A basic tenet of CA is the recognition that social order, evident within the detailed and contingent activities of societal members, exists independently of social scientific inquiry. Irrespective of the possibility of being examined and in some way analytically dissected for purposes of research, interactants simply go about their daily business performing routine and often mundane tasks. Thus, CA gives priority to gaining access to social activities comprising a wide variety of natural settings. However, in order to examine such activities in "real-time" detail (i.e., on their own merits as interesting phenomena), there is a systematic reliance on carefully produced transcriptions of audio and videorecordings. Recordings and transcriptions allow for repeated hearings, viewings, and inspections of "actual and determinate" (Schegloff, 1986) interactional environments. Although neither recordings nor transcriptions are conversations in and of themselves (W. Beach, 1990b; Zimmerman, 1988), they nevertheless preserve and embody the integrity and distinctiveness of many conversational activities. Moreover, as selected fragments of transcriptions are made available for readers' critical inspections, attention can be drawn to specific details and practical consequences of unfolding actions rather than glossed or presumed versions of what might/could have happened (i.e., idealized, intuited, and/or recollected data; see Atkinson & Heritage, 1984, pp. 2–5; Heritage, 1984, pp. 234–238). Direct examinations of recorded and transcribed interactions can begin to remedy the traditional gaps and problems between what people say and what they do (see Drew & Heritage, 1992), in part by analyzing those interactional processes through which persons make available their beliefs, perceptions, and the like to one another. Rather than focusing on personality attributes brought to social occasions, or individuals' beliefs about some reconstructed occasion, attention is given to the talk-in-interaction through which these attributes and beliefs were used and relied on to achieve practical actions and in these ways organize social occasions (see W. Beach, 1989, 1990c, 1995b; Sigman, 1995).

Second, analysis of conversational involvements reveals the omnipresence of patterned orientations to "context." It becomes increasingly evident throughout the G–S analysis that, as originally described by Sacks, Schegloff, and Jefferson (1974) and further elaborated by Schegloff (1987a, 1987c, 1992), "context" is not understood as external to or otherwise exorcized from interaction (see also W. Beach, 1990c; C. Goodwin & Duranti, 1992; Mandelbaum, 1991). On the contrary, context is continually and intrinsically re-achieved as participants display their understandings of specific and locally occasioned moments of conversational involvement: Each emergent action is both *context-shaping* in the way it is tailored to prior and immediate circumstances, and *context-renewing* by means of its contribution to and thus impact on next-positioned actions. Consistent with Schegloff's (1991) reference to CA's concern with "structures of single actions and of series and sequences of them" (p. 47)—the necessity to work closely with single cases and aggregates of recurring phenomena (Schegloff, 1996a, 1996b), and in general how unique interactional circumstances reflect instances of generalized action types (see Atkinson & Drew, 1979; Mandelbaum, 1993; Whalen, Zimmerman, & Whalen, 1988)—it becomes clear that even a minimal understanding of context begins with a compilation of the following: First, whenever participants design and place their utterances within a series of actions, a speaker's current turn projects the relevance of a next turn, such that the range of possible activities accomplished by the second speaker reflect not only an orientation to, but also an understanding of, the emergent character of interaction. Second, in and through the adjacent ordering (see Heritage, 1984, pp. 245–253; Sacks, Schegloff, & Jefferson, 1974; Schegloff, 1996b) of first and second actions, utterances are seen to be "sequentially implicative" (see Schegloff & Sacks, 1973) in the exact ways that speakers systematically organize the occasions in which they are involved. During a series of turns-in-interaction, therefore, speakers design their talk to the occasion of its use and with particular recipients in mind. Finally, just as speakers rely on recipients to display whatever impact(s) speaker's utterance might have in the course of their delivery, so do recipients overwhelmingly design their talk in "conditionally relevant" ways: not just any response will normally suffice because the prior speaker projected the relevance of some range of appropriate and next actions. Of course, as talk has been found to be "sensitive to recipients' design," just how some next turn-at-talk is tailored to some prior action or set of actions becomes the "grist" for analysts' "mills" as speakers contribute to an already unfolding interactional environment.

A third and final set of issues arise from a melding of the dual focus on interaction as structurally organized and contextually oriented: "these two properties inhere in the details of interaction so that no order of detail can be dismissed, a priori, as disorderly, accidental, or irrelevant" (Heritage, 1984, p. 241). However messy and disordered naturally occurring conversations might appear, at least initially, there exists considerable evidence supporting a central tenet of social interaction studies: that there is "order at all points," much of which awaits discovery by analysts, and all of which was produced in the first instance as meaningful and thus in meaningful ways by and for interactants.[7] And considerable effort has been invested toward evidencing the bedrock details underlying the very possibility of an interactionally produced social order (but see also Goffman, 1983). Further, in turning directly to interactional materials to discover how participants

---

[7]M. H. Goodwin (1990, pp. 1–17) traced a neglect of talk-in-interaction through the history of anthropological, sociological, linguistic, and communication research. By ignoring the embedded details of interactional conduct, the diverse range of social actions achieved through talk-in-interaction are systematically excluded. Such a position is, of course, a rejection of Chomsky's (1965, pp. 3–4) well-known but misdirected assessment that "talk" per se is altogether too messy, flawed, and degenerate for studies of phenomena such as "competence."

meaningfully organize conversation, there is an unwillingness to rely on intuited or idealized data, and posit, a priori, that interaction is "driven" by
individuals' motives, needs, or other mentalistic phenomena (as was the case,
e.g., with Garfinkel's original critique and extension of Parson's treatments
of "moral norms," "need dispositions," and "personality"; see Heritage,
1984). Findings emerging from data-driven analyses tend not to be synonymous with a priori theoretical propositions. On the contrary, empirical observations drawn from naturally occurring interactions repeatedly make clear
how "theory construction," when operationalized via indirect measurements
of social processes, is frequently and overwhelmingly premature. Due to its
proclivity toward underspecification, claims and warrants about the detailed
workings of interactional activities are routinely glossed by a priori theoretical propositions and, consequently, incapable of revealing recurrent practices
and patterns of everyday talk. There is, therefore, a decided "off-stage" rather
than "atheoretical" role of theory in CA that includes a set of long-standing
debates and empirical studies (see, e.g., Alexander, Giesen, Münch, & Smelser, 1987; W. Beach, 1990c, 1991c; W. Beach & Lindstrom, 1992; Boden &
Zimmerman, 1991; Drew & Heritage, 1992; Hopper, 1989; Mehan, 1991;
Roger & Bull, 1989; Sacks, 1963, 1984a, 1984b; Schegloff, 1987b, 1991a,
1991b): for example, framing "culture and/or institution" as some externalized causal agents predetermining actions and their consequences, versus situating "culture and/or institution" as ongoing, methodically produced, locally
occasioned, inherently accountable, altogether practical achievements. These
traditional "macro–micro" debates (e.g., involving matters of power, status,
role, gender, class, bureaucracy, or, as with the present analysis, the social
context of bulimic illness and grandparent caregiving) will no doubt continue
to receive considerable attention and are not limited to CA and traditionally
quantitative studies (e.g., see Clayman & Maynard, 1994; Zimmerman &
Boden, 1991). Consistent with concerns regarding premature theory construction, therefore, close inspection of the interaction between G and S has
given rise to subsequent generalizations and broader theoretical discussions.

Toward the Identification of Institutionally Relevant
"Constraint Systems" in Casual (Family) Talk

Having laid grounds for understanding the basic research assumptions of CA,
attention can now be given to previewing centrally important and distinctive
features of the G–S interaction: how medical and thus institutionally relevant
concerns with "bulimia" emerge, and are interactionally managed, between
two family members; the recognizable "constraint systems" at work in the G–S
conversation, what might roughly be characterized as the "bureaucratization
of casual relationships." On the one hand, there is nothing remarkable about
interactions of these sort because it is altogether normal for family members

to talk about and work through medical problems. But on the other hand, these data are remarkable due to the very fact that so little is known about such interactions (i.e., the social organization of family interactions addressing "institutional" matters "informally").

Families represent the elemental and thus primordial societal institution: Family interactions routinely operate as a site for the exercise of "authority" and the pursuit of role-specific, agenda-relevant, task-related activities (see Maynard, 1988; Spear, 1973). Drew and Heritage (1992) clearly articulated how institutional interactions are not restricted to specific kinds of settings:

> Just as people in a workplace may talk together about matters unconnected with their work, so too places not usually considered "institutional," for example a private home, may become the settings for work-related interactions. Thus the institutionality of an interaction is not determined by its setting. Rather, interaction is institutional insofar as participants' institutional or professional identities are somehow made relevant to the work activities in which they are engaged. (pp. 3–4)

Framed in this manner, what is the relevance of G and S's "institutional or professional identities" to "the work activities in which they are engaged"— and what counts as "work"?

It is from family interactions such as G and S that institutional-like conduct can be identified, first and fundamentally by contrast with other forms of casual (informal) conversations. The body of research on these topics has grown substantially since Sacks' pioneering work in the 1960s and 1970s (see Sacks, 1992), and is "brought to bear" throughout this single-case analysis. But with the G–S interaction, useful comparisons can also be made with more recent findings generated from studies within institutional (more formalized, work) occasions (see Drew & Heritage, 1992; Markova & Foppa, 1991): Interactions whose describable features reveal the social organization of marked and specifiable constraints when compared to casual conversations (e.g., see Greatbach, 1992; Heritage & Greatbach, 1991). Particular attention has been given to how "professional–lay" persons (e.g., lawyers–witnesses, judges–defendants, doctors–patients, therapists–clients, news interviewers–interviewees, health visitors–firsttime parents) are routinely caught up in task-related interactions wherein one or more participants is a formal representative of a given organization or bureaucracy. It is an overwhelming and thus distinctive feature of these interactions that professionals work to accomplish the occupational tasks and agendas germane to the institutions they represent. And the more formalized the interactions (e.g., in courts, classrooms, and news interviews), the more restrictive the turn-taking regulations and, consequently, the more "constraints" imposed on lay person's conduct. These constraints reflect the often "asymmetric" and authoritative nature of institutional interactions: Professionals typically engage in such actions as asking more questions, displaying more specialized knowledge and vocabulary than lay persons, and conduct themselves as institutionally priviliged and empowered representatives whose job it is (in part) to "take control" of interaction. This description applies equally well to judges processing cases (see W. Beach, 1995a), doctors managing diagnostic interviews, and news interviewers soliciting information from interviewees. Thus, the interactional work involved in setting and regulating agendas, initiating and restricting elaboration of topics, and imposing "sanctions" (Drew & Heritage, 1992, p. 27) on lay persons' actions that depart from formalized institutional procedures are normalized responsibilities for professionals (and, as becomes evident, concerned family members).

Contrasted with courtroom interaction, for example, where it is typically the case that "modifications to or departures from conversational organization" (Atkinson & Drew, 1979, p. 228) are most clearly evident in recurrent and formalized speech exchange and enforced constraints (e.g., witnesses being instructed to respond directly to lawyers' questions, or being limited in the types of questions they can ask), with G and S what might be described as primordial constraint systems "at work" in the family are evident. Although it was earlier noted that G is also an RN, we can now raise questions (and offer a preview) of how that professional identity is reoccasioned in the family system, and relied on as a resource when laying grounds for the reasonableness of, and need for, S to admit her problem and seek professional (medical) advice and assistance. Just as G's actions can be shown not to be solicited by S but nevertheless (and persistently so) offered by G, so will it become evident that S does not directly request "help." The "interrogation-like" character and quality of portions of the G–S conversation can usefully reveal how G makes it her business to address and resolve S's abnormal family conduct, and how such actions are less formal and constrained than courtroom involvements, but also more formal and constrained than family or other casual interactions wherein agenda, role, and task-specific (e.g., medically relevant) concerns are less apparent. Moreover, when considering the nature of G's queries and S's responses to them, specifically in the ways S can be understood to be avoiding and otherwise discounting G's efforts (e.g., by claiming that Gramma is "so full of shit" and "weird"), it is shown that this family interaction is obviously less restrictive than most formal and even nonformal institutional involvements between professional and lay persons (e.g., see Atkinson & Drew, 1979; Byrne & Long, 1976; Drew & Heritage, 1992; Erickson & Schultz, 1982; Heath, 1986; Sudnow, 1972). And with G and S representing a grandparent–grandchild interaction, not only does no formalized agent–client relationship exist but it is clearly the case that S (allegedly the one "in trouble" due to bulimic tendencies) did not willingly seek out G as a professional whose expertise may aid in remedying or assisting whatever troubles exist. The G–S interaction thus stands in contrast with service encounters (see Jefferson & Lee, 1981), 911 emergency phone calls (see Whalen et al., 1988; Zimmerman, 1992), the possibly unwanted assistance of British Health Visitors visiting firsttime mothers (see Heritage & Sefi, 1992), as well as patients' involuntary visits with psychiatrists during intake interviews (see Bergmann, 1992). Here and elsewhere, there may very well be consequences of unasked-for assistance, such as troubles with offering and receiving diagnosis and advice (see Bergmann, 1992; Heritage & Sefi, 1992; Peräkylä, 1993).

Finally, Labov and Fanshel's (1977) analysis of a 15-minute psychotherapeutic interview, between a therapist and patient clinically diagnosed as anorexic nervosa, offers a germane backdrop for this present study but also a distinct methodological contrast. In an attempt to identify the kinds of speech acts performed by therapist and patient (e.g., admissions, evaluations, challenges, denials), attention was given to how speakers come to understand "surface forms" of the actions achieved through single utterances as well as linkages between utterances. This required the development of (largely unexplicated) "translation rules" to determine utterance functions, including considerable interpretive work involved in assessing speakers' intentions as uttered and as connected with subsequent and thus locally removed actions in the interview. However, a close reading of Labov and Fanshel's (1977) analysis of speech act functions (see also Searle, 1969, 1987) fails, in numerous cases, to provide support for the kinds of claims forwarded (see W. Beach, 1990b; Drew & Heritage, 1992; Levinson, 1980, 1981, 1983, 1992; Schegloff, 1988, 1992; Streeck, 1980): Not only do the constituent features of "challenges" or "counterchallenge" remain largely unexplicated (e.g., see pp. 202–207), but interactional relationships between utterances-in-sequence (as with "assertion–denial") focus on researchers' "translation rules" at the expense of understanding what and how speakers treat specific moments and contingencies as relevant or problematic.

SUMMARY AND IMPLICATIONS FOR STUDY

The evolution of this study represents a shift from specific and local concerns with how G and S interactionally occasioned matters of bulimia and caregiving, toward an understanding of the daily consequences and thus far reaching significance of these inherently social processes for family members as well as researchers, clinicians, and practitioners alike who deal routinely with family medical predicaments. Early on in my search for cumulative research findings it became clear that, aside from gaining a fundamental grasp of and appreciation for extant literature, the need to "find bulimia" by identifying features of social action was mandated. A special concern was with the omnipresence of conversations about illness in everyday life as family members talked through ongoing medical problems, informally, preferably in their home environments. However, an articulation of patterns (i.e., constituent practices) of the everyday interactional activities that bulimics, their families and friends, and caregivers in general (with an eye toward grandparents) get routinely caught up in was noticeably absent. Although specific sorts of puzzles had emerged from direct analysis of the G–S conversation—What specific interactional techniques for raising, avoiding, and being preoccupied with bulimia had been identified? Are other conversations regarding bulimia and caregiving organized in similar fashion? Just how representative and typical was the G–S conversation as an exemplar of how family members work through versions of and concerns about bulimia?—this post hoc search for previously identified features of social action was accutely naive. The upshot of asking these questions was, perhaps, quite predictable: Despite the rich texture of basic and applied research on eating disorders and family caregiving, prior studies had not relied on naturalistic, interactional methodologies for pursuing inherently conversational problems and the often delicate yet complex ways family members sought to remedy them. It is perhaps worth noting that across nearly 300 reviewed sources (only a sampling of which are included in the aforementioned review), not a single study was found that directly examined interactions between either family members expressing bulimic concerns or grandparent–grandchildren conversations on any set of health-care topics. Just as descriptions have thus far been provided of the predominant reliance on psychologically based self-report and field interview data as methods for understanding the social causes and consequences germane to bulimia and caregiving, so should the need for detailed explications of naturally occurring conversations about illness be self-evident.

The fundamental task thus remains to reveal what the study of interaction might offer to understandings of both bulimia and grandparent caregiving as social processes. Attention can now be given to an extended analysis of the G–S conversation, especially how activities characterized in most general terms—for example, initiation, confrontation, avoidance, denial, and preoccupation—are in practice detailed and organized achievements embedded within yet more complex interactional environments.

2

▼▼▼▼▼▼▼

From Troubles to Problems

. . . it's a really non-incidental fact in our society that troubles are formed up as "things happening in a family."

—Sacks (1992a, p. 798)

The following interactional segment occurs 2½ minutes into the conversation between the grandmother and Sissy (see appendix for transcribing conventions and the entire G–S transcript):

Excerpt 1 (SDCL:G/S: 115–122)

```
G:   We:ll Sissy. (0.8) let's ↓ face it no:w
     yo:u kno:w .hh that ch'u are so: e::ager:.
     (.) to be thin:. (0.2) that you sometimes. go in
     the bathroom. (0.2) and throw up your food?
     I kno:w it's tr[ u e ]!
S:                  [GR]AMMA YOU ARE SO:: FULL
     O(F) SHIT! I am so: su:r e.
```

The actions comprising these two turns-at-talk are a microcosm of the G–S conversation; although not exhaustive, this interactional moment reveals typical resources relied on by G and S in the course of displaying contradictory, interactionally asynchronous orientations to this particular matter at hand, but also the central "problem": "throwing up." Even a brief inspection of this excerpt (see also chapter 4) allows for the identification of recurrent issues for G and S, and thus serves as a preview of matters taken up in considerably more detail in this and following chapters.

For example, from Excerpt 1 consider how G makes out S's problem to be one that can be faced by G and S together, constructs common knowledge by attributing knowledge to S while also claiming its truth, attributes S's motive "to be thin," and offers specific observed evidence about S's going into the bathroom to throw up her food. In response, notice that S discounts and claims disbelief, essentially discrediting and challenging the viability of G's assertions; she also avoids the matter at hand by delaying an explanation, neither admitting nor denying "throwing up."

The kinds of actions evident in Excerpt 1 are not uncommon across a wide variety of everyday interactions. On occasions when a first speaker is understood to be alleging wrongdoing toward another, and/or is treated by another as having performed such an utterance, one typical course of action involves a rejection-implicative next response by second speaker (e.g., denying, avoiding, delaying, justifying, counterchallenging/accusing). Early evidence of this type of adjacent response (see Sacks et al., 1974; Schegloff, 1968; Schegloff & Sacks, 1973) has, over time, repeatedly surfaced across rather diverse sets of conversational and institutional interactions, involving a wide variety of naturally occurring activities, and displays an identifiable shape to its organization. Such activities have included, for example, recipient's minimizing responsibility and wrongdoing attributed by first speaker's report of being inconvenienced,[1]

Excerpt 2 (D.Z.:1) (Pomerantz, 1978a, p. 115) ((arrow added))

```
    D:   Yeh that's what yih told me
         Thanks a lot ha ha [hhh
→   Z:                      [N:o no last semester
         they kept it open on Friday night
```

accusation/minimizing response pairs during female gossip confrontations in a corpus of dispute activities among urban Black children,

Excerpt 3 (Maple Street group) (M. H. Goodwin, 1980, p. 677) ((arrow added))

```
    Ter:  Well cuz you- you said that she wrote it.
→   Flo:  UHUH. UHUH CUZ I ONLY WROTE ONE THING IN RED.
```

---

[1]Utterances attributing responsibility and wrongdoing for being inconvenienced have been found to appear prior to turns more fully addressing the problem at hand, just as a shift in attribution focus may occur to an absent third party (e.g., to a professor's negligence in lieu of pursuing cointeractants' responsibility for having been inconvenienced at the computer center; see Pomerantz, 1978a; see also Mandelbaum, 1993). By means of contrast with the case of G and S, although it was not uncommon for S to attempt shifts of focus and topic so as to do "getting off" troubling topics (see chapter 4), G failed to willingly cooperate in such ventures by repeatedly and persistently holding S accountable for her actions.

as well as reciprocal counters among male children such as a challenge/threat with second speaker's counter to it,

> Excerpt 4 (Maple Street Group) (M. H. Goodwin, 1990, p. 242) ((arrow added))
>
> > Chop: Ah you better sh:ut <u>up</u> with your
> > little- <u>di</u>:ngy sneaks.
> > (1.4)
> > → Tony: I'm a <u>dingy your hea:d.=How would you
> > like <u>that</u>.

and the placement of denials in excerpt 5 and counterassertions in Excerpt 6 to prior announcements in children's arguments:

> Excerpt 5 (Wilkinson data) (Maynard, 1985, p. 13) ((arrows added))
>
> > Don: You're a pig, know why
> > Jim: Why
> > Don: You're hoggin' everything
> > → Jim: I am not
> > Don: Yes you are

> Excerpt 6 (p. 20)
>
> > Ralph: Barb you- you don't beg people of-
> > invite- vite you over
> > → Barb: I'm not begging
> > Ralph: Yes you are

And in institutional involvements such as courtroom cross-examination, witnesses provide justifications/excuses,

> Excerpt 7 (ST:96, 16C) (Atkinson & Drew, 1979, p. 137; Drew, 1978)
>
> > C: You saw this newspaper shop being bombed on
> > the front of Davis Street?
> > W: Yes.
> > C: How many petrol bombs were thrown into it?
> > → W: Only a couple. I felt that the window was
> > already broken and that there was part of it
> > burning and this was a re-kindling of the flames.
> > C: What did you do at that point?
> > → W: I was not in a very good position to do
> > anything. We were under gunfire at the time.

and alternative descriptions to what lawyers were understood to be achieving in prior (accusatory) queries:

Excerpt 8 (Da:Ou:45/2B:2) (Drew, 1985, p. 138)

C: An you went to a: uh (0.9) ah you went to a
ba:r? (in) Boston (0.6) iz that correct?
        (1.0)
→ W: It's a clu:b.
     .
     .
     .

C: It's where uh (.) uh (0.3) gi:rls and fella:s
meet, isn't it?
        (0.9)
→ W: People go: there.

The turns marked by arrows reflect a range of circumstances in which second speakers withhold displays of agreement (e.g., by not admitting to and/or apologizing for an alleged wrongdoing) in orientation to their actions having been called into question. In these ways, minimizations of responsibility are recipient designed to what prior speakers were understood to have projected in their initial utterance. In turn, these minimizations are positioned adversarially, oppositionally, or combatively (see Atkinson & Drew, 1979; Drew, 1985; M. H. Goodwin, 1982, 1983; C. Goodwin & Goodwin, 1990; Maynard, 1985; Pomerantz, 1989). Within such sequential environments, second speakers' actions may not only display an orientation to problematic features of prior utterance(s), but also be designed so as to mitigate or even cancel the projected force giving rise to response in the first instance (see Heritage, 1989). Disaffiliative utterances of this type may be oriented to by first speaker as next speaker's unwillingness to agree or defer, but also as functioning to delay and possibly avoid addressing first speaker's concerns (see Pomerantz, 1984a; see also 1978b). These features mark the uniquely disaffiliative, and inevitably collaboratively produced, character of alleging and responding to alleged wrongdoings and/or challenging/threatening as in Excerpt 4.

However, the G–S interaction does possess unique features. For example, although it is not normally just anyone's business what another does with his or her "body," there are circumstances (such as G–S) where claiming intimacy is a matter of making it one's legitimate business to seek and offer concerns about otherwise privatized information. In this way G is making herself out not to be a stranger, but as claiming the right to raise the "problem" she is alleging S to have. In addition, as becomes apparent later, she is also claiming the right to overcome S's displayed resistance and unwillingness to talk about such private "problems" (see Sacks, 1992, p. 194).

This chapter examines the very beginning of the G–S conversation to gain an understanding of how G constructs an accusation of S's "throwing up," as evident in Excerpt 1. The analysis begins by focusing on how G initiates talk about the problem of bulimia by treating S's talk and action as motivated by the desire to lose weight—by asking questions, seeking answers, and/or making observations seeking responses tied to G's concerns regarding S's health. And in the noticeable absence of the sought-after answers or responses from S, G begins to reveal the nature of her difficulty by nevertheless arguing with and countering the alleged bulimic problem evident in Excerpt 1. Attention is drawn to G's initial practices for indirectly bringing her "case" to S, talk ultimately designed to insure that S treats G as informed and takes her seriously (see chapter 3), such that G and S might eventually and mutually identify the existence and problematic nature of bulimia and agree to possible solutions for it.[2] Analysis reveals how G's repeatedly stated concerns with S's health are consequential in shifting from talk about S's troubles to more encompassing "problems" with bulimia (see Jefferson, 1988; Jefferson & Lee, 1981), including S's lack of responsibility in coming to grips with her illness.

From the outset, it thus becomes clear how "troubles" are topically generative and transformed into interactional "problems"—for example, when business as usual (i.e., S's twice inviting G for a walk in the morning) is transformed by G into the business at hand (i.e., as an occasion to initiate pursuit of related matters and particular concerns with S's thinness; see Button & Casey, 1988–1989). But throughout the G–S conversation, this kind of predicament is often reversed. For example, G's articulation of the troubling need for S to seek professional help becomes problematic in the ways S discounts and fails to make a commitment to see a doctor or therapist. It should be made clear, therefore, that each speaker routinely withholds alignment from other's stated concerns and troubles. Ongoing disaffiliations repeatedly illustrate the emergence of interactional problems as both G and S attempt to seek alignment not offered by the other, and thus the shift from troubles to problems is omnipresent as G and S coauthor their orientations to emergent topics.

OCCASIONING "THE PROBLEM"

How did the alleged problem of "throwing up food" in Excerpt 1 emerge interactionally? What gave rise to G's explicit mentioning of this problem,

---

[2]An interesting parallel case to G soliciting S to take her seriously as a necessary means for mobilizing "healthy" actions, is found in Sacks' (1992) analysis of calls to an Emergency Psychiatric Center. However, Sacks reveals how it is the task of suicidal callers to convince call-takers to not only take interest in their case but also to take them seriously, a predominant feature of such agent–client relationships, and as described more fully here a clear reversal of the G–S interaction where S is not directly seeking "help." In regards to a caller's receiving "help" and "feeling better," Sacks (1992) observed: "And the question I've been trying to get to here is, why in the world should he care about that, and how does she bring him to care about that, so that in fact, in the end, the two of them have accomplished that" (p. 395).

and (eventually) to the contradictory and asynchronous courses of action evident in G and S's displayed orientations? The following segment initiated the G/S discussion:

Excerpt 9 (SDCL:G/S:1–16)

```
        G:   Si:ssy what? > time. do you have
             to go to work in the morning. <
                    (1.0)
        S:   I have ta be there at ni::ne.
             > so I think I'll pro(bl)y get up
             a li(tt)le bit < e:arlier. (0.5)
1→           .hh and maybe > i:f I get up e:arly enough <
             you gon(na) go for a ↑ wa:lk with me
                    (0.6)
2→      G:   A wa:lk? (0.5) my goodness (.)
             you're on your feet e:ight hours a d:ay?
             (0.2) > you don't even have a place to sit do(wn)?
             whadda you wanna go for a walk
             that's like the postman goin for a walk
             on (his) day off? <
```

At the outset, G queries S and in so doing requests information regarding what time S is going to work in the morning. Although S's initial response addresses G's query, she then invites G for a walk (1→). As recipient G neither accepts nor rejects S's invitation (2→). Instead, she initiates an alternative course of action, one instance of a rejection-implicative response that, although implicit and therefore indirect, is not necessarily "passive" (Heritage & Sefi, 1992). The (0.6) silence following S's invitation (1→) may be taken to be a signal of potential rejection (Davidson, 1984; Drew, 1984; Pomerantz, 1984a). Similarly, in the way G's repair initiator, "A wa:lk?" (2→), challenges S's prior invitation it may be understood as a "delay device" projecting a disagreement-relevant reponse to the prior utterance (Pomerantz, 1984a, pp. 70–71).

But there is more here. By prefacing what follows with emphasis and even surprise ("my goodness") and moving next to provide supporting evidence of her concerns ("on your feet . . . no place to sit down"), G raises and thus queries S's motivation for walking as a seeming upshot of S's invitation—G leaves it for S to figure out what G might be "up to," failing to make explicit (i.e., to formulate the "upshot"; Drew, 1984, p. 146) of what S's invitation was taken to implicate—as though it were consequential and not a premeditated or purposeful attempt by G to address some problem.[3] However, spe-

---

[3]It is possible that G initially took advantage of the recording session—perhaps as an attempt to generate a "record" of the event, to raise concerns held but not previously articulated, and/or as an aid for soliciting admittance and commitment to seek help from S—by immediately

cifically asking about someone's motivation ("whadda you wanna go for a walk") often involves nontrivial interactional work (see also Heritage & Sorjonen, 1994). On this occasion (but also invoked repeatedly by G, as addressed in subsequent chapters), G asks a question seeking an answer tied to the "problem." As will become clear, the very fact that G may hear S's invitation to "go for a walk" as somehow related to the problem of "throw[ing] up" and thus "bulimia" reveals G's preoccupation (see chapter 5) with a set of circumstances both S and G are variously caught up in. In these ways G's "information seeking" might be understood as purposeful and motivated by some warranting circumstance involving S and her actions (i.e., some problematic or potentially problematic set of conditions with which G is curious about, concerned with, interested in, and/or committed to resolving). And as evident in Excerpt 1, by virtue of the fact that G understands S to be driven by the desire to lose weight, G treats S's invitation as motivationally troubling and thus grounds for challenging what may otherwise appear to be an innocent, even altruistic, invitation to go for a walk.

In Excerpt 2 G (as invitation-recipient) refrains from making "official" her position; she thereby initates a course of action soliciting S to address what G has now occasioned, albeit indirectly and unofficially. One practical and immediate consequence of G questioning S's "walking," now made available for S's consideration, is G's position that going for a walk is unwise in light of S's working on her feet and not being able to sit down and relax. In fact, the very possibility of treating "walking" as a relaxing activity is withheld by G, as is any interest in joining S early the next morning. By withholding an interest in this manner G challenges the legitimacy of S's proposed action, yet also solicits an explanation from S in her following turn ("whadda you wanna go for a walk"; see Pomerantz, 1980, 1988), and by so doing actually intrudes upon and thereby alters S's proposed plans and arrangements.

The construction of G's rejection-implicative turn projects at least three possible inferences made available to S as turn-recipient:

---

challenging S's invitation to go for a walk. However, the unfolding and detailed contingencies of the G/S conversation could not have been fully anticipated and planned for. And there is another parallel, curious feature here, namely, G's possible reliance on what Maynard (1989) identified as a three-part "perspective-display sequence," wherein some opinion or information is requested, provided by recipient, and relied on by asker to offer some subsequent report (see chapter 4). If a case were to be made that the perspective-display was employed by G as a "set-up" because she was previously aware of or bothered by S's walking plans, enacting the query–response in a premeditated fashion due to the "problem" she is concerned about, there would be a need to rely on extrasituational, background, or self-report data that does not exist in this instance; such a case would still require evidencing how these concerns emerged and thus were built into the very contingencies of these interactional moments.

1. The first inference involves G's concern for her granddaughter's health and welfare. Framed in this way, G might be heard as providing a caring response to S's workload;
2. The second and related inference is that G is holding S accountable for her own health and well-being, such that S may very well orient (see Excerpt 10) to G's prior turn as attributing lack of responsibility to S for her own well-being;
3. A third possible inference is that whatever G is up to, she is using her response as an opportunity to set up (i.e., gradually work into) an opportunity to query S more directly and pursue a desired response.

To summarize thus far, G questions S's motivation and thus initiates an orientation to a circumstance she treats as problematic. Her rejection-implicative response to S's invitation can be understood, in part, as relying on the invitation as an opportunity to raise and pursue an alternative course of action designed to address G's concerns regarding S's underlying motives and desires. In this sense, a failure to unequivocally accept or reject S's invitation is nevertheless programmatically relevant to G's reason for soliciting an explanation (i.e., her purpose for asking that remains unarticulated up to this point in the discussion; but see Excerpt 1).

Troubles and Problems

S's immediate response to G appears as (1→):

Excerpt 10 (SDCL:G/S:10–26)

```
        G:   A wa:lk? (0.5) my goodness (.)
             you're on your feet e:ight hours a d:ay?
             > you don't even have a place to sit do(wn)?
             whadda you wanna go for a walk
             that's like the postman goin for a walk
             on (his) day off? <
1→              (0.2)
1→      S:   We[ : : : (ll) ]!
2→      G:      [That's stu]pid
3→      S:   .hh > Ya but gramma you gotta realize
             I work all day out < (.) in the s:tore
             i-it's nice to get outside .hh
             ((clears throat)) where it's (.)
             ↑ you know fresh air and stuff. .hh
4→           come on > j(us)t get up and go for a walk
             we'll have a cup o(f) coffee before we go::? <
```

Marked by a slight delay (0.2) and prefaced "We:::(ll)," this orientation indicates a disagreement-relevant response as well as some degree of reluctance or discomfort on S's part (see Pomerantz, 1984a; also see chapter 4). But even in the absence of a fuller response by S, G's "That's stupid" (2→) (actually tagged onto her prior utterance) displays a strong negative assessment of S's prior (and seemingly innocent) invitation to "go for a walk," an assessment to which S (3→) offers (not surprisingly) an explanation designed to normalize, justify and thus reconcile G's previously stated concerns. In these ways, S's (3→) is but one example of an account (see Atkinson & Drew, 1979; Buttny, 1994; Heritage, 1983, 1988; also see chapter 4), produced in this place and manner so as to mitigate what G was taken to be "up to" in not accepting and even challenging S's walking invitation (i.e., a display of caring for S's workload, holding S accountable for her health). As is the case within cross-examinations in courts (see Excerpts 7 & 8), it is not uncommon for recipients of accusatory utterances (witnesses) to respond to (lawyers') queries with excuses and justifications substantiating their own actions (Atkinson & Drew, 1979; Drew, 1992). Questions are routinely employed as devices for preallocating wrongdoing to recipients, in response to which actions of accountability frequently emerge (see chapter 4). In the case of Excerpt 10 (3→) S's response is positioned accordingly, essentially providing what S clearly takes to be a rational basis for action (i.e., store → walking → fresh air). Rationally, then, S next reissues her invitation to G in the context of Excerpt 10 (4→), as reprinted here,

Excerpt 11 (SDCL:G/S:25–26)

4→   come on > j(us)t get up and go for a walk
      we'll have a cup o(f) coffee before we go::? <

imploring further with "come on" and (for many) the prerequisite "coffee before" technique.

Several additional observations can be offered regarding S's recycled invitation. First, as noted previously, S's original invitation (Excerpt 9, 1→) did not receive a direct or positive response from G. As more fully addressed in chapter 3, failed attempts to achieve desired action can prompt further pursuit (see Pomerantz, 1984c). A subsequent version (by S) to a prior potential rejection (by G) is now offered so as to make the original formulation more desirable and acceptable (see Davidson, 1984). Second, the recycled invitation is latched onto S's account, perhaps as a method for delaying and/or drawing attention away from G's original query: "whadda you wanna go for a walk" (Excerpt 3, 2→). Finally, S's recycled invitation is similar to what Schegloff (1984, pp. 40–41) termed a *redo invitation*: It invites the last speaker to repeat some prior operation and come up with a "different output." One means for S to check whether or not her "rational" account (Excerpt 10, 3→) functioned to satisfy G's query is to once again attempt the invitation.

So doing prompts yet another response from G and, in turn, S's reaction:

Excerpt 12 (SDCL:G/S:25–40)

```
        S:    .

              .
              .
              come on > j(us)t get up and go for a walk
              we'll have a cup o(f) coffee before we go::? <
                    (1.0)
1→      G:    Well honey yer so thin: no:w:
                    (0.6)
2→      G:    I don(t) kno:w (.) I think yer just (0.2)
              °(well you're)° just wearin yourself out
              with all your activity > I think if you
              slo:w down a li(tt)le bit and rest a little bit
              more <
                    (0.4)
3→      S:    GRA:[M M A] YOU'RE SO WEIRD!
        G:        [ Maybe ]
4→      S:    > I don't even know why you say that I- <
              .hh I am f:i::ve thr:ee:: and I still
              weigh a hundred an ten- fifteen po:unds?
```

Following yet another noticeable (1.0) pause and "Well" preface, an acceptance to S's invitation is withheld for the second time. In Excerpt 12 (1→),
however, the rejection-implicative work built into G's response essentially
disregards S's reported trouble (i.e., store → walking → fresh air). In the
absence of a prior answer from S tied to the as yet unarticulated "problem,"
G's observations nevertheless begin to argue with the "problem's" very existence. Although not embedded within a query, G's "Well honey yer so
thin: no:w:" provides, for the first time in the G–S conversation, a candidate
symptom underlying G's concern with S not walking. And though S has
ample opportunity to respond if not altogether deny what such a symptom
might imply, such action is withheld by S in the next (0.6) transition relevant
pause (see also chapter 4). This withholding prompts G to argue further by
offering an additional assessment and advice (Excerpt 12, 2→). Here, an
alternative rationality is proposed: G treats a walk as inappropriate when S
is already too thin, is wearing herself out, and needs rest (i.e., walk → thin
→ wearing herself out → rest). It is in this way that G, as troubles-recipient,
fails to commiserate and align herself with S's trouble telling, essentially fore-
shortening what S treats as troublesome in favor of becoming an advice-giver.
And here it is seen that S is increasingly the unwilling recipient of G's prof-
fered remedies.

   In short, S's redo invitation did prompt different output from G. Although
G's response withheld sympathy and moved toward the giving of advice, it
nevertheless provided further information for S to assess in making sense of

not only G's apparent unwillingness to go for a walk, but also an "odd" information seeking strategy. With slight delay (0.4), S (for the first time) discounts G's concerns in wholesale fashion via "GRA:MMA YOU'RE SO WEIRD!" (3→), followed by a statement of disbelief and S's second account defending her actions (4→). Yet exactly what's "at stake" still remains unexplicated up to this point in the conversation;[4] in Excerpt 12 both G (2→) and S (4→) claim they "don't know." As is obvious, G's purposes for asking remain disguised, as do S's sources of reluctance or discomfort.

Situating the G–S Interaction

It is important to note that transformations from troubles tellings to problems delivering and receiving advice are exceedingly common (see Heritage & Sefi, 1992; Jefferson & Lee, 1981; Maynard, 1988); matters of trouble and help have been a predominant concern of studies focusing on the interactional organization of mundane conversation as well as institutional involvements. Although only limited attention can be given here to otherwise detailed findings, a brief overview allows for a more precise understanding of the distinctive character of the G–S interaction.

Beginning with Sacks' (1992) early examinations of phone calls to a suicide prevention center and an emergency psychiatric clinic, CA attention has been given to how lay persons/clients requiring attention seek out aid and perhaps consolation from others, agents presumably interested in and capable of offering professional assistance in addressing troubling matters, who rely on various techniques for assessing the nature of such troubles and ways of remedying them. Recurring problems, such as how to solicit descriptions about the predicaments of those in need of help, whether or not to take others seriously, and the delicate relationship between problems described and solutions offered, have been shown to involve a host of conversational features designed specifically for just such troubling occasions.

In studies of "talk about troubles," a predominant concern rests with how speakers go about reporting some problematic set of circumstances they have observed, experienced, may have grievances about, and in general have difficulties dealing with. Across a wide variety of mundane conversations, Jefferson (1980a, 1980b, 1984a, 1984b, 1988) extended Sacks' work to convincingly reveal how speakers in some sort of trouble (e.g., going to the dentist, getting hurt, being burglarized), and/or reporting others' troubles with which they are dealing (e.g., domestic problems, terminal illness), voluntarily set-up

---

[4]The expression "at stake" is an unintentional "pun" here; the relationship to "stake/steak" in the midst of writing about "throwing up" and "bulimia" was not purposeful, even though the connection with "food" was later apparent. Although textual, this offers a single instance of the kinds of phenomena addressed in chapter 5 regarding how "preoccupations" find their way into such tasks as "describing" and "explaining."

and subsequently report those troubles. In turn, recipients collaboratively negotiate their degree of receptiveness and "whether or when, and under what auspices (e.g., first or third party) the trouble will be told, thus providing for the recipient's participation in the shaping of the troubles talk" (Jefferson, 1980b, p. 183). As active coparticipants, recipients variably informed about the nature or status of another's predicament may initiate talk by inquiring about the trouble (Jefferson, 1988, pp. 421–422), even attempting to guess the nature of the not-yet-delivered bad news (Schegloff, 1988). In addition to G and S, numerous moments have been identified where recipients provide nonsympathetic hearings by withholding affiliation/alignment (i.e., receptiveness) with actions solicited by troubles tellers, such as when commiseration with a prior complaint is noticeably absent (see Drew & Holt, 1988; Mandelbaum, 1991) and/or even failing to offer advice when requested and thereby withholding collaboration in remedying a reported trouble (see chapter 5).

Taken as a whole, it has thus far been demonstrated that (as with G and S here) although trouble tellers may have difficulty soliciting the nature and degree of affiliation/alignment from recipients of candidate reportings—so as to better insure adequate hearings of their concerns, anxieties, problems, and so on—the source of the candidate troubles being talked about rests not with recipients themselves but with other problematic matters (e.g., trouble teller's "my world" problems with health, money, relatives, being victimized, getting married). Further, although it is apparent that recipients routinely display understanding and identification with trouble-teller's predicaments, at times offering shared experiences (e.g., by means of trouble tellings touched-off or triggered by reported problems, see Jefferson, 1978; or through "recipient-driven" queries; Mandelbaum, 1989), data examined have only begun to reveal how such troubles may also originate with what are constructed as problematic actions enacted by recipient; where the inception and subsequent explicit focus of original recipient of troubling concerns and anxieties (G) become redirected toward troubles teller's (S's) alleged wrongdoings as the trouble source (e.g., with eating disorders, alcoholism, drug abuse).

For example, Jefferson and Lee (1981) demonstrated that, whereas in casual talk the offering of emotional reciprocity by recipient to troubles teller may be accepted, when trouble tellers seek advice in service encounters difficulties may arise. This is especially so when agency personnel attempt to "humanize" the delivery of advice (e.g., "unwarranted affiliation compounded by inept servicing," p. 546). In short:

> Cross-environment profferings of reciprocity or advice turn out to be problematic. Unless, as in the archetypal tribal situation, the advice giver one is consulting happens also to be a proper troubles recipient (e.g., a friend or relative), it appears that adequate management of a "trouble" must be achieved by a shunting between two distinctive but problematically convergent envi-

ronments. And the occurrence of elements of one environment in talk appropriate to the other may constitute attempts to repair perceived inadequacies
of each. (p. 546)

But with G and S, it is due only partially to G self-nominating and thus
taking on the institutional authority both of grandmother and (eventually)
as registered nurse that a "shunting between two distinctive but problemati-
cally convergent environments," as described here by Jefferson and Lee, exists. As a result of G attending not as sympathetic troubles recipient but as
unsolicited advice giver, S must deal with being both advice-recipient and
problem source.

PROBLEMS WITH UNSOLICITED ASSISTANCE

Heritage and Sefi's (1992) analysis of the dilemmas of giving and receiving
advice, involving interactions between community nurses and firsttime mothers, offers a rich resource for understanding basic features of advice giv-
ing/receiving sequences. It also allows for a contrast with more informal family interactions such as G and S wherein, as noted (see chapter 1), G's
institutional authority is not official even though caregiving can and often
does involve the imposition of role, agenda, and task-related activities.

Because it is the institutional directive of health visitors (HVs) to evaluate
and assist mothers, the nurses studied by Heritage and Sefi (1992) are shown
to unilaterally initiate and warrantably occasion unasked-for advice, "as a
central 'ticket of entry' to mothers' homes" (p. 413). Such advice-giving is
initiated as a partial consequence of mothers' replies indicating possible problems requiring attention, but also even when clear-cut problems cannot be
identified in mothers' replies. One predominant and likely counterproductive
upshot of such advice-giving, owing in part to mothers' responses to having
their knowledge and competence questioned and challenged, is "that fully
three-quarters of all the HV-initiated advice met with either passive or active
resistance" (p. 410).

Additional and more specific contrasts with Heritage and Sefi's (1992)
findings regarding giving and receiving advice emerge from consideration of
the basic step-by-step "advice-giving sequence" between HVs and mothers
(p. 379):

Step 1: HV: initial inquiry
Step 2: M: problem-indicative response
Step 3: HV: focusing inquiry into the problem
Step 4: M: response detailing
Step 5: HV: advice giving

An extended instance involving "bathing," appears here:

Excerpt 13 (1C1:39) (Heritage & Sefi, 1992, p. 379) ((arrows as in original format))

```
HV:   1→   And you feel- (0.3) you're alright ba:thing
           (.) her?
M:    2→   I haven't bathed her ye:t.
HV:        Haven't you real[ ly. ]
M:    2→                   [No:.] She had a bath when
      2→   she came home from hospital (0.2) but I top
      2→   and tail her.
HV:        Ye:h=
M:    2→   =but uhm: me mum's coming over tomorro:w (.)
      2→   and I'm gonna ba:th her in front of me mum
      2→   'cos I'm (still) a little bi:t (.) you
      2→   kno:w [(    )]
HV:   3→         [ Did ] they show you how to bath
      3→   her [°(when you were in)°]
M:        [ They di::d but (0.9) ] I: (.) still
      4→   wasn't- I said to me mum you know wuh- when
      4→   you come over tomorrow would you sort'v give
      4→   me a ha:nd you know if I nee:d it.
           (.)
HV:   5→   The main thing is: that you have the things
      5→   all together before you sta:rt.
           ((advice giving continues))
```

To briefly summarize (see Heritage & Sefi, 1992, pp. 379–380), in (1→) it can be seen that although a "no problem" response is solicited by HV's inquiry, M's (2→) reveals an inherent problem and uncertainty about giving her baby a bath. HV then further focuses on the problem (3→) that is elaborated by M (4→), and the HV's advice begins (5→). Through these emergent actions not only is a problem jointly identified, but in the way HV eventually offers advice (5→) a nonadversarial (i.e., noncritical) environment is constructed that falls short of holding M directly accountable for her lack of knowledge and competence in performing a routine mothering task (i.e., bathing her baby). Such is the case even when the organization of advice-giving sequences is abbreviated (as with only two of several variations identified by Heritage & Sefi, 1992, pp. 382, 386):

Step 1: HV: initial inquiry
Step 2: M: problem-indicative response
Step 3: HV: advice giving

———

Step 1: HV: initial inquiry
Step 2: M: "no problem" response
Step 3: HV: advice giving on "possible problem"

From these sequence-types it can be observed that HVs initiated with inquiries and, regardless of whether mothers' response indicated a problem, nevertheless moved next to offer advice. There is, therefore, a certain persistence displayed by these nurses, explained in part by their training (i.e., to identify, diagnose, and treat "problems"). But as Heritage and Sefi (1992, pp. 411–413) argued, a combination of other contributing factors influence the giving and receiving of advice, including an overly pessimistic and defensive stance toward firsttime mothers, a corallary assumption of expertise by nurses, and the inherent equivocality of both the HVs' role and the mothers' orientations to being invaded and under surveillance.

Contrasting these nurse–mother interactions with G and S, focus is drawn to how it is that G pursues and S avoids addressing problems associated with bulimia. Here it is important to reiterate that as a distinctive feature of G and S, the source of G's attention is S's alleged health predicament: G's moving from troubles recipient to advice giver, and attributor of a bulimic problem, is tantamount to building a case for S's responsibility to care for herself having not been fulfilled.

In contrast to G and S, specific features of the HV interactions are significant. First, both G's inquiries/assertions and S's apparent resistance are more directly offered and clearly, in turn, rejection-implicative. Heritage and Sefi (1992), however, characterized HVs' actions as uncritical and, in turn, identified only a single instance where a mother overtly rejected advice offered by nurses. This is a marked contrast to S's description of G as "weird" in Excerpt 5 (3→), "full of shit" response in Excerpt 1, and what are clearly ongoing and recognizably contradictory orientations displayed by S throughout this conversation (see chapters 3 and 4).

Second, the G–S interaction provides clear and relevant markers of "the tribal archetypal situation" alluded to by Jefferson and Lee (1981, p. 456) in two key ways: (a) although clearly family members, a formally designated institutional authority figure is not present in G–S, even though G is a registered nurse by profession and relies on such background and knowledge in the course of attempting to overcome S's resistance (see chapter 3); and (b) compared with nurses who are strangers engaging mothers for the first time, the basic familiarity and thus informality of family interactions is recognizable, even when concerns such as "illness" are vicariously addressed.

Third, in the Heritage and Sefi (1992) corpus mothers do, at times and in various ways, initiate requests for advice from visiting nurses. In contrast, S fails to directly solicit G's advice in this 13-minute conversation. (However, in chapter 4 attention is drawn to how S queries G about her reasons for asking and overall pursuit, and thus can indirectly be heard and seen as seeking some assistance by further topicalizing the "problem.")

Finally, in contrast with the step-by-step emergence of advice-giving apparent between nurses and mothers, G and S display adjacent and contradictory orientations. This is apparent in the initial moments of the conversation (see Excerpt 9) but increasingly throughout. This grandmother–granddaughter interaction involves family members whose actions eventuate in more adversarial position-taking that reflects what was earlier characterized as one version of the "essential problematics of caregiving": Care may be offered for differing motives, and there is no guarantee that expressed concerns for another's health will be accepted and appreciated by allegedly ill recipient.

ESTABLISHING A PATTERN
OF PURSUIT AND AVOIDANCE

We are now in a position to reinspect the beginning moments of the G–S conversation by integrating Excerpts 1 through 5, and to identify the sequence organizations that are beginning to take shape, become established, and thus are distinctive to the interactional work achieved.

S's invitations are used as a point of focus. G has provided rejection-implicative responses to S's two invitations (*→), by either questioning S's motive (1→) or articulating a possible symptom and offering advice (3→):

Excerpt 14 (SDCL:G/S:1–40)

```
        G:   Si:ssy what? > time. do you have
             to go to work in the morning. <
                  (1.0)
        S:   I have ta be there at ni::ne.
             > so I think I'll pro(bl)y get up
             a li(tt)le bit < e:arlier. (0.5)
             .hh and maybe > i:f I get up e:arly enough <
*→           you gon(na) go for a ↑ wa:lk with me
                  (0.6)
        G:   A wa:lk? (0.5) my goodness (.)
             you're on your feet e:ight hours a d:ay?
             (0.2) > you don't even have a place to sit do(wn)?
1→           whadda you wanna go for a walk
             that's like the postman goin for a walk
             on (his) day off? <
                  (0.2)
2→      S:   We[ : : : (ll)  ]!
1→      G:      [That's stu]pid
2→      S:   .hh > Ya but gramma you gotta realize
             I work all day out < (.) in the s:tore
             i-it's nice to get outside .hh
             ((clears throat)) where it's (.)
             ↑ you know fresh air and stuff. .hh
*→           come on > j(us)t get up and go for a walk
             we'll have a cup o(f) coffee before we go::? <
                  (1.0)
3→      G:   Well honey yer so thin: no:w:
                  (0.6)
```

```
3→   G:   I don(t) kno:w (.) I think yer just (0.2)
          °(well you're)° just wearin yourself out
          with all your activity > I think if you
          slo:w down a li(tt)le bit and rest a little bit
          more <
                   (0.4)
4→   S:   GRA:[M  M  A] YOU'RE SO WEIRD!
     G:       [ Maybe ]
4→   S:   > I don't even know why you say that I- <
          .hh I am f:i::ve thr:ee:: and I still
          weigh a hundred an ten- fifteen po:unds?
```

The shape of this compounded (Jefferson & Lee, 1981) organization is analogous to that proposed by Davidson (1984) in her examination of invitations or offers and recipients' responses to "subsequent versions of invitations or offers" (pp. 107–112):

> Initial Version
> Rejection
> Subsequent Version
> → (Possible Response Point)

Focusing on G's utterances (1→ and 3→) as initiating actions in their own right, we can notice how S's responses become increasingly asynchronous: from accountings of her behavior and a recycled or subsequent version of the original invitation in (2→), to an escalated discounting/disbelief of G's displayed orientation in (4→). Thus far both G and S appear to be avoiding and pursuing rejection-implicative courses of action extending beyond, and attending to matters other than, the invitations involved. In this sense, and as noted earlier, G occasions S's invitations as opportunities to initiate a course of action, one eventuating in continued attempts to pursue S's affirmation of wrongdoing and thus movement past denial of bulimia. In the ways G responds to S's invitations, interactional work is being achieved that is programatically relevant to further (and more explicit) attempts to attribute and substantiate S's wrongdoing.

The actions taking shape in Excerpt 14 might be characterized as follows:

*→	S:	Invitation	PURSUIT
1→	G:	Silence/Delay	
		Disagreement Preface	AVOIDANCE
		Solicitation	&
		Negative Assessment	PURSUIT
2→	S:	Silence/Delay	
		Disagreement Preface	AVOIDANCE
		Account	&
*→		Subsequent Version of	PURSUIT
		Invitation	

3→	G:	Silence/Delay	
		Disagreement Preface	AVOIDANCE
		Possible Symptom	&
		Advice	PURSUIT

4→	S:	Silence/Delay	
		Disagreement Preface	AVOIDANCE
		Discounting/Disbelief	&
		Account	PURSUIT

The avoidance–pursuit sequence apparent thus far, collaboratively produced by G and S, is tied to the ongoing construction of disparate responses by both interactants. Just as S pursues the invitation, so does G withhold acceptance; just as G pursues S's being overly thin, so does S account for the appropriateness of her own behavior. In not solely attributing "pursuit" to G and "avoidance" to S, then, it is important to recognize that both engage in each type of activity: To pursue is to avoid some alternative course of action; to avoid is to withhold aligning with the pursuit trajectory made available by prior speaker. As evidenced in chapter 3, G's methods for pursuing and attributing wrongdoing to S simultaneously reflect an unwillingness by G to avoid the problem altogether. Similarly, S's attempts to account for her own behavior and discount G's orientation, indicate the pursuit of a course of avoiding ownership for alleged wrongdoings (see chapter 4).

These contrasting orientations to the same topic/issue, in the ways and to the extent they continue to persist interactionally, do not offer an immediate resolution of an alleged problem (in this particular case S's direct acknowledgment of, unequivocal commitment to eliminating, and promise to seek professional help regarding "throwing up her food"). But do such resolutions emerge? And if so, by what means? How does interaction evolve in environments where "solicitation → failure to directly affirm–confirm → further pursuit" continually develops?

SUMMARY

Analysis of the G–S interaction thus far reveals how G's moving toward attributions of S's lack of responsibility arise not from claims of inconvenience but G's personal concerns with S's health and well-being: There is some set of warranting circumstances G is curious about, interested in, and (as will become increasingly apparent) commited to resolving. Relying on an opportunity to respond to S's first and redo invitations to simply "go for a ↑wa:lk?", G's rejection-implicative responses (e.g., "A wa:lk?") begin to indirectly formulate a not-yet-articulated problem. In the ways that G comes off as not just rejecting a walk, but orienting to other matters at hand, she can be understood as engaging in actions programatically tied to her bulimic preoccupations. Such preoccupations give rise to continued interest in further and more explicit attempts to question S's motives and attribute wrongdoing toward S's actions. Moreover, G's actions are constructed in such a way that it is now the inviter's (S's) problem as well. Not only must S deal with lack of accept-ance to her invitation, but G's response is put forth as an "upshot" of the invitation, although without specific disclosure by G of her concerns at the outset of the conversation. Thus, G leaves it to S to figure out (in due course) what, exactly, she is concerned about and thus "up to."

And it was apparent that S, in having to deal with the absence of either an expected and no doubt preferred response (e.g., acceptance of the invitation) or its outright rejection "for good reasons," must eventually determine just where G was "going" and/or just just how much G "knows" (even though several "clues" were available, e.g. "Well honey yer so <u>thin: no:w:</u>", and various claims of knowledge made). Thus, as both interactants oriented to desired yet contradictory courses of action, G's purpose for asking and S's source of reluctance or discomfort remained unexplicated. This is the case even though both G and S were shown to pursue and avoid matters of relevance to their respective concerns.

Having overviewed how G initiated a course of action by questioning S's motives and beginning to argue with S's unarticulated answer tied to the "problem," we can look more directly at the interactional character of how G develops her case. We are now in a position to analyze a diverse set of resources comprising G's ongoing persistence as she lays ground for the reasonableness of her assertions, proposes solutions, and seeks to mobilize S to treat them seriously as legitimate solutions to the illness bulimia.

3

▼▼▼▼▼▼▼

Overcoming Resistance

Patients with eating disorders are usually secretive and often come to the attention of physicians only at the insistence of others.

—Haller (1992, p. 658)

It has been suggested that direct confrontation is often essential as a means for getting others to face their assumed secretive and therefore private bulimic tendencies, and more generally for soliciting healthy solutions to varied problems associated with eating disorders (see Brisman & Siegel, 1985; Siegel et al., 1988; Vitousek, Daly, & Heiser, 1991). Yet little is known about the interactional organization of such occasions. Understanding how the details of such predicaments get worked out over the course of a conversation requires making explicit G's attempts to substantiate S's bulimia. This interactional work is tailored to S as an individual purportedly "in need of help" (see Sacks, 1992, pp. 376–383), even though S does not initiate, volunteer, or otherwise disclose substantive details regarding her alleged illness. It will become clear that whether or not a "problem" actually exists and if so, just what the "problem" consists of, emerges as an equivocal task in and of itself.

Having initiated talk about the "problem" in chapter 2, the analysis shifts to G's multiple and repeated techniques for attempting to get S to acknowledge and "own" the "problem." An examination of G's resources for overcoming S's resistance to directly admit and seek medical and therapeutic assistance for bulimia reveals how G pursues one set of "problems" in the face of counterevidence provided by S as the very person characterized as "needing help."

Rather than directly attribute responsibility to another for a possible wrongdoing a speaker may, in stepwise fashion, gradually solicit information from recipient regarding alleged problematic actions (see chapter 2 and Heritage & Sefi, 1992). Even at the outset of the G–S interaction, such has been shown to be the case in the ways G initiated a course of action, in part by relying on S's invitations to go for a walk as opportunities to address other problematic issues (e.g., being "so thin"). Because S did not provide the information being solicited in sufficient detail, moving toward remedying the unarticulated "problem" G was beginning to address (as apparent in Excerpt 1, chapter 2 and throughout), G more persistently and directly pursues S's affirmation of responsibility and commitment to seek professional help. And of course how G addresses and pursues the "problem" is therefore contingent on whether, and to what extent, S openly admits and agrees to seek help for alleged bulimic actions and consequences.

One means of understanding the analysis offered in this chapter, therefore, is by framing G's pursuit as a chaining of alternative methods for seeking S's outright affirmation of, and commitment to resolving, the "problem" (i.e., actions qualifying S as "bulimic." Throughout this chapter, however, readers are referred to chapter 4 where more systematic attention is given to S's techniques for "avoiding ownership" of the "problem.") Pursuit of issues directed toward another's alleged wrongdoing is predicated on speaker's ability to provide relevant and compelling "evidence" of claims made (see Atkinson & Drew, 1979; Morris, 1988; Pomerantz, 1984b; Wagner, 1980), especially when participants offer different orientations to, and thus versions of, the issues or events being addressed. In the course of G imputing lack of responsibility in a manner coercing S's remedial action (e.g., admitting wrongdoing, seeking aid, changing/eliminating problematic health behaviors), G must provide and establish a knowledgeable basis for the claims she advances, essentially laying grounds for the reasonableness of her assertions.

In order to clarify the kinds of techniques G invokes, and before turning to more extended analysis, only a selected and abbreviated preview of G's resources appears here. For example, it has been shown that G engages in questioning S's motives prior to G's allegation that S is "throw[ing] up her food" (Excerpt 1 in chapter 2), and such questioning continues:

Excerpt 1 (SDCL:G/S:14)

→   G: <u>wh</u>adda you wanna go for a walk

Excerpt 2 (SDCL:G/S:51)

→   G: ↑ why d'ya wanna be so thi:n!

Excerpt 3 (SDCL:G/S:90)

→   G: > this is ri<u>di</u>culous if you wanna
              look thinner? ↑ why (do) you wanta <u>do</u> that

Excerpt 4 (SDCL:G/S:110)

→   G: .hh so what happens to the food that you eat?

However, as partially evident with "ridiculous" in Excerpt 3, G relies on increasingly direct declarative assertions, replete with extreme case formulations (Pomerantz, 1986), at times by invoking knowledge and questioning S's realization, to depict S's bulimic-related activities as not just consequential but dangerous:

Excerpt 5 (SDCL:G/S:138–140)

→   G: <u>I</u>:? <u>know</u>:. (0.8) that ch'u ar th<u>row</u>ing up
              your food <u>purpose</u>ly. (.) .h > and do you
→   <u>realize</u> that this is a (.) <u>ill</u>:ness <

Excerpt 6 (SDCL:G/S:150–157)

      G: And ↑ you know something (0.4) it's gonna
→   <u>gro:w</u> and <u>gro:w</u> > and you know what it can
              ↑ do (t[o) you] <
      S: [Gram] ma I'm
              [<u>not</u> even gonna (s:t-)]
→   G: [it could ruin your wh]ole life

Excerpt 7 (SDCL:G/S:173–179)

→   G: and <u>tha:t</u> is probl'y the ↑ <u>wor:st</u> thing
              that you could- (.) could ↑<u>ha:pp</u>en.
              to you <u>Sissy</u>
                        (0.6)
→   G: <u>don't</u> you realize what it can do to you:
                        (0.5)
→   G: it can ruin your <u>wh:o::le</u> life.

Excerpt 8 (SDCL:G/S:256–261)

→   G: An(d) ↑ you could just ↑ <u>ruin</u>: your wh<u>ole</u>
              life (.) I'm tellin. ya (0.2) hh
              <u>pritty</u> soon (0.4) > Yu- <u>you</u> don't realize
              it but <u>yer</u> personality's even <u>changin</u> you're gettin
              so: < .hhh <u>picke</u>:: and (0.6) you're
              not (.) you don't seem to be ↑ <u>ha:ppy</u>
              with anything Sissy anymore

A case is made that talk of this sort reveals a particular interactional character; specific kinds of interactional resources are recruited when questioning others' motives and attempting to get another to acknowledge, talk about, and ultimately resolve an alleged health problem. The resources employed by G are designed to legitimize reasons for treating S's actions as worthy of complaint and pursuit, and to portray the consequences of such actions as serious and even dangerous (see Pomerantz, 1984b, 1984c, 1986). And as varied forms of resistance emerge, there are systematic ways of engaging in confrontation not for its own sake, but in the routine course of attempting to help someone come to grips with actions constituting an increasingly disabilitating illness.

In specific consideration of the G–S interaction, therefore, what resources does G use and rely on that repeatedly occasion S's avoidance? How does G persistently topicalize the "problem," and on what basis does G invoke the right to pursue ongoing attempts to remedy S's problem? Analysis proceeds by first overviewing previously identified methods of "pursuing a response" (Pomerantz, 1984c; see also Linnell, Allemyr, & Jonsson, 1993), and briefly establishing whether or not G and S shared common knowledge regarding S's bulimia. Next, in attempting to remedy S's alleged illness, and as continuations of disaffiliative and thus asynchronous responses to S's discountings and withholdings, G's pursuit methods are embedded in the following actions: establishing, asserting, claiming, and imputing knowledge; laying out consequences of S's actions; citing sources and offering evidence of and for G's claims.

VARIATIONS OF "PURSUING A RESPONSE"

Individuals with whom problems allegedly reside are, not surprisingly, often less than forthcoming about such details. Individuals claimed by others to have a problem may seek to avoid discussing it altogether, yet if somehow coerced into talking about a problem, repeatedly offer outright or mitigated denials. These denials minimize and discount the severity of alleged problems, and in general display an unwillingness to own up to problems as described. In the face of such contradictory orientations to issues raised and matters addressed, individuals initiating a course of action involving a problem may be made out to be not only presumptuous but unequivocally misdirected and uninformed. As noted, the burden of proof is therefore incumbent on the speaker initiating and pursuing the problem to construct grounds for the reasonableness of the assertions. The interactional task is to provide a compelling case that the problem actually exists—is not simply a figment of speaker's imagination, which the other claimed to have the problem may very well make it out to be—and to do so in a manner capable of withstanding counterevidence designed to reveal the fallibility of any such claims.

Such efforts reflect delicate orientations to the problem, negotiations that do not always come off without a hitch. Ways must be found to not only occasion and somehow raise the "problem" in the first instance (see chapter 2), but to continually draw attention to a particular set of concerns—issues that are potentially stigmatizing for, and degrading to, the identity and status of family and/or friends (see Garfinkel, 1956; Goffman, 1963). Not infrequently, there are disaffiliative aftershocks for initiating such courses of action; varied and complex consequences brought on by how speakers initiate and pursue a problem, on the one hand, and how recipients may facilitate and/or display contradictory orientations to issues raised and matters addressed on the other hand.

Pomerantz (1984c) overviewed three "procedures through which speakers pursue responses to their assertions [which have failed] to get a coherent confirmation or disconfirmation from the recipient" (p. 152). Each method of pursuit is designed to resolve particular kinds of problems. For example, a speaker may seek to remedy recipient's lack of understanding by scanning for and replacing troublesome pronoun and/or vocabulary usages (e.g., see discussions of Excerpt 15, 3→; Excerpt 26, 2→). The two remaining methods are examined in direct contrast to the G–S interaction—G's reviewing of facts and information, and altering pursuit techniques rather than treating them as inadequate—although neither addresses exactly the contingencies that arise. The two methods addressed by Pomerantz (1984c) are summarized here, followed by a contrast with G–S contingencies:

1. A speaker may wrongly assume recipient knows about the matter being discussed, leading to recipient's confusion and attempts by speaker to review facts and information to create shared knowledge before proceeding (Pomerantz, 1984c, pp. 156–159). In contrast: Throughout G–S it will first be shown that the recipient (S) does recognize what the speaker (G) is addressing (e.g., bulimia), thus some adequate degree of shared knowledge apparently already exists. However, even though it becomes obvious that S comprehends the talk of which she is a focus, she withholds granting the articulated responses G is pursuing (i.e., directly admitting, confessing, apologizing, unequivocally committing to seeking professional help). Consequently, G proceeds by constructing and in these ways reviewing facts and information as a means of soliciting responses (rather than, e.g., simply attempting to create shared knowledge).[1]

---

[1] It is on this basis that Pomerantz (1984c) seems to address, in closing and thus as a future implication of her analysis, the operating conditions most applicable to the G–S interaction investigated herein:

> To find out where the breakdown occurs, a speaker can present to the recipient each relevant fact upon which he or she based the assertion. They may find they have different versions of events. *On the other hand*, a recipient may be unable to deny convincingly or disclaim knowledge of the facts as presented. By laying out the grounds or the basis of an assertion to a recipient, a speaker may determine whether the recipient's difficulty in responding is based on rational grounds, for example, having different information, or is based on other grounds such as conflicting interests or *some emotional commitment*. (p. 162, italics added)

2. A speaker may review and evaluate assertions, when and if recipient's response is hesitant due to lack of support and agreement. If speaker finds own assertions to be inadequate, positions may be modified (Pomerantz, 1984c, pp. 159–161). In contrast: Recipient (S) does fail to provide the articulated responses identified by Pomerantz, noticeably falling short of supporting and outrightly agreeing with speaker's (G's) assertions. In turn, however, and in lieu of formulating her own assertions as inaccurate, G relies on a variety of resources for altering her pursuit techniques rather than reversing or treating own position as not credible.

Common Knowledge? Getting Another to Acknowledge and "Own" the "Problem"

The initial task is to address if, how, and to what extent G and S display common knowledge. Does S display confusion and/or inability to understand G's claims? A variety of interactional moments suggest this is not the case. Even though S consistently discounts, withholds, and otherwise avoids detailed considerations of the problems (and their consequences) raised by G (see chapter 4), she does not offer straightforward denials of the "problem" (but see Excerpt 14 in this chapter). Repeatedly, S's actions can be understood as mitigated confessions (1→), treated next by G (2→) in declarative, rejection-implicative fashion:

Excerpt 9 (SDCL:G/S:198–202)

```
1→   S:   You look at me. I do no:t look skinny
          and withdra::wn from soci:ety? ((staccato))
          .hh fi:n:e I eat a little bit (0.4) too much
          I- I feel stuffed .hhh ↑ and I'll jis:-
2→   G:   O:h:: > ↓ come off it < ((continues))
```

Excerpt 10 (SDCL:G/S:248–251)

```
1→   S:   .hh Gra:mma look at me I'm not
          gonna let it get any worse =
2→   G:   = They a:ll said, the ↑ sa:me thing
          °when they° started dear. ((continues))
```

Excerpt 11 (SDCL:G/S:295–299)

```
1→   S:   = I won't do it anymo::re
2→   G:   Oh they ↑ always say
          I won't do it anymore ((continues))
```

Excerpt 12 (SDCL:G/S:348–352)

```
1→   S:   Well why (.) > well why do we have to go
          to a doctor let's < .hh le(t)'s jus(t)
          try to handle it here.
```

2→   G: You have to have pro<u>fess</u>ional help
           .hh you have to go to a <u>co:unseler</u> ((continues))

Excerpt 13 (SDCL:G/S:390–394)

1→   S: > Yeah but Gramma I don't want < anybody
           to ↓ <u>kno::w</u> I'm ↑ so: <u>su:re</u>!
2→   G: Your > <u>doctor</u> <u>certainly</u> isn't gonna
           <u>pub</u>lish it in the <u>p</u>aper yuh kno:w. <
           (.) h(e) isn't gonna <u>te</u>:ll anybody

In Excerpts 9 through 13, the deictic "it" refers, of course, to what was established earlier (Excerpt 1, chapter 2): S's throwing up her food and the more encompassing problem of bulimia, only alluded to by S in Excerpt 9. Although G and S clearly orient to "it" as a basis for common knowledge, S's offerings— to not let "it" happen anymore, to not let "it" get worse, to handle "it" here—as well as expressing anxiety should anyone learn about her problem (Excerpt 13), are not displays of confusion about the issues G is pursuing. Nor are G's responses (Excerpts 9–13, 2→) attempts to create common knowledge via reviews of facts or information. Rather, G displays unwillingness to treat S's offerings as sufficient; she immediately discounts the very positions employed by S when mitigating and indirectly formulating her "confessions."

And of course there is more in Excerpts 9 through 13 about the ways G treats S as essentially incompetent to make her own decisions regarding an illness she appears unwilling to admit and seek help for. These very kinds of interactional predicaments were forecast by Parsons (1975; see also 1951) when examining the concept of "sick role."[2] By addressing the kinds of deviant and thus dysfunctional behaviors adopted by those who are ill as they respond to social pressures and evade social responsibilities, and in general the social systemic consequences of being and acting "sick," it can be seen how there are assumed obligations that unhealthy persons will attempt to get well, in part by admitting problems and seeking technically competent professional help. This is apparent in the following (and also cited at the outset of Heath's, 1992, analysis of general practice consultations):

> By the same institutional definition the sick person is not, of course, competent to help himself, or what he can do is, except for trivial illness, not adequate. But in our culture there is a special definition of the kind of help he needs, namely, professional, technically competent help. The nature of this help imposes a further disability or handicap upon him. He is not only generally not in a position to do what needs to be done, but does now "know" what needs to be done or how to do it. . . . There is, that is to say, a "communication gap." (Parsons, 1951, p. 441)[3]

---

[2] Thanks to Brian Spitzberg for early discussions of "sick role."
[3] Perhaps the kinds of features comprising such a "communication gap" are apparent in SDCL:G/S:276–299 and 348–352 (see appendix).

By reinspecting Excerpts 9 through 13, it is seen that G treats as inadequate S's prior responses, setting up further pursuit by G toward alternatives put forth as better suited to resolving the alleged bulimic problems (the specific resources relied on by G, e.g., "citing sources" as in the "Oh-prefaced" response in Excerpt 11, and "offering evidence," are addressed more directly in the final section of this chapter). Not uncommonly in the G–S interaction, these kinds of activities contribute to what was previously described as a "chaining" of paired actions (see Frankel, 1990), reflecting in these moments disaffiliative, asynchronous environments collaboratively produced by G and S. This is apparent once again in Excerpt 14:

Excerpt 14 (SDCL:G/S:158–167)

```
G:    ·
      ·
      ·
      > ↑ Don't tell me that now.
      you just better stop < (.) [ denyin(g) ]
S:                               [ Gra:mma ]
      I've ↓ o::nly done that a couple a ti:m:es,
G:    ↓ A couple [°of ti::(mes)°]
S:                [ > It's not? ] that big of a deal.
      my friends used to do it in the sorority $ all
      the t(hh)i:me. $ <
```

where it is perhaps not surprising that G, through reprimand and warning, treats S's actions as "denying" (see later and also chapter 4) rather than indirectly formulated ("that") admittance as in S's next "a couple a ti:m:es," and where contradictory courses of action continue to chain out despite what has emerged as clearly established, recognizable common knowledge shared by G and S regarding the "problem."

PURSUIT: LAYING GROUNDS
FOR REASONABLE ASSERTION

Having established that confusions surrounding common knowledge are minimal, that instead contradictory orientations to the severity of the "problem" of bulimia and means for its resolution underly the G–S interaction, attention can now be more directly drawn to G's resources (as in Excerpts 9–13, 2→, and 14) for extending and thus achieving pursuit. As previously overviewed, these resources are addressed within the general categories of: claiming and imputing knowledge, laying out consequences, and citing sources and offering evidence.

Claiming and Imputing Knowledge

Claims of knowledge are employed by G, at times without directly imputing S's knowledge, and are embedded within more complex sets of actions involving "troubles" and "problems" as an early moment in the interaction reveals:

Excerpt 15 (SDCL:G/S:60–77)

```
1→   S:   = Gra:mma. (.) I a:te good the other nite.
          didn't I you an(d) I both went out for a big
          salad an:(d) s:oup. (.) why are you: sittin
          here sayi:n my:- ( ) (0.4) > should be with
          exerci:se. <
                  (0.7)
2→   G:   Well now Sissy with your ↑ foo:d. (1.2)
          uh:: you don't always get the benefit of what
*→        ch'u eat? > now I happen to know °that <
*→        (.) that's true°
                  (0.8)
3→   S:   ↑ We:ll: ((high pitched voice)) (0.6)
          ↑ I know it's hard. right no:w
          > I mean I'm tryin to look good for my wedding? <
          and ↑ I might not e[ at (as)   ]
4→   G:                      [> Well Sis]sy do you? think
          you're gonna look good < (.) when you're so: thin:
```

In (1→) S makes reference to a meal shared with G. It is curious that in mentioning "a big salad an:(d) s:oup." S works toward offering a "no problem" response by minimizing G's concerns with exercise, followed by a query actually soliciting G's response (see chapter 4). Yet in so doing S actually, and no doubt unknowingly, makes available to G an "eating → food" relationship: eating "big" and healthy meals may at times be necessary, but clearly not sufficient, if and when "you don't always get the benefit of what ch'u eat?" (2→). Here G occasions S's "big" as unarticulated grounds for the very possibility of "binging," and in (2→) indirectly raises, but does not explicitly confront S with the "problem" of "purging."

This manner of making obvious the "binge → purge" cycle reveals G's preoccupation with the "problem" and an altogether delicate counter to S's reconstruction of eating together. But next, and more explicitly (*→), G moves to assert and thereby upgrade this problematic state of affairs with a claim of its truth. Notice, however, that G's "happen to know" is constructed as an upshot of more or less random occurrence, rather than a consequence of G's systematic and thus deliberate monitoring and observation of S's "bulimic" actions—owing perhaps to the "early" location in the G–S conversation. In (2→), G's tag-positioned claim of knowledge regarding S's actions illustrates one means of attempting to "establish the facts" *as* the "truth," further substantiating the response to S's query as authoritative and thus defensible.

In Excerpt 15, 3→ what can now be established as a standard mode of response from S (i.e., silence/delay, disagreement preface, account/reporting of "trouble") fails to specifically address G's "binge/purging" orientation, even though token acknowledgment is given in the form of "it's ha̲rd. right no:w." Instead, S initiates a "trouble" by repairing with "I mean," and in this way respecifies a more precise version of her concerns (see Schegloff, 1992), by offering a reason for eating less: "I'm trying to look good for my wedding?" And in (4→) G's inquiry refocuses on the "problem" ("so̲: thi̲n:"), essentially rejecting S's "trouble" by withholding alignment and failing to commiserate with S's stated concerns.

Although in Excerpt 15, G's responses fall short of directly addressing S as knowledgeable of what are made out to be problematic actions, such is not always the case. One way G explicitly treats S as knowledgeable is by asserting and drawing attention to S's "knowing," the implication being that even though S is aware of her bulimic actions she nevertheless engages in what G construes as wrongful behavior(s). A reinspection of what gave rise to Excerpt 1 at the outset of this analysis (chapter 2), however, reveals how G's claiming of knowledge has not only shifted from the indirect formulation in Excerpt 15, but is clearly preparatory to later imputations and observations regarding S's actions (see Excerpt 17). In Excerpt 16, G extends the "eating → food" relationship, and thus the "binge → purge" preoccupation, by treating S's weight as "amazing" prior to more directly inquiring about "what happens to the food that you eat?":

Excerpt 16 (SDCL:G/S:108–122)

```
1→   G:   Well you al:ways eat just fine?
          it's amazing that you don't weigh? more.
          .hh so what happens to the food that you eat?
               (1.1)
     G:   You- > you're not getting any bigger? but. <
               (1.0)
     S:   What do you mean by tha:t?
     G:   We:ll Sissy. (0.8) let's ↓ face it no:w
2→        yo:u kno:w .hh that ch'u are so: e::ager:.
          (.) to be thin:. (0.2) that you sometimes. go in
          the bathroom. (0.2) and throw up your food?
3→        I kno:w it's [ true!  ]
     S:              [GRAM ]MA YOU ARE SO:: FULL
          O(F) SHIT! I am so: su:r e.
```

Following (1→), when S fails to respond, G reassesses S's weight by moving to an observation of size ("bigger"). It is then in response to S's query (see chapter 4) that G both attributes S's knowledge (2→) and emphasizes the confidence of her assertion in (3→). Even though S overlaps, it is clear in her response that G's claims have not gone unattended as evident in the wholesale discounting S provides (see chapter 4), actions failing to directly address G's concerns, and in this way providing sufficient cause for G's continued pursuit.

In Excerpts 15 and 16, G more directly claims and imputes knowledge as means for substantiating her position, relying on these alternative resources in responding to S's discountings and withholdings and thereby legitimizing her pursuit. As this G–S interaction unfolds, parallels exist across recurring and longer interactional environments in which increasingly direct knowledge claims and attributions are utilized. For example, an extended glimpse of the interactional "aftershocks" following Excerpt 16 provides yet another set of moments where G both claims and imputes knowledge so as to establish the "truth value" of her assertions:

Excerpt 17 (SDCL:G/S:121–140)

```
       S:  GRAM MA YOU ARE SO:: FULL
           O(F) SHIT! I am so: su:r[e. ]
*→     G:                          [(S]i::ssy stop) ↑ sa:ying
           such a thing as tha[ t. ]
       S:                     [↑ W]E:LL: I can't believe
           > that ch'u would even say something like tha:t. <
1→     G:  Well it's tru:e isn't it?
2→             (0.4)
3→     G:  You know I:? know more about this than you
           think? I know.
               (0.5)
       S:  Gra:mma. you (a)re so we::ird (.hh aghhh)
               (1.0)
*→     G:  °Sissy I wanna tell you something°
               (0.8)
4→     G:  I:? know:. (0.8) that ch'u ar throwing up
           your food purposely. (.) .h > and do you
           realize that this is a (.) ill:ness <
```

Before we address (1→ – 4→), one initial observation regarding certain paired actions within this extended segment involves how G responds (*→) to S's discountings that Gramma is "so full of shit" and "so weird." Here, as throughout, G attempts to keep interaction focused and "on track," working to align S (and by so doing monitoring, adjusting, and thus impacting the sequential progression of the interaction) with the trajectory G is pursuing (see also W. Beach, 1990c, 1995a, 1995b). In the first instance, G moves to disallow and thus constrain S's prior name-calling, and in the second she uses one form of prefaced announcement ("°Sissy I wanna tell you something°") (see W. Beach & Dunning, 1982; Schegloff, 1980; Terasaki, 1976). This presequence is designed by G to not only garner a particular kind of attention from S as recipient but also to foreshadow the importance or sensitivity of the matters addressed.

In terms of (1→ – 3→) in Excerpt 17, it is seen that G's straightforward query (1→, "Well it's tru:e isn't it?") is responsive to S's restated and elaborated statement of disbelief (i.e., that G would both impute and claim knowledge of S's "throwing up"). Although S passes on the oppportunity to answer and perhaps refute G's assertion in (2→), such a withholding is meaningful and consequential for G's continued pursuit in the way it is heard and treated as "admission" (see chapter 4). In (3→), then, G moves forward as though S admitted "bulimia," now reasserting knowledge imputed to be greater than what S may have believed and/or acted on in constructing positions rooted in discountings and disbelief.

It is thus apparent that, when S discounts in the very next turn via a disgruntled "Gra:mma. you (a)re so we::ird (.hh aghhh)", G is uniquely positioned to rely on a presequence to foreshadow and then deliver what eventuates in (4→). Here, G again claims knowledge about S's purposeful "throwing up," but also works toward a tagged-question of S's realization that her actions constitute "an illness." Through this upgrading inquiry, the potential seriousness of the "problem" is refocused; it is made yet further apparent when G can be heard and seen as basically chiding S to "realize" and accept the consequences of her actions. But there is more here, namely, how G's utterance (4→) is built in such a manner that it invites S to consider the ramifications of her actions, attempting to constrain next response. For S to assert "lack of realization" as a legitimate excuse for having engaged in, or continuing what has now been substantiated as shared knowledge and put forth by G as "an illness," sets S up for further inquiry and contradiction by G.

Laying Out Consequences

Just as G's attributing and claiming knowledge emerged gradually and more directly in Excerpts 15–17, so is it the case that G escalates the pursuit in response to S's unwillingness to directly admit the problem. By articulating possible consequences (→ below), G more tenaciously seeks specific affirmation from S:

Excerpt 18 (SDCL:G/S:138–167)

```
       G:   I:? know:. (0.8) that ch'u are throwing up
  →          your food purposely. (.) .h > and do you realize
             that this is a (.) ill:ness <
                       (0.4)
  →    G:   and the m:ore > you do it (up) <
             [   (if) you don't stop right now    ]
       S:   [↑ You'r::e so: FUNNY GRAMMA!]
             .hh this is an ill:ness I can't believe
             you're throwing up your food. ((mimmick voice))
```

```
*→   G:    °Well you ar:e°?
            (1.2)
 →   G:    And ↑ you know something (0.4) it's gonna
            gro:w and gro:w > and you know what it can
            ↑ do (t[ o) you ] <
     S:              [ Gram ] ma I'm
            [no t even gonna (s:t-)]
 →   G:    [it could ruin your wh]ole life
            > ↑ Don't tell me that now.
            you just better stop < (.) [ denyin(g) ]
     S:                          [ Gra:mma ]
            I've ↓ o::nly done that a couple a ti:m:es
     G:    ° ↓ A couple [ of times° ]
     S:                 [ > It's not?] that big of a deal.
            my friends used to do it in the sorority $ all
            the ti:me. $ <
```

At the outset of Excerpt 18, when S characterizes G as "FUNNY" and mimics G's position (see chapter 4), G once again resorts to refocusing the "problem"—similar to "Well it's tru:e isn't it?" (Excerpt 17, 1→)—by declaring "°Well you ar:e°?" (Excerpt 18, *→), which once again gives rise to G's upgraded pursuit following S's silence (see chapter 4).

By laying out possible consequences that S appears unable and/or unwilling to consider or confront, G now creates negative case scenarios built to portray unpleasant outcomes: "It could ruin your whole life". These and related extreme case formulations are clearly offered in anticipation of S's nonsympathetic hearings (see Pomerantz, 1986), as not just possible but likely consequences of S's discountings and unwillingness to alleviate the damage "it" could do—as though the bulimic tendencies being addressed (e.g., "so thin," "throwing up") have an externalized life of their own *causing*, not just implicated within, S's actions. In these ways, G formulates "it" as S's opposition as well, now not simply a figment constructed by S of G's imagination, but an "enemy" of sufficient force compelling G and S to join forces and battle together (as with Excerpt 16, 2→ "let's ↓ face it no:w"). And G does not portray the opposition S is facing as displaying "steady state" tendencies, but as some malignant entity that will "gro:w and gro:w" until "it" ruins S's "whole life."

Although dramatic in character, G's mode of pursuit is nevertheless treated by S in Excerpt 18 as both hypothetical and overly paranoid: S's continual downgradings persist, and the extreme seriousness of the matters as constructed by G appear to have little impact on S's "teaming up" with G to fight the invisible assailant. But G is equally persistent, and the extreme case formulations evident in Excerpt 18—amounting to worse case scenarios and a challenging of S's own lack of realization of the "problem"—are by no means abandoned:

Excerpt 19 (SDCL:G/S:165–179)

```
     S:    > It's not? that big of a deal.
           my friends used to do it in the sorority $ all
           the ti:me. $ <
 *→  G:    °Well listen? your friends used to do a lot
           of things in the sorority that you didn't
           have to pattern after I'm quite sure?°
                 (0.6)
  →  G:    and tha:t is probl'y the ↑ wor:st thing
           that you could- (.) could ↑ha:ppen.
           to you Sissy
                 (0.6)
  →  G:    don't you realize what it can do to you:
                 (0.5)
  →  G:    it can ruin your wh:o::le life.
```

Excerpt 20 (SDCL:G/S:248–257)

```
     S:    ·
           ·
           ·
           .hh Gra:mma look at me I'm not
           gonna let it get any worse =
 *→  G:    = They a:ll said, the ↑ sa:me thing
           °when they° started dear.
                 (.)
  →  G:    Don't ch'a realize this sorta thing
           just grows on ya an grows on ya an
           gro:ws on ya
                 (1.0)
  →  G:    An ↑ you could just ↑ ruin: your whole
           life (.) I'm tellin. ya (0.2) hh ((continues))
```

Both Excerpts 19 and 20 begin with two types of discountings routinely employed by S, an account and a promise, and in each instance G's responses (*→) immediately transform S's offerings—each designed to minimize the "problem"—into failed attempts on the basis that "friends" and "they" are themselves subject to similar or same wrongdoings. And next, in each instance, G reasserts and seeks to further substantiate her position by constructing variations of previously employed options: In Excerpt 19 from "↑ wor:st thing" → "don't you realize" → "it can ruin your wh:o::le life.", and in Excerpt 20 from "Don't ch'a realize" → "grows on ya an grows on ya an gro:ws on ya" → "And ↑ you could just ↑ ruin: your whole life." Here, G's "grows on ya an grows on ya an gro:ws on ya" reveals what, on initial inspection, may be heard and seen quite literally as a preoccupation with "size and weight." But G's orientation is also a reformulation both of S's prior "I'm not gonna let it get any worse" and G's "°when they° started dear": it is in reference to "bulimia" as an illness, one incapable of being healed by self-directed monitoring alone, that G is addressing. And in this sense of inversion, as the illness "grows" not only does the ability to manage bingeing and purging decline, but so does "size and weight" of the ill person.

A comparison of Excerpts 18 and 19 to the later Excerpt 20, however, reveals that G even further upgrades the consequences she is laying out: from "it's gonna gro:w and gro:w" in Excerpt 18 to a more personalized and triplicate "grows on ya an grows on ya an gro:ws on ya" in Excerpt 20; from "it can ruin your wh:o::le life" in Excerpts 18 and 19 to, again, a more personal "And ↑ you could just ↑ ruin: your whole life" in Excerpt 20. At times, the consequences G is laying out amount to unequivocal "threats," as when G suggests that she will do something "desperate" such as telling S's fiancé (Bill) about the "problem"—an informing that may eventuate in "break[ing] off this engagement" (see also Excerpt 29, this chapter; Excerpt 7, chapter 4; Excerpt 319–324 in the appendix).

Citing Sources and Offering Evidence

The course of action discussed here, one designed by G to increasingly invoke the seriousness of "bulimia," is further diversified by an additional and related means of establishing credibility for knowledge claims: referencing other "sources" (see Pomerantz, 1984b) and offering "observations" (e.g., about S's physical appearance and moods) as evidence. Sources and observations are offered by G in order to increase the breadth and depth of knowledge claims, and to transform what might be treated by S as simply ungrounded opinion into "factual" evidence. Just as "facts" are inherently an upshot of their social construction (see Garfinkel, 1967) in reporting and telling about ambiguous and essentially incomplete circumstances and events, so is it the case that G relies on sources and observations as a means of better insuring coercion by substantiating that G is not alone in becoming informed about, and taking positions on, the "problem." As becomes obvious, cited sources and observations may also, in turn, function as resources for refuting attempts to discount S's emergent and counterclaims that G is biased, idiosyncratic, uninformed, less than accurate and, as noted, building a fictional rather than factual case.

In pursuit of S's affirmation of wrongdoing, G cites and thus recruits several sources and forms of evidence: reconstructed behavioral observations put forth as "evidence," reconstructions of others' written and spoken assessments of S, and/or additional individuals struggling with "bulimia."

Beginning with early moments in the G–S conversation, it can be observed that citing sources and offering "physical" evidence, often in unison, were possible options for G—resources that continued to be utilized as S's resistance continued. In Excerpts 21 through 23, G's nonsympathetic and thus disaffiliative responses to S's immediately prior assertion of "facts" (or in

Excerpt 23, S's "promise," "= I won't do it anymo::re") are repeatedly established:

Excerpt 21 (SDCL:G/S:38–51)

```
1→   S:   > I don't even know why you say that I- <
          t.hh I am f:i::ve thr:ee:: and I still
          weigh a hundred an ten- fifteen po:unds?
               (0.6)
2→   G:   O:h ↓ you don't weigh a hundred an
2→        fifteen ↑ pounds .hh all your clothes
2→        are fallin off of ya everybody tells you
          ya look thi::n?
     S:   Ya:: but fin[ ally I  ]
2→   G:               [You're b]o:ny look at acrossed
2→        your chest an yer .hh co:llar bo:nes
2→        stickin o::ut > ↑ why d'ya wanna be so thi:n! <
```

Excerpt 22 (SDCL:G/S:198–207)

```
1→   S:   You look at me. I do no:t look skinny
          and withdra::wn from soci:ety? ((staccato))
          .hh fi:n:e I eat a little bit (0.4) too much
          I- I feel stuffed .hhh ↑ and I'll jis:-
2→   G:   O:h:: > ↓ come off it < (0.2) (eh-)
2→        look at everybody else. they eat
2→        [and they o:vereat and they don't run in the]
     S:   [Gra:mma I got plenty? of friends. that do- ]
2→   G:   bathroom and throw it up
```

Excerpt 23 (SDCL:G/S:295–317)

```
1→   S:   = I won't do it anymo::re
2→   G:   Oh they ↑ always say
          I won't do it anymore
          > you do it all the time
          I know you do <
               (1.0)
     G:   > An d'yu know what <
               (0.5)
     G:   this might- (0.4) y'know you lo:ve perfume
          (1.0) and you spend a lotta > money on it <
→         do you know that you have a cert(ain)
          o:dor about ch'u
               (2.0)
     G:   from this
               (1.0)
→    G:   when I'm aroun(d) ↑ you every so often
          I get this (0.5) this jus(t) little
          aro:ma: of (.) uh vomitis
               (1.5)
```

```
*→   G:   I honest to God do Sissy.
               (2.0)
*→   G:   °And I uh an it jus(t), it just kills me.
          because° > you know how dear you are to me <
          and I just can't sta:nd to see you
          destroy your life like this
```

In each instance, but also collectively, the pattern of action co-authored by G and S may be depicted as follows:

```
1→   S:   Assertion of physical/social "facts" (Excerpts 21–22)
          Promise (Excerpt 23)
2→   G:   Oh-prefaced (inapposite) response
          Re-assertion of position via citing sources/physical observations
```

Heritage (1984) convincingly showed how placements of "oh" in conversation routinely display user's change-of-state in knowledge and/or orientation to what is being attended to and thereby noticed (e.g., as a response to informing actions). In cases such as (2→, 21–23) where an "oh" is built into a turn-initial response, however, Heritage (1990) further evidenced alternative, yet nevertheless systematic, deployments of "oh-prefaces." Several recurrent features originally noted by Heritage are of particular relevance to the present analysis, speaking both to the universality of employment across diverse social occasions but also to the situated character of "problems" addressed in (Excerpts 21–23) and throughout G–S:

First, "oh-prefaces" are embedded within turn-initial positions by recipients treating prior inquiries and/or questions as inappropriate, inapposite, or even as "questioning the unquestionable" (p. 4);

Second, "ohs" can be heard to preface what turn out to be not only "my world" proposals by recipients, but also reassertions designed to "hold a position" rather than display alignment with what was taken to have been projected by prior inquiry and/or question (pp. 6–8);

Finally, "oh-prefaces" may project a subsequent topic shift, as though recipient is unwilling to consider or address issues occasioned by first speaker.

The resemblances to G–S are striking. In Excerpt 21, following S's statement of disbelief and self-generated description of height and weight (1→), G discounts the reasonableness of S's claim with "Oh-prefaced" response + citing "everybody" else not "throw[ing] it up." In Excerpt 22, S implores G to "look at me." prior to declaring herself as neither skinny nor withdrawn from society, work preparatory to offering a partial admission of her binging and purging. Here G's turn-initial "O:h:: > ↓ come off it <" (2→) quickly rejects, and in wholesale fashion, S's version of the "problem," thus displaying both G's trouble and unwillingness to "give ground" on positions being constructed. And in a more extended instance as Excerpt 23, S's "promise" (1→) is discounted by G via "Oh + citing a source" in a manner categorizing

S's prior action as typical of "they" (i.e., other "bulimics") and thus not to be believed. Note also, however, that as G continues and S withholds further response, G not only elaborates (→) by claiming a certain "odor or aroma" that S spends so much money on perfume to avoid (see also G's citing of such symptoms as "personality" and "pink toothbrush" in Excerpts 27 and 28) but further upgrades her "sincerity" by explicitly stating her commitment to S and basic unwillingness to allow the illness to continue.

As with Excerpt 23, and as G aptly summarizes at a later point in the discussion,

Excerpt 24 (SDCL:G/S:369–372)

G: Now ↑ I can't stand idly <u>by:</u> and see
  you de<u>stroy</u> yourself.
   (1.2)
G: > There isn't any <u>way</u>. <

she is unwilling to refrain from attempting to resolve this "illness." It would be an oversimplification, however, to suggest that such sincere commitment reflects only "grandmotherly" altruism on G's part. As noted previously, the very fact that G is by trade a registered nurse—trained and socialized to observe, recognize, describe, and remedy symptomatic behaviors promoting and constituting illness—should not be treated as coincidental to the talk-in-interaction.

In Excerpt 25, this nursing background does get invoked by G (1→) as "I-world" constructions, in unison with citing two additional sources involving "reading" (2→) and other "people" G has "personally known" (3→):

Excerpt 25 (SDCL:G/S:229–242)

   G: ·
     ·
     ·

1→ I: (1.2) am a nur:se? (0.2)
   I <u>kno:w</u>? > what I'm talk in about <
2→ I have r:ead a great deal?
3→ (.) [I have (known personally)]
*→ S: [Oka:y Gramma it's <u>not</u>:? ↓ go]nna
   happen ag[a:in]
*→ G: [Now] you? be <u>quiet</u> for a moment
     (0.4)
3→ G: I have kno:wn <u>three people personally</u>
   (1.0) °<u>that</u>. have the <u>same</u> problem°
    (0.5)
3→ G: <u>You know</u> (.) <u>you know</u> (wa) ↑ <u>Ja:net</u> .hh an

Although in (*→) S does rely on "Okay + [promise]" in moving to curtail G's trajectory, get off of this troubling topic, and thus close down pursuit activities (see W. Beach, 1993b, 1995b), G immediately (*→) squelches S's attempt ("be quiet") and begins to elaborate on others she has known who "have the same problem." And Excerpt 25 is not an isolated instance; a set of moments occurring immediately prior to Excerpt 22 also draws attention to S's alleged failure to keep informed of "the news" (1→),

Excerpt 26 (SDCL:G/S:181–207)

```
        G:    your h:e:alth (0.2) your teeth
              > d'you do you (av) you ever? s:een. <
1→            .hh have you (h)aven't ch'u been
              keepin up with the news?
              a:l[l: the things that's written and] published?
        S:        [  But GRA::mma. I don't  ]
              fee:l ba::d:!
                   (1.5)
2→      G:    Well why? are ya so tir:ed
              an can-[(canky)]
        S:           [ Beca:u]se I have to
              ↓ work such [  long hours ](.) [ G r a] mma
                          [((tape noise))]   [ ((tn)) ]
                   (0.2)
        S:    You look at me. I do no:t look skinny
              and withdra::wn from soci:ety? ((staccato))
              .hh fi:n:e I eat a little bit (0.4) too much
              I- I feel stuffed .hhh ↑ and I'll jis:-
        G:    O:h:: > ↓ come off it < (0.2) (eh-)
              look at everybody else. they eat
              [and they o:vereat and they don't run in the]
        S:    [ Gra:mma I got plenty? of friends. that do-]
        G:    bathroom and throw it up
```

an implication that S vehemently contradicts with alternative evidence (not feeling bad), and in queried response to which G (2→) counters by citing further behavioral symptoms of "tir:ed an can- (canky)."[4]

It is clear that G repeatedly cites sources and offers observations as evidence connecting her particularized concerns with "publically available" consequences (i.e., "what anyone might/could see" as symptomatic of the health problems S is creating). Yet as with the earlier discussion of "laying out consequences," G also works to appeal to S by personally tailoring her observations to S's situation and predicament. In Excerpt 27, G moves from a general behavior (a change of personality) to a specific one (getting picky), then back to a general symptom (not being happy anymore):

---

[4] The latter repair, "can- (canky)," is one example of "conversational poetics" (cf. W. Beach, 1993b; Hopper, 1992a; Jefferson, 1977, 1996; Sacks, 1992). This "speech error" displays just what G was orienting to, and thus preoccupied with: attempting, although failing, to generate a description of S as both "cantankerous" and "cranky" within an oppositional and otherwise disaffiliative interactional environment (see also chapter 5).

Excerpt 27 (SDCL:G/S:256–261)

```
        G:    An(d) ↑ you could just ↑ ruin: your whole
              life (.) I'm tellin. ya (0.2) hh
              pritty soon (0.4) > Yu- you don't realize
   →          it but yer personality's even changin you're
   →          gettin so: < .hhh picke:: and (0.6) you're
   →          not (.) you don't seem to be ↑ ha:ppy
   →          with anything Sissy anymore
```

And other specific symptoms include a "pink toothbrush," prefaced by an explicit plea for S to admit the consequences of the "problem":

Excerpt 28 (SDCL:G/S:511–516)

```
        G:    Now admit just a little bit to me
              .hhh they'll (.) you do go in and-
   →          have you noticed that your teeth
   →          (.) I noticed your toothbrush has
   →          a lot of ↑ pink like you're (l'ke)
   →          you're kinda bleeding?
```

Finally, it should not be overlooked that S was soon to be married, and that G's continued references to "everybody" also includes an early citing of S's fiancé:

Excerpt 29 (SDCL:G/S:96–104)

```
   1→   G:    What does ↓ Bill think about you getting
              so thin=
   2→   S:    =He thinks I look great.
                     (0.2)
   2→   S:    he doesn't wa[ (nt)  ]
   3→   G:               [He do]es no:t I heard him
              say Sissy? ↓ don't you lose another POUND!
              ((staccato delivery))
```

That G cites Bill as a source for substantiating her concerns and justifying her mode of pursuit is but one interesting feature of this segment. Perhaps more importantly, it is consequential that G does not directly announce Bill's opinion, but "delivers the news" only following S's reply. In this way, the organization of Excerpt 29 bears strong resemblance to what Maynard (1989; see also 1991, 1992) describes as a three-part "perspective-display sequence":

A different strategy, which appears more cautious and interactionally safer, is to solicit another party's opinion and to then produce one's own report or assessment in a way that takes the other's into account. This can be done through a three-part "perspective-display sequence" consisting of (1) an opinion or query or "perspective-display invitation," (2) the reply or recipient's opinion, and (3) asker's subsequent report. . . . In all, the sequence appears tightly organized to prefer affiliation between recipient's and asker's positions. In so doing, the sequence allows asker's report and the position it implies both to confirm and to be affirmed by recipient's perspective. (pp. 91, 110)

In the case of Excerpt 29, however, it is obvious that G was well aware of Bill's opinion prior to soliciting S's report. And by first inviting S to display her perspective, G next and quickly determined that S's report was contradictory to her own knowledge regarding Bill's opinion (put forth in 3→ as "reported speech"). The interjective and overlapped result was straightforward refutation: G had simply "caught S in the act" and, in so doing, substantiated Bill as a concerned source whose opinion fit well within the overall course of action G was pursuing.

SUMMARY

In this chapter, previously unexplicted notions such as "insistence," "confrontation," and "overcoming resistance" have been characterized as interactional achievements by G and S. Particular attention has been given to activities designed by G for soliciting S's directly talking about "problems" (acknowledging, admitting, committing to seeking help for "bulimia") that she remains unwilling to "own." It was established that both G and S knew, and displayed recognition, that "bulimia" was the source of G's concerns and allegations toward S. Nevertheless, S continued to withhold relevant details and failed to agree with the positions G constructed.

It was shown that G's attempts to overcome S's resistance must be understood as occasioned from within the interactional contingencies that arose, and may vary over the course of a conversation. Just as the giving of "advice" was shown to emerge in step-by-step fashion by both Heritage and Sefi (1992) and G–S in chapter 2, so has preliminary attention been given in this chapter to how emergent shifts occurred within each of the three methods of pursuit employed by G (i.e., claiming and imputing knowledge, laying out consequences, citing sources and offering evidence) but also more generally across these resources. As S's resistance emerged (see chapter 4), so did G chain together alternative methods of pursuit en route to building relevant and compelling grounds and thus "evidence" for claims made—activities designed to substantiate her position as knowing and factual, not unknowing and fictional, and thus to coerce S toward confronting and healing her own illness.

First, from an understanding of G's actions, it is clear that as speakers attempt to establish themselves as knowledgeable and informed, they have available to them opportunities to both claim and attribute knowledge to others with whom problems allegedly reside. By asserting and upgrading the truth of a claim, questioning another's motives, or reviewing information about bulimia as social constructions amounting to "facts" rather than a matter of personal opinion, speakers' pursuit techniques may be altered—to solicit particular kinds of responses from recipients, and to legitimize the reasonableness of their actions.

Second, one means of escalating such pursuit is to lay out the consequences of failed action. When and if another disattends the "facts" being constructed, not only may their lack of realization be challenged, but attempts to "team up" to fight the problem may be offered. Further, negative and extreme case scenarios can be built on-the-spot, as with G's "It could ruin your whole life": the "It" here representing bulimia, which was also replaced with a more personalized "you" by G in a subsequent interactional moment. Of interest here is the ways G indirectly draws relationship between S's illness ("it") and the lack of control S appears to have on bulimia's consequences ("you"). This recurring feature of the G–S interaction is apparent in the ways consequences were reasserted and variably offered by G, in part to bolster her position, but also as a means for continuing to seek withheld affirmation from S about the problem and its severity.

Finally, the seriousness of bulimia was yet further substantiated as G worked to cite sources and offer observations as evidence of claims. Several references were made to S's physical appearance and moods as symptomatic of bulimia, including a "pink toothbrush." Also, specific examination was made of how G invoked S's fiancé as essentially agreeing with her concerned position, thereby disagreeing with S's reconstruction ("=He thinks I look great."), by first soliciting S's report before informing S that she had contradictory information regarding Bill's opinion. This kind of interactional predicament reveals how speakers, as with those pursuing another's alleged wrongdoing, may rely on prior knowledge of a "source" to refute the very positions taken by the person failing to "own" the problem.

Thus far, however, only minimal attention has been given to the kinds of responses produced by S, in orientation to which it is now clear that G quite tenaciously pursued and attempted to overcome S's resistance. The details of S's varied techniques for avoiding ownership of the bulimic problem are addressed in the following chapter.

4
▼▼▼▼▼▼▼

Avoiding Ownership

SDCL: G/S: 158–159; 335–338

G: > ↑ *Don't tell me that now.*
    you just better <u>stop</u> < (.) denyin(g)
    .

    .
    .

G: *everything that I <u>sa:</u>y (0.2) <u>you</u> <u>you:</u> (.) you <u>deny:</u>,*
    (0.5) just because of this <u>very</u> reason that
    ch'u (eh) are <u>not? willing.</u> (0.4) to <u>be::</u> (0.3)
    honest with your<u>self</u>

On two different occasions, G attributes "denial" to S's actions: first, as an activity that S "just better <u>stop</u>" doing; next, as repeatedly offered responses to "<u>everything that I sa:y</u>," reactions explained by G because she makes S out as unwilling to be "honest with your<u>self</u>." These actions are attributed by G even though it has thus far been shown that outright "denial" is an untapped resource for S. Several moments have revealed S's actions as more closely akin to a series of mitigated confessions (i.e., less than direct admissions of "bulimia"). Her actions also reveal a host of passed-by opportunities to be forthright and thus align with G by more fully disclosing her "problem" and committing to professional (medical/therapeutic) assistance.

In the following discussion, *denial* is shown to be a predominant clinical explanation of bulimics' behaviors. And, as stated earlier, G has attributed "denial" by warning of the dangers of S's being less than honest in coming to grips with the "problem." However, the interactions examined in this chapter reveal as insufficient the tendency to subsume S's actions under the rubric "denial." Straightforward "denial" does not adequately describe the more diverse set of orientations produced by S, responses typifying her "resistance" to G's persistence. Rather, S employs at least five methods that approximate denial by "avoiding ownership" of the "problem": discountings, providing accounts or explanations to minimize wrongdoing, withholding response through no-talk (silence), seeking closure on troubling topics (i.e., the focus of the alleged wrongdoing), and downgrading the seriousness of attribution through humor.

Before turning directly to these avoidance techniques, it is useful to briefly consider that although denial has emerged as a central concern for researchers and clinicians dealing with eating-disordered individuals, just how such descriptions may or may not apply to S's often remarkably subtle actions remains problematic.

First, as described by both researchers and clinicians, dealing with forms of denial is altogether routine in clinical encounters. Eating-disordered individuals are often understood to display behaviors indicative of a "lifelong pattern of denial of affect and illness" (Bulik, Carter, & Sullivan, 1994, p. 297). Denial and distortion in self-reports about internal experiences and bulimic actions (deliberately or inadvertantly) are also exceedingly common (see Vitousek & Manke, 1994). And specific kinds of symptomatic denials are commonplace (see Butler & Newton, 1989; Newton, Butler, & Slade, 1988), including "hunger" (see Heatherington & Rolls, 1989). Consequently, denial has been put forth as a key attribute of "resistance to treatment" (see Richards, 1989; Smaldino, 1991; Williamson, Davis, & Duchmann, 1992).

For example, a recurring difficulty for clinicians are patients who offer what are treated as denials to questions "about taking laxatives, diuretics, or amphetamines to lose weight" (Baker, 1993, p. 172). Unless directly asked by physicians, "patients do not usually reveal their bulimic behavior" (Yanovski, 1991, p. 1231), perhaps not even then—a theme and set of interaction possiblities initially raised in chapter 3.

Second, not all of S's actions can easily be seen as instances of denial. For example, it cannot be overlooked that, early on, S twice queries G about matters raised and by so doing further topicalizes the "problem":

Excerpt 1 (SDCL:G/S:62–64)

S: why are you: sittin here sayi:n my: - ( )
      (0.4) > should be with <u>exerci:se</u>. <

Excerpt 2 (SDCL:G/S:114)

S: What do you mean by <u>tha:t</u>?

These two attempts fall noticeably short of directly asking for G's advice, yet may nevertheless exemplify efforts not to deny but to mobilize assistance and, perhaps, build a partnership for helping S uncover and cope with her maladaptive lifestyle (see Smaldino, 1991). Moreover, S does (finally) agree to see the "doctor":

Excerpt 3 (SDCL:G/S:405–406)

S: I will go o:ne time an(d) I'm not going
      after that

yet it is clear that a single visit is commensurate with a token, bandaid remedy for a considerably more serious "problem" requiring (minimally) individual commitment, a program of clinical treatment, and when available strong family support. And even under these circumstances, unequivocal healing of often long-term addictions (not just with eating disorders, but also, e.g., alcoholism, drug abuse, smoking, and additional "problems") cannot be guaranteed. Thus, agreement to see the doctor, but only on S's terms, reflects yet another display of avoidance in coming to grips with the seriousness and consequences of her bulimic illness.

Finally, even Excerpt 4 can be understood as S avoiding direct ownership of the problem. Consider the following delicately constructed segment where S, for the third time, cycles back to invite G to go for a "walk" (see chapter 2 for analysis of the prior two "invitations," and G's responses to them as means for initiating the "problem"):

Excerpt 4 (SDCL:G/S:419–423)

        S: .hh hhhh I'm exhausted I hafta work tomorrow are
1→   you still gonna go walk with me tomorrow:?
                    (0.2)
2→   S: .hh And it's not because I'm a buli:mic
              I just like to get out with some fresh air:.

In stating "still gonna go" (1→), S treats as a prior established agreement what G has, in marked contrast, noticeably withheld and thus failed to agree to do in prior two invitations. In this way, S is re-inviting as though G's prior rejection-implicative responses can now justifiably be understood as something other than unequivocal rejections, with the possibility left open via "still" that G's "acceptance" remained a viable option worth of S's pursuit: S treats as unfinished business her concerns with "walking," but also reformulates and noticeably disregards G's earlier stated "problems" occasioned at the very outset of the G–S conversation. This is one remarkably subtle way of shifting focus, by "beginning anew" her own pursuit of response for an acceptance which G had thus far not provided, an attempted return to "business as usual" rather than "problems" associated with "business at hand" as initiated by G (see Button & Casey, 1988–1989).

And in (2→) S next explicitly mentions that a good reason for walking is "<u>not</u> because I'm a buli:mic," but rather that she simply wants "to get out with some <u>fresh</u> air:." Notice here that it is S who now raises "bulimia" as a topic that G earlier initiated, but does so once again in a remarkably subtle manner, an action falling short of self-criticism: not by denying in wholesale fashion that she engages in bulimic actions, to which she has repeatedly "confessed" in mitigated fashion, but by more singularly dismissing "bulimia" as a "reason for walking."

APPROXIMATING DENIAL

The kinds of actions apparent in Excerpts 1 through 4 cannot be sufficiently explained by subsuming S's actions into "denial," nor can a more diverse set of S's orientations to G's persistence.

Discounting

In Excerpt 5, originally addressed in chapter 2, G proffers an unsolicited evaluation and explicitly claims knowledge of S's motivations and actions:

Excerpt 5 (SDCL:G/S:139–148)

```
      G:   We:ll Sissy. (0.8) let's ↓ face it no:w (.)
           yo:u kno:w .hh that ch'u are so: e::ager:. (.)
           to be thin:. (0.2) that you sometimes. go
           in the bathroom. (0.2) and throw up your food?
           I kno:w it's tr[ ue! ]
1→    S:                  [GR ]AMMA YOU ARE SO:: FULL O(F)
2→         SHIT! I am so: su:re.
```

Aside from the fact that the response "YOU ARE <u>SO::</u> FULL O(F) SHIT!" might be construed as an exceptional and perhaps novel way for granddaughters to speak with grandmothers, what interactional work is being achieved in this instance?

First, S offers what is clearly a straightforward and exclamated discounting of the knowledge G is claiming to possess. By so "denying" the legitimacy of G as a viable source, one whose grounds for assertion are deemed inadequate, S forestalls (at least for the moment) being held accountable for the "problems" G has projected in prior turn. In effect, the responsibility not assumed by G to be taken up by S is nevertheless dismissed by S: in countering, S reciprocally attributes G's lack of responsibility via "full of shit"— literally satiated with displeasing and/or unsuitable information, and labeled as such in derogatory fashion. In Excerpt 5, S is therefore not compelled to "face" a problematic circumstance that is treated as fundamentally excremental, such as the imputed motive that S is purposely "throwing up" because she is "<u>so: e::ager:</u>. (.) to be th<u>in:</u>." Instead, S's discounting is upgraded by claiming disbelief with a tag-positioned "I am <u>so: su:re</u>." This tag casts additional doubt on the truth value of G's description and assessment, but also on the relevance and appropriateness of even raising such possibilities in the first instance.

Second, by discounting and claiming disbelief as in Excerpt 5, S is noticeably not offering an explanation (but see subsequent section), explicitly admitting guilt, nor straightforwardly "denying" alleged wrongdoings. As noted, such withholdings effectively delay, however briefly, further consideration of the "problem"—throwing up food and taking responsibility for such actions. Yet withholdings of this sort also display S's unwillingness to address the truth and/or falsity of G's alleged wrongdoings, as one form of disputation involving return and exchange moves (see M. H. Goodwin, 1980, 1990), in favor of drawing attention back to the original source. By discounting (1→) and displaying disbelief (2→), however, S also engages in an activity other than counteraccusation: it is not G's unhealthy actions that occasion S's next actions, but the substantive basis on which G makes her claims.

On examination of the environment of interaction subsequent to Excerpt 5, S's actions are themselves found to be implicative for G's response. It is now G, who first alleged S's wrongdoing, who reprimands the apparent inappropriateness of S's discounting via "full of shit":

Excerpt 6 (SDCL:G/S:117–134)

```
       G:    ·
             .
             .
             (0.2) that you sometimes. go
             in the bathroom. (0.2) and throw up your food?
             I kno:w it's tr[ue!  ]
1→     S:              [GR ]AMMA YOU ARE SO:: FULL (O)F
             SHIT! I am so: su:r[e.]
       G:                     [(S]i::ssy stop) ↑ sa:ying
             such a thing as tha[t.  ]
2→     S:                   [↑ W]E:LL: I can't believe
             > that ch'u would even say something like
             tha:t. <
                     (0.2)
       G:    Well it's tru:e isn't it?
                     (0.4)
       G:    You know I:? know more about this than you
             think? I know.
                     (0.5)
3→     S:    Gra:mma. you (a)re so we::ird (.hh aghhh)
```

In overlap (2→), S now elaborates and further specifies the disbelief initiated in (1→), in lieu of offering what reprimands hearably project (e.g., deferring, apologizing). This is met with G's query and noticeable, transitional silence (addressed in a subsequent section), followed by what is yet another attempt by G to substantiate a knowledgeable basis for pursuing the "problem." Once again, however, S orients to G as illegitimate in (3→), thereby laying grounds for withholding response to G's claiming and imputing knowledge. Here it is seen that S's description of "weirdness" to G precedes a disgruntled reaction (.hh aghhh), one noticeably provided by S in the course of discounting and continuing to delay direct consideration of the "problem" as G constructs it.

In short, G's claims for viability as a knowledgeable source, and positioning through an attempted reprimand, are transformed by S into a focus of G's own culpability. By making G out to be "full of shit" and "weird," the initial wrongdoing attributed to S is discountable by means of refocusing on G's inadequacies—a shift from self to other as responsibility gets negotiated turn-by-turn (see Goffman, 1955, 1967). In these ways, discountings may involve explicit refocusings on other's vulnerabilities while remaining void of self-evaluation.

Such a self–other shift is explicitly marked in Excerpt 7 as S responds to G's preannouncement (see Terasaki, 1976), a recommendation to see a doctor, and an attempt to inform her of activities comprising such a visit:

Excerpt 7 (SDCL:G/S:263–281)

```
        G:   You know what I would li:ke to do:.
             (.) I would like to take you. (0.8)
             to a doctor. and we'll talk it over and
             you can tell em:
                     (0.8)
        G:   You know they have [ways of]
1→      S:                      [Wha::-!] Oh Ga-
2→           .hh Gramma you are s:o weird
3→           I can't believe that you'd even think that
4→           .hh Y:ou wanta go to a doctor you take
             yourself to a doctor
                     (1.8)
        G:   Sissy (.) I'm tellin ya (.) .hhh you
             need HELP .hhh and I mean big help (.)
             [      you need ↑ ther:apy      ] =
5→      S:   > [I need help fer my grandmother] <
```

In overlap, S's "Wha::(t) Oh Ga-" (1→) treats G's prior turn as problematic, mitigates the essential force of the recommendation offered, and as with G's "Oh-prefaced" actions in chapter 3 (Excerpts 21–23) reasserts her position with yet another upgraded "weird" discounting in (2→) and an elaborated statement of disbelief in (3→). These moves in a series are prefatory, in this instance, to S's counterrecommendation in (4→): an unwillingness to seriously consider G's recommendation by reflecting G's advising as best followed by the source of the recommendation, constructed so as to imply that G could benefit from the same solutions available for S's "problem." Regardless of G's subsequent attempt to stress the critical nature of S's predicament, an escalated three-part list construction (help → big help → therapy) (see Jefferson, 1990), in (5→), S overlaps and once again discounts by framing herself as the one needing help to deal with her grandmother.

To summarize, S's discounting of what G is "up to" in the pursuit of information can be understood as one means of forestalling direct consideration of alleged wrongdoings. By casting doubt on the viability of claims offered and shifting the focus of inadequacy back on the very constructions attributed by G toward S, S displays an unwillingness to align and thus take seriously the "problems" projected by G. This is not to say that explanations are always withheld by S in the course of receipting alleged wrongdoings, however, as is evident in the following set of instances.

Accounting

As Heritage (1989) observed, and initially overviewed in chapter 2, a range of instances have been identified wherein "a second speaker's failure to accomplish a projected, or looked for, action is accompanied by an explanation or account of some kind" (p. 133). Such instances include, for example, mitigated rejections of invitations (see Drew, 1984) and the absence of an expected answer to a question (including ignorance as an account, e.g., "I don't know"; see Schegloff, 1984). In these and related instances, accounts are often provided in ways that frustrate, delay, and/or avoid first speaker's pursuit of a response, which was itself constructed so as to elicit from second speaker descriptions and/or confirmations of "problems" addressed.

In and through the production of an account in Excerpt 8, S seeks to reconcile the trajectory of G's utterance (e.g., S's excusing or justifying actions) by treating her actions as normal and thus morally and ethically acceptable (see Heritage, 1983; Mills, 1940):

Excerpt 8 (SDCL:G/S:190–194)

```
    G:   Well why? are ya so tir:ed
         an can- [ (canky)]
→   S:            [ Beca:u ]se? I have to
         ↓ work such long hours (.) Gramma
```

It is worth noting that S is not simply providing an answer to a question, but accounting for the actions attended to by G (see Atkinson & Drew, 1979; Schegloff, 1984). S's response is not designed as a denial, however, but rather a provisional acceptance to what G's query is noticeably asserting. In confirming being "tir:ed an can- (canky)," S also provides, for G's consideration, an acceptable activity consequential to and thus responsible for such behavior—working long hours. By offering this activity as a reasonable and legitimate explanation, S can be heard to minimize wrongdoing by averting attention away from alternative and perhaps illegitimate reasons for behaving in this manner (i.e., behaving "for no good reason").

Similar to Excerpt 7, where G attempts to recommend that S visit a doctor, in Excerpt 9 G's description of S's "activity" and subsequent recommendation is once again receipted with a discounting (1→) and statement of disbelief (2→) (see also chapter 2, Excerpt 12). However, S next provides an explanation or account in (3→), thus the sequence is organized as follows: Discounting → Disbelief → **Account**:

Excerpt 9 (SDCL:G/S:28–40)

```
        G:   Well honey yer so thin: no:w:
                  (0.6)
        G:   I don'(t) know (.) I think yer just (0.2)
             °(well you're)° just wearin yourself out
             with all your activity > I think if you
             slo:w down a li(tt)le bit and rest a little
             bit more <
                  (0.4)
 1→  S:   GRA:[M M A] YOU'RE SO WEIRD!
        G:       [ Maybe ]
 2→  S:   > I don't even know why you say that I- <
 3→       .hh I am f:i::ve thr:ee:: and I still
             weigh a hundred an ten- fifteen po:unds?
```

Actions such as G's unsolicited recommendations needn't be taken seriously, when and if S acts as though she fails to recognize the import (e.g., displays an inability to grasp the relevance) of G's reasons for offering advice-relevant information. This appears to be the case through S's discounting and claiming disbelief in Excerpt 9, actions functioning to forestall attention given to G's focus on the "problem." Yet in (3→) it is evident that S seeks to further substantiate both G's concerns as unnecessary on the one hand, and the basis on which discounting and disbelief are legitimately offered on the other. Although (3→) functions as a counter to G's initial assertion ("honey yer so thin: no:w:"), the counter is substantiated by explaining or accounting for "height" and "weight" as indices of "normality."

Thus far, S's explanations or accounts have been shown to occur in immediate response to G's assertions in Excerpt 8, and/or as apparent upgrades to discountings and statements of disbelief in Excerpt 9. In essence, S's reliance on "working long hours" and "height and weight" appear as offerings of suitable evidence for effacing what G is noticeably orienting to. However, it should be made clear that neither placement guarantees the suspension nor automatic deletion of concerns held by a speaker such as G. Accounts can themselves occur as moves-in-a-series (see 1→ – 4→), provided by S in evolving fashion as continued responses to G's hearable failures to accept the viability of explanations offered (a→, b→, c→):

Excerpt 10 (SDCL:G/S:38–64)

```
1→  S:   > I don't even know why you say that I- <
         .hh I am f:i::ve thr:ee:: and I still
         weigh a hundred an te[ n- fif ]teen po:unds?
                            [ ((noise))]
              (0.6)
a→  G:   O:h ↓ you don't weigh a hundred an
         fifteen ↑ pounds .hh all your clothes
         are fallin off of ya everybody tells you
         ya look thi::n?
2→  S:   Ya:: but fin[ ally I  ]
b→  G:             [You're b]o:ny look at acrossed
         your chest an yer .hh your co:llar bo:nes
         stickin o::ut > ↑ why d'ya wanna be so thi:n! <
3→  S:   Gra:mma:. ↑ it's not: .hh if I could lo::se
         more weight an git it off my thi::ghs?
         I wouldn't. .hhh I wouldn't wanna lose any
         more weight > but I ↑ can't help it if
         my shoulders look. ba:re! < =
c→  G    = Well dear < (.) You do that with exercise.
         no:t di::eting (an le) an not getting the
         right foods? =
4→  S:   = Gra:mma. (.) I a:te good the other night
         didn't I you an(d) I both went out for a big
         salad an:(d) s:oup. (.) why are you: sitting
         here sayi:n my:- ( ) (0.4) > should be
         with exerci:se. <
```

In Excerpt 10, S and G collaboratively produce a series of two-turn sequences, chained-out in such a manner that each utterance reoccasions the relevance and subsequent placement of a next positioned, reciprocal counter. In (a→), for example, G's turn-initial "oh" and subsequent response (marked with disagreement and reference to "everybody") clearly renders S's prior utterance as untenable. And although S relies on a transitional moment to begin offering what would appear to be a preface to an account in (2→), G elaborates in (b→) by countering with further "evidence" and offering a tag-positioned "why d'ya wanna be so thi:n!". In turn, S explains via a partial excuse and minimization of responsibility ("but I ↑ can't help it . . .") in (3→). As the interaction unfolds with G's disagreement-relevant (c→), S once again receipts prior turn by attempting to explain actions called into question (i.e., by referencing an occasion of eating appropriately, as examined in more detail in chapter 3, Excerpt 15).

From Excerpts 8 to 10 it is clear that interaction can proceed through ongoing attempts to defend actions as understandable and acceptable orientations to alleged wrongdoings. Explanations or accounts are, in the ways S utilizes them, one set of resources for situating motives, actions, and/or occasions in attempting to legitimize what may otherwise be treated as problematic.

Withholding Response: No-Talk (Silence)

The previous examination of discountings and accounts provides an opportunity to inspect two explicit techniques for minimizing and/or avoiding ownership for G's allegations and attempts to substantiate "problems" typifying wrongdoings. By discounting the viability of claims and offering explanations to legitimate actions, S withheld alignment by failing to agree with and/or affirm G's projected concerns.

In contrast, withholdings may also occur not from what S explicitly provides as a response, but rather the noticeable absence of responses such as discountings and accounts (i.e., through "no-talk" or silence):

Excerpt 11 (SDCL:G/S:127–132)

S:	↑ WE:LL: I can't believe > that ch'u would even say something like tha:t. <
G:	Well it's tru:e isn't it?
→	(0.4)
G:	You know I:? know more about this than you think? I know.

Silence is itself a response that has been shown to signal both delay and/or potential rejection following assertions (Pomerantz, 1984a), invitations and offers (Davidson, 1984). By failing to provide an explicit answer to G's query in Excerpt 11, S averts (if only momentarily) owning up to what G suspects is true nonetheless. Yet S's silence may nevertheless be heard and treated as "admission." This suspicion is further substantiated as G resumes speaking following S's failure to provide affirmation. Through G's resumption it becomes evident that, even though silence may display a problematic orientation to prior turn and thus trouble with what prior utterance projects, it need not constrain G's orientation to silence as noncompliant action. As Heritage (1989) observed:

> At all events, *the failure is treated as requiring explanation* and, indeed, it is a positive signal for us to initiate a search for an explanation that is appropriate to the circumstances. The explanations which may be arrived at under such circumstances are almost always negative in their implications for nonresponding parties and this factor may be a major motivation for them to produce either compliant actions or, alternatively to produce their own accounts for non-compliance which forestall the negative conclusions which might otherwise be drawn. (p. 139)

It is through G's resumption of speaking following silence, and what is achieved via resumption, that an affirmation and/or explanation may be treated as noticeably absent and thus "due."

In Excerpts 11 and 12 to 13, withholdings via silence recurrently appeared within a three-part sequence: specific queries by G (1→) were followed by S's withholding of explicit reponses (2→), which were themselves receipted by G as further substantiation of the correctness of her assertions in the search for information *and* alignment/confession (3→), thus:

1→ G: Queries
2→ S: Silent Withholding
3→ G: Resumption of Pursuit

Excerpt 12 (SDCL:G/S:92–96)

```
1→    G:  > Well Sissy do you? think you're gonna
              look good < (.) when you're so: thin:
2→                  (1.6)
3→    G:  that chu'll be > pretty in your wedding on
              that beautiful wedding gown ((continues))
```

Excerpt 13 (SDCL:G/S:108–112)

```
1→    G:  Well you al:ways eat just fine?
              it's amazing that you don't weigh? more.
              .hh so what happens to the food that you eat?
2→                  (1.1)
3→    G:  you- > you're not getting any bigger? but. <
```

In Excerpts 11 to 13 "well" is employed as a disagreement-relevant preface. In the following Excerpt 14, an alternative preface in the form of a preannouncement (see Terasaki, 1976) is employed. This preface is also receipted silently, however, followed with a similar three-part sequence:

Excerpt 14 (SDCL:G/S:136–142)

```
      G:  °Sissy I wanna tell you something°
                  (0.8)
1→    G:  I:? know:. (0.8) that ch'u are throwing up
              your food purposely. (.) .hh > and do you
              realize that this is a (.) ill:ness <
2→                  (0.4)
3→    G:  and the m:ore > you do it (up) <
              ((continues))
```

In the absence of an articulated response to prior query, S's failure to explicitly deny, admit, and/or display common knowledge contributes to G's orienting to the contingencies of the moment as "unfinished business." By

S's withholding of possible "incriminating evidence" (see Heritage, 1989), however, G may nevertheless display an understanding of what was not offered, as though information withheld is "hearable" in its absence. Consider, for example, a continuation of (Excerpt 8):

Excerpt 15 (SDCL:G/S:190–219)

```
        G:    Well why? are ya so tir:ed
              an can- [ (canky)]
        S:              [ Beca:u] se? I have to
              ↓ work such [ long hours ] (.)[G r a ]mma
                         [((tape noise))]   [ (((tn)) ]
                 (0.2)
        S:    you look at me. I do not look skinny and
              withdra::wn from soci:ety? ((staccato))
 1→           .hh fi:n:e I eat a little bit (0.4) too much
              I- I feel stuffed .hhh ↑ and I'll jis:-
                 (0.5)
 2→     G:    O:h:: ((low voice)) >↓ come off it <
              (0.2) (eh-) look at everybody else. they eat
              [and they o:vereat and they don't run in the] =
 3→     S:    [Gra:mma I got plenty? of friends. that do- ]
 2→     G:    = bathroom and [ throw it up  ]
 3→     S:                   [ Yeah and yu-] oh you don't
              think? they do:.
                 (0.4)
 3→     S:    H:o:ney > I got so many friends that do it
              you don't even [ know. < ]
        G:                   [Do you thi]nk
              you're [(            )]
 3→     S:          > [How do you] think I lear:ned?
              it Gramma? <
```

Following an explanation or account in (1→), S fails to complete her turn by stating "I- I feel stuffed .hhh ↑ and I'll jis:-." Although withheld by S, G nevertheless is able to understand exactly what was not offered. This understanding is displayed in (2→), where G's "oh-prefaced" response challenges the legitimacy of S's explanation. By reasserting and providing counterevidence, G both maintains a position and completes what S withheld ("run in the bathroom and throw it up"). Although G made explicit in next turn what S left unspecified, as one form of "collaborative completion" (see Lerner, 1989), and despite the fact that S indirectly admits engaging in the activity ("throwing up") that G hearably treats as problematic, immediately following overlap S's oh-prefaced response nevertheless invokes friends' actions as justification for her behavior as the interaction unfolds (3→). By reciprocally countering G's reference to "everybody else" and "they" in (2→), S displays further unwillingness to assume responsibility for such actions (i.e., due to her own citing sources and invoking, at least in part, a "safety in numbers" rationality), yet also leaves open the possibility that friends were responsible for her "learning" the activity in the first instance. This is indeed an interesting turn of events when considering that G's initial query, "Well why? are ya so tir:ed an can- (canky)," was immediately treated by S as problematic and, by implication, tied to "throwing up her food."

Topic Closure

It has been suggested that topic shifts may occur following user's placement of "oh-prefaces," in line with Heritage's (1990) analysis of features built into sequential activities possessing an "inapposite character." The interactional work of terminating a problematic, and initiating an alternative topic evidences yet an additional resource used and relied on by S: explicit attempts to coerce G to change and perhaps even terminate the problematic topics being addressed.

Although the conversational organization of "topic" has received considerable attention (see W. Beach, 1990a, 1993a, 1993b, 1995a, 1995b; Button, 1987, 1990; Button & Casey, 1984, 1985, 1988–1989; Drummond & Hopper, 1993; Hopper & Drummond, 1993; Jefferson, 1980, 1981, 1993; Maynard, 1980), of particular relevance to the present analysis is consideration of moving away from a topic involving "troubles talk" (see W. Beach, 1990a; Jefferson, 1984b; Sacks, 1976). In cases when talk about troubles is problematic for one or more interactants, as described in chapter 2, it is normal to enter into a closing of current topic by restarting an alternative one:

Excerpt 16 (JG:II:(a):3–4) (Jefferson, 1984b, p.193)

```
M:    But anyway I figure that maybe he can,
      hh give me something to: uh (.) you know
      bring this do:wn. Cause God I can't afford
      to you know. (0.2) get like tha:t?
           (0.3)
S:    Ye:ah
           (0.6)
→  M:    hhh tch How are you.
```

In referencing Sacks's work on getting off troubling topics in conversation, Jefferson (1984b) noted how a variety of devices are employed by interactants on entry into closings, each of which not only displays an orientation to new topic but "but as proposing to start the conversation afresh; thus the name 'conversation restart' " (p. 193). A particularly marked instance appears in Excerpt 17, where G seeks S's commitment to keep an appointment through a "promise":

Excerpt 17 (SDCL:G/S:410–423)

```
  G:   O:ne > step at a time < Sissy
            (0.5)
       We'll go the one ti:me (0.7) that ch'u (0.4)
       promise me [that I'll make the appointment ( )]
1→ S:             [  OKA:::Y ALright (.) OKAY  ]
       I'LL GO n- le(t)'s just drop it for t'night
       okay? (.) I don't wanta talk about it anymore.
            (1.5)
2→ S:  .hh hhhh I'm exhausted I havta work tomorrow
       are you still gonna go walk with me tomorrow:
       (.) .hh and it's not because I'm a buli:mic
       I just like to get out with some fresh air:.
```

Prior to her request to "drop it," in (1→) S overlaps G's prior turn by making a concession to the appointment ("I'LL GO"). She then explicitly references a dispreference to continue on topic. With heightened emphasis (see Goodwin, 1980), S's "OKA:::Y ALright (.) OKAY" thus evidences not just an attempt to close down G's concerns with making the "appointment," but *all* discussion about the "problem" initiated by G at the outset of the conversation (see chapter 2). One universal feature of speakers' "Okay" usages involves their recruitment to treat as sufficient prior speakers' contributions and elaborations on a given set of issues, clearing the way for transition and thus shift to next-positioned (although in "casual" interactions, typically "on topic") matters (see W. Beach, 1990a, 1993b, 1995a, 1995b). In Excerpt 17, however, it is clear that S is initiating a more terminal shift; her trimarked response, as is common with "Okays-in-a-series," displays a definitive and escalated attempt toward closure not only by means of S raising her voice and paralinguistically emphasizing each word, and by the insertion of "ALright" as an upgrade toward termination of topic (see W. Beach, 1993b, 1995b), but also by her immediately next and explicit formulation of not wanting to "talk about it anymore." S's "OKA:::Y ALright (.) OKAY" is designed to unequivocally achieve a "conversation restart." Even S's final "okay?" in (1→) can be understood as a topic terminal inquiry seeking G's alignment toward and affirmation of closure. As preclosing devices toward topic *attrition*, therefore, this is consistent with Jefferson's (1981) analysis of those systematic procedures that interactants rely on, such as "acknowledgment tokens" (e.g., um hmm, uh huh, yeah), during movement toward speaker readiness and preparedness to shift topic.

Following G's noticeable withholding of response, the interactional environment previously examined in Excerpt 4 can now be understood in yet further detail: in (2→) S initiates a new topic by returning to what amounts to her third attempt to invite G to go for a walk.

S's attempts to delimit re-emergence of G's concerns with the "problem," however, may involve considerable effort with no guarantee of "success." The following instance occurred less than one minute following Excerpt 17:

Excerpt 18 (SDCL:G/S:446–460)

```
        G:   Okay. (.) wher- where are you getting any
             nourishment to do all these [(                    )]
1→      S:                               [ Grandma I thought ]
             we weren't
             gonna [ talk    about    it    anymor:::e   ]
        G:         [You go out there and lift twenty five]
             pound weights of
                        (0.4)
        G:   of
2→      S:   Grandma I don't wanna ta- ↑ look do you wa-
             > do you want me to go: < see that doctor? fine.
                        (0.4)
3→      S:   Now let's just drop it for tonite.
```

In response to G's persistence, S first announces surprise to topic reinitiation (1→) and then proceeds in (2→) to offer compliance (to see a doctor) conditionally on the topic once again being dropped. In (2→), it can be seen that S's restart and emphasized "↑ look", and second restart, indicate her frustration with the repeated topicalization by G—a frustration giving rise, following G's failure to assume speakership at this (0.4) transitional moment, to S's reiteration of "Now let's just drop it for tonite" in (3→; see also Excerpt 17, 1→). As with G's treatment of S's silence described earlier, this interactional work involves, minimally, S's query, a noticeably absent response by G through silence, and S's speakership resumption reasserting her position.

And in Excerpt 19 this sequence organization reappears yet again as G explicitly seeks admittance, but is subsequently receipted by S (1→):

Excerpt 19 (SDCL:G/S:511–537)

```
        G:   Now admit just a little bit to me
             .hhh they'll (.) you do go in and-
             have you noticed that your teeth
             (.) I noticed your toothbrush has
             a lot of ↑ pink like your (I'ke) you're
             kinda bleeding?
                        (2.2)
        G:   Uh: (.) do you [ think that maybe this]
1→      S:                  [ Grandma I thought  ]
             you said we were gonna change the subject.
                        (0.6)
2→      S:   Oka:y? =
        G:   = Allright well (wh'ya) talk about.
3→      S:   Well I dunno but I'm not gonna stay up here
             if you keep talkin about that.
                        (0.6)
        G:   ↑ Well=
4→      S:   =Well let's [    turn (.) let's turn the t-    ] =
        G:              [Okay you've ↑ made a promise]
```

```
5→    S:    = ↑ Oka::y (le-) forget it let's drop that
            .hhh let's (.) let's turn the TV on:.
                  (2.0)
      S:    ↑ Okay just turn- go ahead and turn the TV on.
6→    G:    Well tell me Sissy (.) now how much longer
            is it before (.) uh the wedding?
```

Throughout this extended exchange, S again seeks to hold G accountable for reinitiating the "problem" (1→). In (2→), S's "Oka:y?" functions as a solicitation device for G's confirmation in response to G's withholding, and in (3→), S counters with a "threat" en route to turning the TV on (an apparent distraction ploy in lieu of self-selecting new and/or alternative topic). Once again, however, G's persistent concern with S's "promise" is receipted by S through concession and a recycled attempt to terminate the topic with "let's drop that" (5→). Finally, in (6→) G formally initiates a new and different topic, one apparently designed so as to engender S's interest and willingness to further engage in interaction—a move that initiates talk about "the wedding" for a period of time which G, although in more indirect fashion, occasions as yet a further opportunity to pursue the "problem" (see chapter 5).

Additional resources are no doubt available to interactants for moving out of troublesome topics (see Jefferson, 1984b), and/or for drawing attention to specific "agendas" (see W. Beach, 1990b, 1993b, 1995a, 1995b), each indexing the specific occasion of use and thus participants' orientations to moment-by-moment contingencies of interaction. Yet it is clear from the instances above that while topic and thus "problem" closure can be addressed through specific and explicit references to "dropping" a topic, such attempts by S do not, by fiat, eliminate or guarantee that particular issues or concerns, once mutually "dropped" by shifting onto a new or different topic, will remain suppressed. In fact, G works to make sure such is not the case throughout the remainder of the G–S conversation (see chapter 5). Attempts toward topical closure by S, therefore, turn out to be only momentary solutions to G's preoccupation with the bulimic problem.

Humor: Downgrading Seriousness of Attributions

At times, S responds to G humorously, particularly in moments when she attempts to downgrade the relative impact and seriousness of G's attributions. Prior attention has been given to situations where a troubles-teller laughs so as to indicate an ability to take the trouble lightly (see Jefferson, 1984a). A modified version of this appears in the following:

Excerpt 20 (SDCL:G/S:192–211)

```
      G:    > ↑ Don't tell me that now.
            you just better stop < (.) [ denyin(g) ]
1→    S:                               [ Gra:mma ]
            I've ↓ o::nly done that a couple a ti:m:es,
```

```
       G:   ↓ ° A couple [ of ti::(mes)] °
       S:              [ It's not? ] that big of a deal.
2→          my friends used to do it in the sorority $ all
            the t(hh)i:me. $
                       (1.0)
3→     G:   ° Well listen? ° your friends used to do a lot
            of things in the sorority that you didn't
            have to pattern after I'm quite sure?
```

In response to G's initial and explicit assertion that S should quit "denyin(g)," addressed at the outset of this chapter, S provides a qualified admittance (1→). With a reciprocal counter G challenges this qualified admittance in disbelieving fashion by repeating a portion of S's prior utterance in next turn ("↓ ° A couple of ti::(mes) °"). In (2→) S overlaps and continues to elaborate by seeking to minimize and thus discount her wrongdoing. This response is recipient-designed to G's prior position of disbelief by first downgrading and invoking a well-known excuse of "safety in numbers" (see Excerpt 15), but also by S's "$ all the t(hh)i:me. $" In this way, S's admitted "couple of times" is offered in pale comparison with sorority friends who used to do it "all the time." The quickened and heightened delivery of S's laughing voice treats the seriousness of G's concerns as, literally, a laughing matter so as to add further impetus to the downgrading force of the utterance. Notice, however, that G's next disagreement-relevant response (3→) fails to treat S's laughing voice humorously. Instead, G provides one version of a "po-faced" (see Drew, 1987) and thus serious response to what, alternatively, might have been treated as an accepted invitation to share S's laughter (see Glenn, 1989; Jefferson, 1979).

The final instance displays comparable features:

Excerpt 21 (SDCL:G/S:136–150)

```
       G:   ° Sissy I wanna tell you something °
                       (0.8)
       G:   I:? know:. (0.8) that ch'u are throwing
            up your food purposely. (.) .hh and
            do you realize that this is a (.) ill:ness <
                       (0.4)
       G:   and the m:ore > you do it (up) <
            [    (if) you don't stop right now     ]
1→     S:   [ ↑ You'r::e so: FUNNY GRAMMA! ]
            .hh this is an ill:ness I can't believe
            you're throwing up your food ((mimmick voice))
2→     G:   Well you ar:e ?
                       (1.2)
       G:   and ↑ you know something ((continues))
```

Following G's preannouncement, as earlier noted G claims and attributes knowledge to S, moving next to question and seek affirmation regarding

"<u>ill</u>:ness" before continuing to lay out consequences for S's actions. In overlap, however, S withholds affirmation and treats G's concerns lightly. In
(1→) G's altogether serious concerns are initially transformed by S's char-
acterization of G as "<u>so</u>: FUNNY", an action preparatory to mimicking G's
own delivery and orientation. Once again, however, this humorous discounting is treated seriously as G queries S in (2→) and is receipted with silence.
Of interest here is the cyclic transformation from seriousness to attempted
humor and back again, quickly emerging transitions further perpetuating
the interactionally asynchronous environment occurring throughout the G–S
conversation.

SUMMARY

Focusing on a series of actions not adequately captured by the term *denial*,
this chapter examined how S attempts to avoid ownership for, and otherwise
mitigate the attribution and pursuit by G, of a "problem" portrayed as a
consequence of S's wrongdoing. It has been shown that S's persistence is
apparent in a variety of subsequent responses which withhold affiliation and
agreement: discountings (and claims of disbelief); accounts or explanations;
no-talk (silence); attempts to close prior and restart alternative topics; and
humorous responses to problematic and otherwise serious allegations. As
interactional techniques for achieving avoidance, S's responses function to
forestall, excuse, and even formulate the normalcy of actions purported to
be the very source of G's expressed concerns. As noted, however, S's responses do not necessarily minimize nor guarantee G's voluntarily "dropping" the topic.

From the data examined herein it should be evident that "avoidance" is
thoroughly an interactional achievement, thus collaboratively produced by
speakers. It is sensitive to and arises within the ordinary circumstances of
everyday family life such as the G–S conversation. In this sense, taking responsibility for one's actions need not be, and frequently is not, an individual
task: S does not display a willingness to directly admit, or even grant the
plausibility, that a "problem" exists mirroring the attention given to it by
G. S's actions are locally and thus contingently built as responsive to what
G offers as reasonable assertions, just as S's responses occasion, in their
course, how G proceeds to solicit S's owning up to (and hopefully resolving)
her bulimic problems.

In addition to S's five methods for avoiding ownership noted earlier, it
is important to stress that actions of "denial" are not always apparent when
dealing with a problem such as bulimia. Although G twice and explicitly
describes S as essentially being in denial, it has been shown that S engages
in alternative actions—mitigated confessions, passing by opportunities to dis-

close and commit to seeking professional assistance (although only a "token" commitment was offered), indirectly mobilizing G's assistance, and dismissing bulimia as a "reason for walking" rather than denying the illness altogether. Collectively, these moments reveal how the work involved in "not denying" appears in many guises and is thus implicated across manifold interactional trajectories.

There is now sufficient evidence to indicate that the detailed and often subtle actions S and G are *preoccupied* with actually comprise the very circumstances they have co-constructed. As with "denial" discussed at the outset of this chapter, however, it remains to be more fully demonstrated that and how "preoccupations" are, first and foremost, embedded within participants' orientations to interactional contingencies. The interactional organization of "preoccupations" is addressed in the following chapter.

5
▼▼▼▼▼▼▼

Preoccupations

I'm not yet convinced that we don't have all these delicates going on constantly and continuingly. But we just don't yet know how delicate. . . . And now we're all catching each other do it a lot, because we just skim away the surface a bit.

—Jefferson (1977)

Claims that bulimics are constantly "preoccupied" with food, thinness, shape, weight, and appearance remain largely mentalistic in scope, owing in part to how both researchers and clinicians have systematically failed to take into account the kinds of interactional circumstances (such as G and S) that talk about bulimic problems may very well generate.[1] As with "confrontation" or "denial," the altogether detailed and often subtle actions on which a case for preoccupations in interaction might be built cannot be understood by attending solely to reports and reconstructions by individuals. In this chapter, despite the fact that S has resisted G's attempts to solicit admittance and commitment to remedy bulimia, a case is made that her actions nevertheless reveal preoccupations with some of the very issues and concerns raised by G.

It is shown here that S's wedding is one extremely important social occasion of relevance to S's bulimia, and that as G and S focus on the wedding

---

[1]Whenever everyday conversations are examined on their own merits, including occasions such as G and S where problems with bulimia are interactionally constituted, mentalistic concerns become transformed into social predicaments: "So don't worry about the brains that these persons couldn't have but which the objects seem to require. Our task, in this sense, is to build their brains. . . . one has to come to terms with the fact that from one's appearances the activities one has engaged in are observable" (Sacks, 1985, pp. 16, 22).

plans, S's illness remains a focal point of concern. An examination of the coauthored details of an extended segment, occurring late in the G–S conversation, is offered. This conversational fragment involves S's reported troubles with planning her wedding, and interactional problems arising from G's disaffiliative and sarcastic responses about S's predicament. These actions are thus situated within an environment of potential conflict, where G continues to withhold affiliation and alignment with S's stated concerns and troubles (see also chapters 2 and 3).

But what does S, having initiated some trouble or complaint that fails to solicit affiliation from G, do next? Through analysis of her "descriptive language" and "speech errors" (see Excerpt 1), apparent within S's next-positioned responses to G, attention is given to how S is preoccupied with both bulimia and her upcoming wedding. In the midst of dealing with problems generated by G's withholdings and pursuit, it becomes clear that S's language is tailored to the very circumstances she is, visibly and contingently, "caught up in" and thus "occupied with": S's actions are a direct reflection of the interactional problems G and S have coproduced, and S's preoccupations are apparent within the situation she is attempting to describe. Such absorption eventuates in tailormade characterizations of interrelationships among activities and events of central importance in S's life (i.e., bulimia and her wedding).

Specific attention is drawn to S's utterances 1→ and 2→:

Excerpt 1 (SDCL:G/S:559–605)

```
        S:   I don't know: to tell ya the truth::
             I kinda wanted a black 'n white wedding
             but everybody else has been saying
             (.) .hh "Do:n't have a black 'n white wedding."
             (.) maybe I'll have a fuc:ia or real pretty pink:.
                  (1.2)
        G:   °(Uh huh)°
             [[
1→      S:   God:: it's hard fittin everyone in my
1→           wedding? .hh Grandma there's so many
1→           people different sizes?
        G:   Well of ↑ course (.) there's the nic:e
             plump (.) > normal looking people <
             and then there are the skinny people?
                  (0.8)
        S:   Grandma?
        G:   that look $like$ they're undernourished?
                  (1.0)
        G:   Then (.) now [ I ]
2→      S:                [Uh] huh [ huh huh  ]
        G:                         [but (at) first] (.)
             [ if the ] bride's
2→      S:   [uh huh.] there's always? a clown:.
                  (0.4)
```

```
2→   S:   there's always a c:lown in the party
2→        er: in the [cro::wd]
     G:            [You kn]ow what?
                   (0.6)
     G:   If the bride looks pretty no::body else
          cares about how the rest of em look (.)
          Bride is the star:::=
     S:   =You know I'll look prettier than
          anybody else so we don't havta
          [ worry about that]
     G:   [   Well I sure   ]ly do ↑ hope you ↑ will:
                   (1.0)
     G:   If we havta pad ya up a bit
          here and [  ( t h e r e )  ]
     S:            [ Hah hah hah::] (.) such a comedian:.
                   (1.2)
     G:   When's Bill comin home?
```

By seeking to extend mentalistic conceptions that bulimic individuals are preoccupied with their bodies, understandings are sought of the ubiquitous and noncoincidental nature of preoccupations in the G–S conversation— those closer to the surface and thus easily identified, and others more likely to go unnoticed until analysis reveals them as delicately tied to the interactional (unwitting, unintentional) moments in which they arise (e.g., as with S's "descriptive language" and "speech errors" when responding to G's withholdings and sarcasm). Through such analysis it becomes possible to address whether and how poetics emerge and are conversationally organized in everyday talk; situated examination of the details of social interaction is prerequisite to addressing whether and how poetics emerge rapidly, spontaneously, and are delicately organized as interactional achievements. This is a preliminary step toward comprehending the kinds of phenomena Sacks (1992b) was getting at in noting "we're trying to find out things we don't know about how delicately people use their language. Then, any possible extended delicacy is something to look into" (p. 292). And these are the kinds of candidate phenomena Sacks (1985) had "in mind" when observing that, simply because certain features of talk are produced quickly and (more or less) effortlessly, this does not necessarily mean there are simple analytic answers to their production. We are concerned here with the most intricate and delicate resources for locating and describing, not just preoccupations, but more generally the "poetics of everyday talk." Sacks (1992) and Jefferson (1977, 1996) gave early and detailed attention to various arrangements of "sounds, categories, words, utterances, and errors" that are "not 'exceptional' nor 'incidental' nor 'constantly suppressed' in normal talk. Rather, they are constantly embedded in and masked by a range of syntactic, sequential, interactional structures" (Jefferson, 1977, p. 19). Jefferson's (1977,

1996) basic description of "errors" is also a fundamental point of departure for the ensuing analysis (as it was for Hopper, 1992a; see also Motley, 1985), especially in the ways they

> provide a break in the conversation's surface which permits easy observation of the phenomena . . . which only emerge when the talk is not taken at "face-value," when the "plausible" surface is disregarded. And one easy way to get past the surface is to have it already disturbed for us, as is the case with errors.
> We'll be using errors, then, as a window into some of the mechanisms via which words are selected in the course of an utterance. (Jefferson, 1977, pp. 2–3)

To summarize, as reflective of the "troubles" and "problems" apparent throughout the G–S conversation (but also see Drew & Holt, 1988; Jefferson, 1984a, 1984b), G consistently withholds affiliation and/or sympathy from S's expressed anxieties or concerns. From Excerpt 1, it is argued that two solutions to such predicaments are provided by S (involving her "descriptive language" and "speech errors"), each revealing preoccupations with bulimia and the wedding. Further, an expanded notion of the word *error* includes predicaments emerging when the interactional work of G and S is understood as hearably and doubly problematic: descriptions and errors produced in an environment of having been found "in error"—one version of *double trouble* (see also Jefferson, 1996, pp. 11–12).

Analysis begins with an overview of how preoccupations might be recognized in language generally, although particularly and next within disaffiliative sequential environments where responses to prior complaints can give rise to "idiomatic expressions" uniquely tailored to interactional circumstances. We then return to G and S to make the case for preoccupations with bulimia and its consequences in their conversation.

THE DELICACY OF PREOCCUPATIONS: AN OVERVIEW

In "favorable circumstances" language has been shown to be recruited and shaped to intentionally achieve what Freud (1963) described as "double meaning proper, or play upon words," as with the following seditious witticism:[2]

---

[2]Notice that this instance does not reflect a typical Freudian slip (i.e., when some utterance is purported to display "deeply hidden meanings" rooted in subconscious [latent, suppressed] thoughts, feelings, motives, needs, and the like).

Excerpt 2

One of Napoleon III's first acts when he assumed power was to seize the property of the House of Orleans. This excellent play upon current words was current at the time: "C'est le premier vol de l'aigle." ["It is the eagle's first *vol*."] "**Vol**" means "flight" but also "theft." (p. 37)

Or a speaker may appear preoccupied when assessing surrounding circumstances that go unnoticed, but only for a brief moment:

Excerpt 3

San Diego Tribune, January 27, 1992
[During one of several interviews with runners, immediately following the U.S. Olympic Women's Marathon Trials in Houston]:
Francie Larrieu Smith looked at Janis Klecker and said, "For Janis, running a marathon is like *brushing your teeth.*"
Then, realizing that she had unwittingly made a play on words about Klecker's profession, Larrieu Smith said, "Funny I should say that about a *dentist.*" (italics added)

But then again, speakers in ordinary talk commonly make available what they are orienting to without realizing how the just produced utterance was or was not tailored to, or triggered by, immediately prior topics or activities. And in next turn, recipients do not seem to make the connection either. A preoccupation is later available for analysts to point out and make something out of, yet in the course of its "real-time" production the talk appears taken for granted by participants—used and recruited to get specific work done, but apparently unseen/unheard and thus passed by—in favor of moving onto some next positioned matter. One such case appears in (*1→) (but see also W. Beach, 1993a):

Excerpt 4 (NB:IV:10:36) (from Drew & Holt, 1988, p. 401) ((arrows added))

```
        Emma:   Wel you know we were there in Ju:ne
                yihknow Bud played go:lf inna (.)
  1→            when the air c'nditioner went o::ff?
                .hhh En we're about (.) th'only ones
                that ha:d'n air conditioned room the
                rest of'm were bro:ken. .hhh An'we
  1→            went down to breakfast 'n there was only
                about two people to help for breakfast
                with all these guys goina pla:y go:lf.
 *1→            They were a:ll teed o:ff:.
        Lottie: Ye[:ah?
        Emma:      [Becuz (.) Bud couldn't e:ven eat his
  1→            breakfast. He o:rdered he waited forty
                five minutes'n he'a:dtuh be out there
 *1→            tuh tee off so I gave it to uh: (.)
                Karen's: liddle bo:y.
  2→                    (0.7)
        Emma:   ((swallow)) I mean that's how bad the
```

3→   service was .hhh (.) I̲t's gone tuh p̲o̲t.
       Lottie: u-O̲h̲::: (.) e- Y̲ e : ̲: a h.

Part of Emma's telling about their trip involved multiple complaints (1→) with the hotel's poor facilities and bad service. The sequential environment within which these complaints get constructed, not taken up by Lottie (2→), and further solicited by Emma (3→) are central to the ensuing analysis and are addressed later. However, notice first how Emma displays what appears to be her dual preoccupation with the practical consequences of the complained about matters. Emma reports they were "all teed off" with the unfortunate circumstances they were caught up in because Bud and "these guys" might be late to "tee off" a round of golf: "teed off/tee off" are clearly connected. Now, did "teed off" simply get moved up and/or did "tee off" get triggered by Emma's dual preoccupations? This dual use can most likely be added to Jefferson's (1977) collection of how sounds and noises get "moved up," and how prior words give rise to something produced next as "father to a thought" (p. 10).

Yet there is more to be addressed here. Neither Emma nor Lottie attended to "goina play golf ←→ They were all teed off" as something special, more than a coincidence, a "play on words." They were, in the first instance, occupied with other encompassing matters; they apparently were not aware of the poetics of their conversational preoccupations.

As analysts, we can post hoc skim the surface away a bit and make something of these kinds of delicacies: the intentionally constructed "Vol → flight/theft" in Excerpt 2, the unwittingly produced yet immediately recognized "brushing your teeth/dentist" in Excerpt 3, the altogether unnoticed "teed off/tee off" in Excerpt 4. These utterances get occasioned as descriptive resources, revealing just what these participants were and were not treating as significant. Clearly, as with Excerpt 4, used but unnoticed features of talk can become the grist for analysts' mills, even if the participants being analyzed appear to make nothing of them. This leads to a consideration of just how ordinary talk is routinely and unwittingly produced—without forethought, void of some a priori or externalized "script" designed to configure a social interaction toward specific effects and desired consequences. Rather, preoccupations arise from and are embedded within momentary and contingent types of actions, such as the seditious witticism in Excerpt 2, the assessment in Excerpt 3, and the complaint in Excerpt 4. They are thus features of evolving usages of language and interaction, not detached mental states.

DISAFFILIATIONS AND THEIR CONSEQUENCES

More can be said about these poetic features, especially with regard to the occasioning of their use. Returning to Excerpt 4, what were Emma and Lottie caught up in producing that so captured and drew their attention away from what analysts can recognize as delicate and poetic connections? What are these other "matters" emerging within the turn-by-turn evolution of these particular interactional circumstances? Extending the discussion initiated in chapter 2, a variety of researchers have evidenced how a considerable corpus of conversational materials includes moments of potential interpersonal conflict, most notably during ongoing alignment difficulties manifest in such activities as *complaining* and *receipting a complaint* (but also agreeing and disagreeing, anticipating nonsympathetic hearings, inviting and rejecting an invitation, and so on). Relying on the Emma–Lottie interaction in Excerpt 4, and a collection of similar instances, Drew and Holt (1988) showed how idiomatic expressions (e.g., "It's gone tuh pot," "banging your head against a brick wall," "down the tubes," "throw me off the deep end," and so on) are often employed in sequential environments involving complainable matters. As central to G and S, when an individual provides otherwise private troubles and/or anxieties for another's inspection and response (i.e., a "trouble-telling"), recipients may produce and/or withhold sympathizing and/or affiliating with the complainer. In cases where withholdings occur and where potential resistance to sympathizing with a prior complaint is displayed (as in Excerpt 4, 2→), it is not uncommon for initial complainers to pursue affiliation by use of *idiomatic expressions* (as in Excerpt 6, 3→ "It's gone tuh pot").

To summarize Excerpt 4, then, it can be seen that on completion of Emma's telling and complaint formulations (1→/*1→), Lottie fails to provide sympathy or affiliation (2→). In seeking to legitimize, summarize, and bring her complaints to a close (3→), Emma's idiomatic "It's gone tuh pot." effectively solicits what was previously and noticeably absent: Lottie's affiliative "u-Oh::: (.) e- Y e : : a h." Although idioms do vary, they can generally be identified as (a) formulaic constructions, (b) whose meaning is largely figurative, and (c) designed to summarize and/or complain about others' treatment of them (see Drew & Holt, 1988).

Within "inauspicious" or potentially disaffiliative environments as these, it is thus common for actions to be organized in the following canonical manner:

1→   Complainable Matters
                        ↓
2→   Withholding(s) of Affiliation/Sympathy
                        ↓
3→   **Idiomatic Expression**

In Excerpt 4, Emma's unwittingly employed descriptions were tailored to such interactional circumstances. The questions remain: Are such unwitting descriptions evident in similar troublesome environments? If so, what peculiar shapes might they take?

Unwitting and Tailored Descriptions

With this brief backdrop in mind, the analysis proceeds by considering whether and how S produces unwitting and tailored descriptions: (a) as responsive to G having withheld sympathy or affiliation to S's prior reported trouble; and (b) as delicately tied to the circumstances S reveals herself to be caught up in—responding to G's persistent orientation to bulimic problems and the wedding itself.

Excerpt 5 occurs shortly after what might roughly be characterized as an "agreement" between G and S to "drop" the topic (see Excerpt 19, chapter 4). Here G can be seen as initiating a new, although related "wedding topic" by twice querying S about the "bridesmaid's dresses":

Excerpt 5 (SDCL:G/S:552–568)

```
        G:    Well (th- ) eh h- ha- have you really
              decided on on the. bridesmaid's s-
              dresses [ (    )]
        S:            [ Well ] (.) [ I- ]
        G:                         [Did] you find anything?
  1→    S:    I don't know: to tell ya the truth::
              I kinda wanted a black 'n white wedding
              but everybody else has been saying
              (.) .hh do:n't have a black 'n white wedding.
              (.) maybe I'll have a fuch:sia or real pretty pink:.
  2→          (1.2)
  2→    G:    °(Uh huh)°
              [[
 *3→    S:    God:: it's hard fittin everyone in my
              wedding? .hh Grandma there's so many
              people different sizes?
```

In (1→) S does not offer an affirmative response to G's questions about the "dresses." Instead, her "I don't know" prefaces an expression of uncertainty and thus some concern or trouble. What is next reported is one version of a "my side telling" (Pomerantz, 1980), an experience involving a potential conflict between her preference for a "black 'n white wedding" and "everybody else" standing in opposition to such a choice. Although S is the bride and could likely thwart wedding plans not to her liking, this reported conflict makes clear that others' opinions are not only taken into serious consideration but also allowed to impact the choices S makes. Yet no choice is immediately forthcoming.

Rather, it is within this environment of having received others' opinions, and attempting to figure out what to do with them, that S next appears to reflect on further alternatives: "maybe I'll have a fuchsia or real pretty pink." But in so designing her talk, and by refraining from further speaking, S also offers these alternatives up for G's consideration—one "delicately and circuitously handled" "fishing" device (Pomerantz, 1980, p. 197) for indirectly soliciting rather than directly asking for G's opinion. Indirectly, S provides an oppportunity for G to tell what she thinks, from a different point of view, and thus to collaborate in solving what S has put forth as a current trouble—the "bridesmaid's dresses" predicament raised at the outset and thus occasioned via G's two queries. These queries revealed G as possessing some, but not updated, knowledge about wedding plans.

In these ways, S's (1→) should not necessarily be heard as a complaint seeking commiseration by appealing to G for sympathy; instead, (1→) is an attempt to make available to G one of many predicaments S has "presented the evidence for" and is facing in planning the wedding, and to indirectly solicit G's opinion or advice. Or, as Drew and Holt (1988) put it, summarizing Emerson and Messinger's (1977) conceptual interests in the "micropolitics of trouble," actions of this sort can be understood as an "effort to mobilize help in remedying the trouble" (p. 399).

In (2→), however, such affiliation is not forthcoming. As the noticeable (1.2) silence indicates, G withholds by passing on the opportunity to collaborate in talking about, perhaps even solving, this particular problem at hand. As recipient to S's attempt to elicit information and involvement, G fails to offer some information or opinion of relevance to S's stated problem. Only G's soft-spoken "°(Uh huh)°" follows the lengthy silence, a token that neither directly acknowledges S's solicitation nor reveals movement toward fuller speakership.

We are now in a position to examine how S, in next turn, deals with G's implicit unwillingness to affiliate by not responding substantively to the predicament S's telling had put forth:

Excerpt 6 (SDCL:G/S:567–568)

*3→   S: God:: it's hard fittin everyone in my wedding?
            .hh Grandma there's so many people different sizes?

What is S attending to (i.e., the nature of the trouble at hand) at this interactional moment? Might "God" have some relationship to other features of this utterance? Is there a sense in which these reported troubles consist of more than S's concerns with others in her wedding (e.g., "but everybody else has been saying," "fitting everyone in," "so many people")?

First, answers to these questions might begin with considering whether S's (*3→), produced simultaneously with G's minimal "°Uh huh°" following the (1.2) silence, treats G as having declined S's solicitation with a displayed unwillingness to talk further about "bridesmaid's dresses." It seems such a case can be made, especially when considering how G's attempts to achieve unequivocal alignment from S prompts further pursuit (see chapters 2 and 3). In response to G's withholding, one taken to be treating S's initial telling and indirect solicitation as ineffectual, S now produces a second and related source of troubles for G's consideration. Essentially, S's second telling can be understood as a "redo" troubles reporting, once again and indirectly soliciting G to produce a "different output" (see Schegloff, 1987c, pp. 40–41).

Yet the manner in which S constructs (*3→) does more than resolicit G to affiliate and, at this moment, provide sympathy for S's problems; it also adds further *legitimation* to the worthiness of her tellings in the first instance (see Drew & Holt, 1988; Pomerantz, 1980). Here S's telling rests not with a single or several persons, but progresses from "everybody else" in (1→) to "everyone" and "so many people" in (*3→). These descriptors increasingly assert S's problematic circumstances as S seeks response from G. But notice that in (1→) and especially (*3→) S reports details representing more or less "literal descriptions" of her circumstances (e.g., "people different sizes"), not figurative or metaphorical versions of the problems at hand. Thus, although S's (*3→) can be understood as an escalated attempt to formulate the extremity of her situation and detail her problematic circumstances, it is not "idiomatic" per se, as with Emma's "It's gone tuh pot" in Excerpt 4, and thus does not possess "a certain resistance to being tested or challenged on the empirical facts of the matter" (Drew & Holt, 1988, pp. 405–406).

Second, it is obvious at first glance that S prefaces her response with "God": What might be noted about S's usage of the expletive "God" in the environment of reporting troubles about her "wedding"? Is "God" simply another means for drawing G's attention to further wedding problems, yet an additional "solicitation device" employed in the course of re-formulating the difficulties she is caught up within?[3] That is one version. Another possibility is this: "God ←→ wedding" connections are categorically relevant in many, if not most, matrimonial events. Both Sacks (1992, pp. 291–293) and Jefferson (1977, endnote 17) have noted families of relationships (e.g., semantic, sound) between "God" and other words occurring in close proximity to this and other expletives. For example, they consider how a portion of an utterance, "God there wasn't a soul in we were the only ones at the bar . . . ," involves "God and soul" close together, with "only ones" roughly synonymous with "sole." Similarly, "God ←→ Wedding" may fit within a collection of categorical relevance and family relationships.

Third, is it coincidental that S's dual description of the problem "God it's hard fittin everyone in my wedding?", and "Grandma there's so many people different sizes?" are themselves mirrored images of S's own predica-

---

[3]But there might be more here. Given the disjunctive character of the talk throughout this interactional event and G's withholding above, could it also be that S's "God" expletive is an unwitting call to the "deity"—as an entity beyond and/or greater than one's self, more encompassing than the situation at hand—for deliverance, help, and even restitution? As Sacks (1965–1975 Winter, 1971 lecture) put it: "Well, who knows? Noticing it, you get the possibility of investigating it. Laughing it off in the first instance, or not even allowing yourself to notice it, of course it becomes impossible to find out whether there is anything to it" (p. 292).

ment, namely: (a) fitting into her own wedding dress; and (b) accommodating everyone's concerns and priorities (notably, but not exclusively, G's) into the planning and organization of the wedding? And what of S's lexical choices: it's "[hard] fitting everyone in" following the exact moment it was [hard] getting a response from G?; the address term [Grandma] prefacing people [different] sizes, following an extended discussion between G and S over their [different] concerns with bulimia? At least these threads appear woven throughout S's utterance, "God → hard → wedding," "Grandma → people different." Perhaps these categorical and descriptive resemblances are a matter of random occurrence and should be analytically treated as such. Conversely, it is perhaps just these sorts of "delicacies" that Sacks (1992, pp. 87–97; 291–302) calls attention to in evidencing how immediately and spontaneously interactants perform operations on the materials of the moment—without forethought, apparently void of intentional projection, and possible only in the confines of such rapid construction—yet nevertheless with amazing sensitivity to the troubles and/or topics at hand. In this way, S's offering her concerns with fitting everyone else in, and with other peoples' sizes, displays her preoccupation with the more encompassing problem of achieving her own desired size and dress-fit for the wedding. And this preoccupation affects the manner in which the problems presented by S are embedded, and thus made available, in the talk.[4]

Topical Puns

In Excerpt 6, S's constructions of reported troubles with the wedding, and as responsive to G's prior nonsympathetic hearing, can be seen as displaying

---

[4]This is the kind of "parallel" that Sacks (1992, pp. 263–266) found compelling, "at the edge of overt punning" (1965–1975, Winter 1969 lecture), in examining a data segment from a New York radio call-in show involving a blind caller's complaint about "the lack of courtesy that people pay to blind people" (1965–1975, Winter 1969 lecture, p. 1). In uttering (Sacks, 1992, p. 263),

   A: Uh::, You see what happens, wit:h- specially with
       New Yorkers, i:s? thet they get a::l preoccupie::d
       with their own problems

Sacks described how the host of the show produced an explanation precisely fitted to the blind person's circumstances: though you can't see and are complaining about it, realize that others don't notice things due to their own problems, including noticing the blind. The issue is framed by asking how did the host of the show produce an explanation, "on the spur of the moment," that so delicately paralleled the blind person's problem (i.e., that persons have problems preventing them from "seeing")?:

   Of interest in that [i.e., moderator's explanation that New Yorkers "get all preoccupied
   with their own problems"] is this: Roughly, how fine is the relationship between an explanation and the thing it explains? . . . Its compellingness turns on its relationship to
   the presented complaint; in the series of ways in which it fits and parallels and turns on
   her [i.e., the caller's] circumstances. (Sacks, 1965–1971, Winter 1969 lecture, pp. 1–2)

an altogether delicate connection to the circumstances she is caught up within: S's unwitting utterance turns out to be a direct, even elegant, description of the wedding and illness problems she is preoccupied with (i.e., "fittin," "sizes"). As interactional resources these problems find their way into, and are captured by, the language poetics used to organize just this occasion. In particular, understanding how the categorical and descriptive resemblances of S's Excerpt 8 (*3→) might be understood as tailored to, parallel with, and mirror images of S's own predicament provides the opportunity to raise several issues of relevance to "making the case for" the possible existence of such poetic phenomena in everyday conversation.

Although no "speech errors" are apparent in the construction of S's utterance, a case might be made for the existence of a "sound row" [d] (see Jefferson, 1977, 1996):

    *3→ S: Go[d::] it's har[d] fittin everyone in my we[dd]ing?
              .hh Gran[d]ma there's so many people [d]ifferent sizes?

This instance might fit within a larger "sound row" collection; the series of [d] sounds could partially explain S's construction of this utterance. But there is much more here, as has been argued, closely akin to what Sacks (1992) and Jefferson (1977, p. 21) refer to as *topical puns*, involving "words selected in talking about something that are especially apt for the thing being talked about." Clearly, the present analysis of what S is preoccupied with hinges less on noticeable speech errors and sound rows than on various combinations and categories of words as embodied reflections of surrounding circumstances. The interactional orientations displayed by S, and thus the social actions achieved, are more convincing as "poetic" evidence than the seemingly endless search for "deep hidden meanings."[5]

A related issue of "evidence" involves consideration of how S's (*3→) is itself implicative for G's next response. A careful consideration of G's subsequent turn-at-talk and its consequences provides yet further details regarding what G is herself preoccupied with, the serious yet playful nature of her concerns, and what (if any) poetic features emerge as this conversation unfolds. These achievements have much to do with the ongoing organization of the interactional environment within which S's complaint is first put forth and receipted by G, and its impact on subsequent talk-in-interaction as addressed here.

---

[5]Having now provided the argument that S's (*→3) is not incidental nor exceptional, the issue arises as to how "normal talk" may nevertheless, at times, be hooked up with "pathological processes." Following Jefferson's (1977, p. 19) substantive extension of Sacks's lecture notes, it must be kept in mind that by simply raising such possibilities, it may very well be the analyst who comes off as "screwy" in providing evidence for the organized nature of such materials. Or, as Jefferson (1977, cover page) informally reported a written note from Sacks regarding "a rather elaborate proposed case of poetic talk": "Not for circulation; they'll think we're both batty."

A Sarcastic Withholding

The utterances produced by S in Excerpt 5 (1→ and *3→) have a commis-
erative character; they are complaint-like in the way she seeks to mobilize
G's sympathy and affiliation. But as evident here, although G's straightfaced
and topic initial "Well of ↑ course" in (2→) initially comes off as aligning
with S's complainable matter, drawing attention to the normalcy of S's concerns, it actually serves as a preface or set-up to a noticeable and second
withholding of sympathy or affiliation in (2→):

Excerpt 7 (SDCL:G/S:567–574)

```
1→   S:   God:: it's hard fittin everyone in my
           wedding? .hh Grandma there's so many
           people different sizes?
2→   G:   Well of ↑ course (.) there's the nic:e
           plump (.) > normal looking people <
           and then there are the skinny people?
                (0.8)
     S:   Grandma?
2→   G:   that look $like$ they're undernourished?
```

There is obviously something more to G's (2→) than a mere declination or
withholding, however; something sly, sneaky, and inherently sarcastic in its
paired categorizations of "plump → normal / skinny → undernourished."
This is one form of a "tease" initially coming off as *playful* but, at root,
employed to address *serious* concerns and consequences (see Drew, 1987).
Without explicitly mentioning which "category" is most applicable to S, G
constructs her turn somewhat innocently—and recognizably so, as though
G does not have S "in mind"—yet in a manner uniquely designed for, and
accessible to, S's hearing and understanding. This understanding is achieved
and offered by S's upward-intoned "Grandma?", a "po-faced," serious response to the "serious" side of G's prior tease (see Drew, 1987). As a passing
warning, S treats G as engaging in an activity beyond S's tolerance threshold,
effectively "trying her patience." Not only is (2→) misaligned with prior turn
(1→) (i.e., once again withholding affiliation), but more pointedly it signals
a *breach* of a prior agreement (and even promise) to "change the subject"
(see Excerpt 19, chapter 2). Through G's continuation and smile voice
"$like$" in (2→), G does give herself away (at least momentarily) to the
humor of the moment. But it is important to note that in so revealing her
orientation to having just subtly breached, and been warned for breaching
by S, G needn't sacrifice the seriousness of her concerns with S's health and
behavior (i.e., vomiting her food prior to the wedding). In fact, it is the
serious nature of these health issues that explains, in no uncertain terms,
G's persistence in the pursuit of S's alleged wrongdoing.

In short, G is clearly unwilling to refrain from once again "making her point" in (2→). Yet in exactly the way the point is made, G also displays a sensitivity and awareness of the potential enforcement of an agreement she promised to keep. Her solution to this double-binded problem—of being unwilling to totally refrain from expressing her opinion, yet at the same time abiding (at least somewhat) to an earlier promise—is apparent in the way she successfully gets her point across by packaging her concerns in "sarcastic comparison." The working order of such a comparison turns, inevitably, on the anticipation and requirement that S "fill in" the unspoken, but nevertheless intended and projected "meaning," that was noticeably withheld by G in the first instance.

THE POETIC CONSTRUCTION
OF AN IDIOMATIC EXPRESSION

Attention can now be drawn to how S responds "idiomatically" (*3→) to G's second withholding of affiliation via sarcastic comparison:

Excerpt 8 (SDCL:G/S:567–586)

```
1→   S:   God:: it's hard fittin everyone in my
          wedding? .hh Grandma there's so many
          people different sizes?
2→   G:   Well of ↑ course (.) there's the nic:e
          plump (.) > normal looking people <
          and then there are the skinny people?
               (0.8)
     S:   Grandma?
2→   G:   that look $like$ they're undernourished?
               (1.0)
     G:   Then (.) now [ I ]
*3→  S:                [Uh] huh [  huh huh  ]
     G:                         [but (at) first] (.)
          [ if the ] bride's
*3→  S:   [uh huh.] there's always? a clown:.
               (0.4)
*3→  S:   there's always a c:lown in the party
*3→       er: in the [cro::wd]
```

Following (2→), a (1.0) pause occurs marking G and S's failure to expand either the sarcasm or additional warnings about the "breach." Next, it appears that G attempts to initiate a shift in "footing" (Goffman, 1981) via "Then (.) now I"—work involving "getting off troubling topics," similar to what was addressed in chapter 4 in terms of S's actions, and described by Jefferson (1984b) as "conversation restarts" where speakers enter into the task of shifting and closing down topics so as "to start the conversation afresh" (p. 193). It can be further observed that G's "Then (.) now I", and "but (at) first (.) if the <u>bride's</u>" are attempts to produce what eventuates in Excerpt 10, 4→.

Yet these attempts to shift both footing and topic are overlapped, somewhat interjectively and thus in overriding fashion, as S begins (*3→) with what is hearable as fake laughter. These tokens are recipient designed to G's prior sarcasm, decidedly offered so as to not be taken "at face value" but as insincere responses to G's laugh token "$like$" in (2→). By means of these counterfeit tokens S negatively assesses this moment, displaying a recognition of what G was "up to" by moving to reject G's actions—drawing attention away from G's being "funny" and toward S's unappreciative treatment of G's previous sarcasm. Just as G's (2→) was employed to produce seriousness humorously, so do S's fake laughter tokens.

Further, these tokens are consequential in additional ways: G is now shown to be constrained by the "aftershocks" of what she occasioned in her prior sarcastic withholding (2→). This is apparently the case even though G initiates a closing down of troubles talk and topic shift; she is now being held accountable by S for what she initiated in the construction of (2→), caught midstream between her immediately prior sarcasm and the sincerity apparent in the not yet produced (4→).

But in what precise sense is S's (*3→), following the fake laughter tokens, also recipient designed to G's (2→)?:

Excerpt 9 (SDCL:G/S:583–586)

```
*3→  S:   uh huh. there's always? a clown:.
              (0.4)
*3→  S:   there's always a c:lown in the party
          er: in the [cro::wd]
```

Before directly examining S's preoccupations embodied within the speech error "er: in the [cro::wd]," we begin by noting basic features. This particular turn (*3→) possesses multiple units (see Sacks et al., 1974), comprised of four constructional elements: (a) fake laughter tokens, (b) "there's always? a clown:.", (c) "there's always a c:lown in the party", and (d) "er: in the cro::wd"—with a (0.4) pause between (b) and (c). The question here is: What is being achieved through this figurative/metaphorical multiunit turn-at-talk? Answers to this question are predicated, initially, on a series of observations available from (*3→) itself. First, prior to the pause, S's "there's always? a clown:." does not appear to project completion but rather an upcoming and extended turn—to which G orients by withholding response at the transition-relevant pause of (0.4). Second, S's "there's always a c:lown in the party" recycles (see Schegloff, 1987c) the initial portion of the turn, after which S completes what was projected prior to the pause. Third, it is within S's completion, an apparent increment added to the turn, that the speech error ("er: in the [cro::wd]") occurs.

Similar to the question raised earlier focusing on poetic relationships between "explanations and the things they explain" (Sacks, 1965–1971, 1992), so is it the case that idiomatic expressions (such as S's *3→ in Excerpts 11–12) offer summarized versions of just what the trouble is taken to be (i.e., as constitutive and regulative features of the very troubles they report; see Drew & Holt, 1988). And two additional key features are evident in (*3→) that appear quite universally when "idioms" are employed in conversation. First, (*3→) fails to articulate the exact nature of S's grievance toward G. By so doing S also refrains from directly responding to, and/or expanding on, what G's utterance (2→) projected (i.e., "plump → normal," "skinny → undernourished"). It is, in this sense, only a summarized version of the empirical details put forth by G in (2→): an idiomatic "way out" of (or solution to) having to address, literally, her being "skinny → undernourished." Second, in providing the figurative or metaphorical "gist" of her reaction, but no more, S's (*3→) works to *terminate* and thus close down the topic/activity rather than pursue its elaboration. This is in alignment with G's "en route" shift of footing and topic discussed earlier, as well as an enforcement G's earlier "promise" to not "talk about that" anymore.

And there are distinct "poetic" qualities of S's (*3→), a consideration of which can add meaningfully to an enhanced understanding of how S's preoccupations are embedded in this particular idiomatic expression.[6] As S constructs her multiunit turn there is an apparent ambiguity between "clown/party/crowd," each of which is drawn from several idiomatic or colloquial expressions (e.g., clichés). Jefferson (1977) observed how speakers, when attempting to correct and otherwise treat a word or portions of an utterance as a possible error, necessarily rely on "a gross selection mechanism that delivers up a category, but not the specific member within that category, such that it is a matter of pot luck whether the correct member is uttered" (p. 5).

With S's (*3→), several idiomatic expressions are possible (categorical) resources—"Stop clowning around," "Class clown," "Life of the party," "Party pooper," and/or "There's one in every crowd." It is clear that the

---

[6]A comparison with the song "Send in the Clowns" by Stephen Sondheim (originally from the Broadway show *A Little Night Music*, and later sung by Judy Collins, 1975), provides an altogether coincidental yet seemingly tailored parallel:

> Don't you love fights?
> My fault I fear
> I thought that you'd want what I want
> Sorry, my Dear
> But where are the clowns?
> Send in the clowns
> Don't bother, they're here

ambiguity may be rooted in S's attempt to employ an appropriate cliche, such as a one-liner that "fits the situation" at hand, but in this instance different clichés simply get mixed up following the (0.4) pause. An explanation for this mix-up can be enhanced by further considering S's delicate use of "party" versus "crowd" in her utterance. Although the possibility exists that these descriptors are a "result of more or less random choices between various ways of saying something" (Drew & Holt, 1988, p. 399), it should not be overlooked that "party/crowd" may very well represent inherent contradictions in both this interactional moment and S's situation in general: A wedding is a party, therefore a celebrative event; A wedding has a crowd, and therefore involves the stress of "appearing good" as well as the responsibility of working to make the event run smoothly (i.e., to "come off without a hitch"). This involves taking others' needs into consideration. In (*3→), S displays ambiguity as to which of the above ("party" or "crowd") G may best be "categorized" into (i.e., "treated as a member of"). At just this moment of rapid construction, S's "encoding" task is shown to be inherently problematic: Is G a celebrative partner with whom S can intimately share (i.e, "party → close"), and/or a source of stress and discomfort (i.e., "crowd → distant")? It is on the cusp of closeness/intimacy versus distance/discomfort that S appears to be wavering; indeed, a tenuous (although likely not uncommon) position to be negotiating in the midst of planning a wedding. Moreover, the dual orientation of "appearance/looking good" and "planning/organization" are central to an explanation that relies, as warrants for claims, on materials comprising a single turn-at-talk (such as the words "party/crowd" in *3→).

Poetic Aftershocks

In overlap with S's Excerpt 13 (*3→), it is seen that G's "You know what?" is yet another attention gainer or general "pre" (see Schegloff, 1980; Terasaki, 1976). It is employed so as to set up and garner a particular kind of attention from S, better insuring that S will align herself with G's upcoming turn—an attempt to get the floor (as with earlier described attempts such as "°Sissy I wanna tell you something°", and "Now you? be quiet for a moment") that was previously unsuccessful due to the interjective character of S's fake laughter:

Excerpt 10 (SDCL:G/S:583–595)

```
*3→   S:   uh huh. there's always? a clown:.
                 (0.4)
*3→   S:   there's always a c:lown in the party
           er: in the [cro::wd ]
      G:              [You kn]ow what?
                 (0.6)
```

```
4→   G:   If the bride looks pretty no::body else
          cares about how the rest of em look (.)
          Bride is the star:::=
     S:   =You know I'll look prettier than
          anybody else wo we don't havta
          worry about that
```

The subsequent (0.6) pause marks a noticeable absence of a response by S to G's prior "what?", and is significant in two ways. First, it marks S's failure to respond to G's "pre" by withholding alignment and facilitation of what G is attempting to accomplish, particularly at this juncture of the conversation (i.e., an apparent "serious" shift of topic immediately following S's idiomatic expression in *3→). Second, S does align and facilitate G's pursuit by withholding response (compared, e.g., with explicit topic shift and/or outright refusal to listen further to what G has to say).

In (4→), then, G's "If the bride" is both a recycled turn-beginning (see Schegloff, 1987c) and an initiation of a hypothetical "If/then" turn-construction—one uniquely built toward G's advantage. What comes off as a somewhat idyllic ("dream like") vision designed to edify and support S, can alternatively be heard and seen as evidence offered by G to bolster her previous utterance in Excerpt 8, 2→. Although G attempted to construct a version of (4→) following (2→), an attempt that failed as a result of S's fake laughter, G's (4→) is yet a further attempt to garner S's consensus: *If* S is "plump/normal" rather than "skinny/undernourished," *then* "no::body else cares about how the rest of em look"; *If* Sissy is "plump/normal," *then* she will be the "star." Of interest here is not only G's overall manner of inducing consensus, but also her specific use of "Bride is the star:::". From this grand illusion to "star" additional "aesthetic poetics" are implied, where "star" is roughly analogous with: Heavenly or celestial "body"; Center of attention or status; Leading or prominent "lady."

It is in response to what might be referred to as the "poetics of dream-like visions" in G's (4→) that S, in next turn, makes use of what she takes to be G's knowledge ("You know I'll look prettier than anybody else") and also speaks for G in downgrading the seriousness of the situation ("so we don't havta worry about that"). As apparent in Excerpt 11, 5→, however, G proceeds to reveal to S the "hypothetical baiting" of (4→)—an "if/then" not yet directly applicable nor available to S—by once again failing to affiliate with S's stated assumptions or "trouble-telling":

Excerpt 11 (SDCL:G/S:593–605)

```
     S:   =You know I'll look prettier than
          anybody else so we don't havta
          [worry about that]
5→   G:   [ Well I sure  ]ly do ↑ hope you.↑ will:
               (1.0)
```

```
5→    G:    If we havta pad ya up a bit
            here and [(  t h e r e  )]
6→    S:               [Hah hah hah::] (.) such a comedian:.
            (1.2)
      G:    When's Bill comin home?
```

It is in (5→) that G displays how S's stated concerns or (at this moment, potential) anxieties remain inherently problematic. By overlapping interjectively, G herself produces a multiturn unit strikingly similar to her earlier withholding of affiliation and sarcastic comparison in (2→). Immediately following a complainable matter or trouble-telling by S, G's "Well I surely do ↑ hope you.↑ will:" offers a topic initial, straightfaced response that, in this instance, withholds full agreement by casting positive aspersions. However, these aspersions also cast doubt, by means of "hope," rather than certainty about S's predicament. That this turn projects noncompletion is evident in S's not taking up the floor during the (1.0) pause, and also the next positioned increment in G's "If we havta pad ya up a bit here and (t h e r e)". Notice here that G's sarcastic "pad" is a shorthand version, yet in its brevity, one that nevertheless provides a solution to what G construes as a significant feature of S's "problem": an apparent unwillingness to make a transition from "skinny/undernourished" → plump/normal".

Finally, in (6→) it can be observed that through such rapid construction S relies on a second, appropriately and recurrently positioned, idiomatic expression. As with (*3→), S's "fake laughter + [idiom]" is relied on as a resource for dealing, then and there, with not having received sympathy nor affiliation from G. But here the idiom "such a comedian:." comes off as a final assessment designed to close down current topic (Jefferson, 1981; Pomerantz, 1984a). As abbreviated, it is perhaps a simplified version of "Everybody's a comedian," itself being a likely member of the category from which "clown" in Excerpts 8–9, *3→ was originally drawn. These sequential environments, both inauspicious, are strikingly similar in shape and outcome. Of course, there is no speech error in (6→), as S fails to extend her turn and attempt to complete what "such a comedian:." leaves unspecified. Yet quite possibly S's failure to extend the utterance signals "enough is enough," a message to which G's "When's Bill comin home" appears recipient designed in its unequivocal shift toward another (seemingly unrelated) topic.

SUMMARY

An analysis of an extended Excerpt 1 was offered in this chapter to exemplify how the very circumstances S is caught up in and thus preoccupied with, bulimia and her wedding, are apparent within selected environments of the G–S conversation. A case for "preoccupations" has been forwarded, not as an upshot of mentalistic conceptions derived from individuals' predispositions and reports, but as embedded within language and interactional contingencies. Descriptively and through a speech error, S's responses reveal delicate orientations to G's disaffiliative and sarcastic utterances, actions extending withholdings of commiseration and sympathy from S's troubles-tellings (e.g., as with S's reporting the difficulty of fitting different sized people into her wedding). Although delicate and tailormade characterizations were offered by S mirroring the predicaments she faced, such utterances were unwittingly produced within contingencies of potential conflict. It is therefore not necessary to attribute conscious awareness to S's actions, as though S intentionally and thus strategically reflected on and/or chartered her way through interrelationships among bulimic and wedding problems. Rather, as indicative of a wide variety of "sounds, categories, words, utterances, and errors" (Jefferson, 1977, p. 19), conversational poetics emerge rapidly and spontaneously across a wide variety of everyday interactions and are valuable analytic resources for explicating how participants, such as G and S, attend to emergent situations in delicate ways.

From examination of S's utterance,

S: God:: it's hard fitting everyone in my wedding?
      .hh Grandma there's so many people different sizes?

it was shown that when S finally does solicit G's advice or opinion, it emerged from a prior withholding from G and is not about dealing with bulimia per se. Rather, this utterance was constructed and employed by S as a solicitation device to receive, from G, a noticeably absent and affiliative response regarding troubles in planning her wedding. However, from invoking "God::", to unwittingly building into her wedding description details of relevance to bulimic tendencies, S's actions are without forethought but not a matter of random occurrence as she deals on the spot with momentary details and in these ways displays her preoccupations with bulimia.

Attention was also given to S's following utterance,

S: uh huh. there's always? a clown:.
           (0.4)
      there's always a c:lown in the party
      er: in the cro::wd

particularly what S appeared to be preoccupied with, in unison with an oddly placed "error" involving what initial inspection may reveal as somewhat strange word choices ("er: in the cro::wd"). On further analysis, however, this error was itself found to be embedded in the construction of an idiomatic expression. Produced rapidly and in the midst of ongoing trouble, S's utterance was shown to be one technique and thus solution for both addressing and further avoiding the empirical details of G's sarcastic comparison—a universal feature of the use of idioms in sequential environments involving complainable matters (see Drew & Holt, 1988), as well as in reponding seriously to being "teased" (see Drew, 1987). In this sense, there is an unavoidable interrelationship between S's "speech error" on the one hand, and its use and emergence in the course of "being found in error" by G on the other hand—what has been described as one form of "double trouble" in ordinary conversational events as participants are dealing spontaneously with problematic interactional circumstances (bulimic problems being one example).

Moreover, additional forms of "double trouble" have emerged, both in Excerpt 3 and throughout the G–S conversation: Numerous contrasting orientations are evident in the delicate organization of the talk by G and S. Combined, these inherent contradictions or "tensions" are embedded in ongoing troubles and problems as G consistently draws attention to S's bulimic condition—matters routinely avoided by S, but concerns S nevertheless displays preoccupations with through her words, tailored explanations, and speech errors produced in an environment of being found "in error" by G. I am referring here to such noticeable "both/and" relationships as the following: Wedding as Party/Celebration *and* Wedding as Stressor; Seriousness *and* Play; Making *and* Breaking a Promise; (Fake) Laughter *and* (Real) Problems; Grand Illusions *and* (Bare) Facts of "Reality"; Looking Good *and* Feeling Bad; Skinny/Undernourished *and* Plump/Normal; Hope *and* Doubt; Bulimia *and* a Wedding. It is the collaborative working out of these and clearly other, equally apparent priorities and concerns that have been shown to be of particular relevance to G and S. Of course such pairings, while suggestive, do not adequately account for the interactional contingencies examined in this and previous chapters. They remain summarized and categorical versions of practical actions, not unlike generalized references to bulimics being "preoccupied" with food, weight, shape, thinness, and appearance. By focusing on the *social* shapes and consequences of such preoccupations, the focus of this chapter has been to provide alternative, *interactional* understandings of preoccupations as resources for organizing talk about bulimia and, in most simple terms, as ways of dealing with emergent conversational circumstances. Perhaps that's just the point: Intuition and imagination alone cannot be relied on to conceive or describe the working nature of such delicacies in everyday conversation.

6
▼▼▼▼▼▼

Interaction and
Social Problems

De gustibus non disputandum.
(In matters of taste one should not argue.)[1]

Although data-driven observations provided unmotivated impetus for investigating the G–S conversation, recognition of bulimia and grandparent caregiving as predominant family and thus societal problems became increasingly apparent as extant literature was reviewed and synthesized in chapter 1. Having offered examinations of the interactional organization of troubles and problems apparent throughout the G–S conversation, the task remains to determine how or if the predicaments and solutions cogenerated by G and S provide heuristic explanations of social behavior noticeably absent from prior theoretical and empirical attempts to understand bulimia and grandparent caregiving: What understandings of the "social contexts" of bulimia and caregiving currently exist, and are they sufficient for coming to grips with ordinary family relationships and ongoing predicaments? As a point of departure for understanding conversations about illness in families and institutional settings alike, how might a grandmother–granddaughter interaction (and the cross-situational materials employed as resources for making sense of G and S) reveal preliminary findings and knowledge claims pointing directions for possible avenues of research?

---

[1]Thanks to Michael Real for bringing this expression to my attention, and his translation from Latin to English.

TOWARD INTERACTIONAL UNDERSTANDINGS
OF SOCIAL PROBLEMS

First, regarding bulimia, it should be recalled that despite considerable attention given to biomedical, developmental, family dynamic, and psychosocial explanations of the causes and consequences of eating disorders, not a single study was located focusing directly on naturally occurring interaction. The research literature's proclivity toward individuals' reconstructions of social events and relationships results in explanations of otherwise locally occasioned courses of practical action, but solely in terms of personality attributes and profiles. The diverse interactional circumstances and contingencies of social relationships are transformed into individualistic insights: inherent problems emerge regarding the goodness-of-fit between what people "say" they do and how (or if) they actually engage in described activities; what persons may reasonably be expected to report about their behavior, others' actions, and jointly produced interactions requiring coordination rather than unilateral orientations remains a source of confusion.

It may very well be the case that major causal factors for bulimic tendencies are identifiable—for example, low self-esteem, the overwhelming desire to please others, excessive need for external approval, high pressure, and dysfunctional family interactions—but it remains to be established how such factors might be at work and recognized as meaningful resources in interaction. Even when more specific findings such as "lack of social support and less affective involvement," "poor communication," and "negative and conflicting interactions" in the family (and more) are put forth, little reflexivity is evident in recognizing that such categorical descriptions emerge from researcher-imposed constructions of removed events and, simply, that matters of "saying" versus "doing" require attention. An unequivocal need exists for taking into account marked differences between significantly reported "dimensions" of scaled measurements and responses to interview protocols, on the one hand, and displayed (rather than idealized) orientations by participants in real time interactions on the other. There is no escaping the fact that individually based characterizations of interactions, eventuating in "themes" mentioned or "dimensions" shown to be significant, are at best glossed representations of family members' conversational involvements and the social actions comprising them.

Second, regarding grandparent caregiving, gaining access to the kinds of activities grandparents do is similarly problematic as increasing attention is being given to processes underlying the facilitation and development of relationships with grandchildren. As grandparenting has emerged in part as a subset of concerns with overall family caregiving, particularly caregivers' subjective well-being, overemphasis on reported lived experiences leaves barren understandings of caregiving tasks and responsibilities as interactional achievements. Grandparents are, no doubt, important influences in the lives of grandchildren by means of actually spending considerable time with them, making decisions for/with, guiding and directing the growth and development of their childrens' children. As with research on bulimia, however, little is known about the kinds of social activities undergirding "caretaking" situations—such as "normative yet stressful burdens" and "dealing with difficult situations"—beyond descriptions offered by individuals in consideration of circumstances (voluntarily or otherwise) they have and/or are currently caught up in and thus preoccupied with.

Social Contexts?

Attempts to gain access to collaborative relational processes that avoid the contextual and thus situated nature of talk and action reflect, by fiat (see Cicourel, 1964; Phillipson, 1972; Schrag, 1980), an inability to demonstrate the social organization of human interaction in its manifest and multifarious forms. Seeking answers to innately social problems by sole reliance on pooled individuals' conceptions—gaining access to the infamous "black box" in order to understand individuals' interior and interpretive practices (Drew & Heritage, 1992, p. 5), ultimately searching outside of actual situations via multiple participants' self-reported "meanings" about those events—inevitably treats social occasions (implicitly or explicitly) as encapsulated, inaccessible entities. What is irretrievably lost is the ability to uncover what participants themselves come to display and treat as interactionally meaningful in commonsense "environments of the moment" (C. Goodwin & Duranti, 1992, p. 5). A focus on participants' perceptual orientations to a given event or situation remain disembodied if and when the indigenous activities they actually perform in those events and situations, including but not limited to interaction itself, are not shown to be invoked, designed, and shaped by those persons whose in-progress understandings require constant monitoring and updating.

Locating and analyzing social meanings apart from situated actions thus amounts to the utilization of "context-stripping methods" (Mishler, 1979). For example, in reference to work on language acquisition versus language socialization (see Schieffelin & Ochs, 1986), C. Goodwin and Duranti (1992) argued that attempts to understand how children develop competencies apart from speaking and membership involvements in actual communities are problematic: "Such research has made it clear that it would be blatantly absurd to propose that one could provide a comprehensive analysis of human social organization without paying close attention to the details of how human beings employ language to build the social and cultural worlds that they inhabit" (pp. 1–2). Similarly, examinations of the "social context" of bulimia in family environments—and for that matter, any illness—cannot escape the inevitable reliance on language and social interaction as vehicular for members experiencing and inhabiting such "problem" environments. If the understandings sought are indeed social in nature and consequence; if priority is actually given to the kinds of indigenous activities family members systemically produce that are, at root, nonsummative and thus incapable of being constructed by individuals alone throughout the often variegated course of an illness, then it is necessary to develop and utilize methods capable of revealing participants' methods for organizing interaction. In the analysis of G and S throughout this book, "bulimia" and "grandparent caregiving" are treated neither as distinct entities nor as adequate categorical descriptions of the kinds of actions comprising, and in these ways attended to as relevant and momentary features of, emergent troubles and "problems."

In consideration of extant approaches to both "bulimia" and "grandparent caregiving," therefore, there is little option but to conclude that approaches to behavior in context are only beginning to receive attention but are not yet substantiated as methods of inquiry. Across a wide variety of orientations to "context" by social scientists representing diverse disciplines and interests, "talk of some type [is typically] the behavior that context is being invoked to interpret" (C. Goodwin & Duranti, 1992, p. 3). Because talk per se is often reported about but is not accessed in any detail as a set of resources for participants and in these ways for researchers, the complicated search for a "theory of social action" is indeed in its infant stages.

CONVERSATIONS ABOUT ILLNESS

The detailed and meaningful resources employed by G and S to organize their conversation are exactly the kinds of actions overlooked by employing research methods that solicit only reports about interaction and relationships. In consideration of the G–S findings available in preceding chapters, implications exist for future inquiries that, although only sketched here, provide diverse possibilities for coming to grips with basic features of conversations about illness.

First, and most generally, in situations where family members and/or friends assume the responsibility of taking on and working through concerns with another's health and well being, it is inevitable that contradictory and perhaps disaffiliative orientations to "problems" will emerge. Courses of actions as those described herein—raising and addressing the "problem," attempting to overcome resistance by laying grounds for reasonable concern and assertion, avoiding ownership of problems described, and the altogether delicate ways preoccupations with an illness and related circumstances (such as an upcoming wedding) are evident within the participants' orientations—are no doubt coenacted throughout a wide variety of illness predicaments.

The seeming omnipresence of these patterns of interaction in G and S clearly evidence the ongoing and negotiated character of nonalignment; at least with S's orientation to the illness bulimia, it indeed appears to be the case that (as noted in the epigraph at the outset of this chapter) "in matters of taste one should not argue." And although this conversation may appear as an extreme case on these asynchronous grounds, it is important to note the essentially "civil" character of this talk. In marked contrast, there no doubt exist a multiplicity of encounters where, in the end, the "problems" being addressed and avoided are considerably more difficult and hostile—for example, where those treated as needing help and assistance refuse altogether to discuss the "problems" raised (even by physically removing themselves from the environment), and on occasions where escalated expressions of anger and emotional outbursts promote altogether counterproductive results, creating additional "problems" in their own right.

But then again, it should not be overlooked that many discussions about illness are (for all practical purposes) wholly cooperative and mutually compassionate, where participants in interaction openly agree and align with one another's concerns and suggestions regarding "problems" and what might be done (as best possible) to deal with and remedy them—working predominantly toward shared resolutions rather than being consistently at odds—all of which qualify as versions of home-based "medical teams." Over time, just how these lay "teams" move in and out of different versions of the often contrasting phases of decision making and action, including working with and making sense of advanced technologies and medical experts (e.g., see Hyde, 1990, 1993), remains to be specified. And of course it also awaits to be evidenced, in a convincing manner, just how any given set of previously described actions are practically and interactionally accomplished, not to mention achieved over time (although see later discussion).

Second, it is counterintuitive and perhaps unnerving to recognize, at least initially, that caregiving may often involve consistent withholdings of commiseration and sympathy from the person struggling with an illness. At face value, this "tough love" approach to offering assistance seems itself to be contradictory and perhaps ingenuous. Yet from the outset of this G–S analysis and throughout, it became clear that G constructed bulimic "problems" out of S's trouble-tellings (i.e., regarding work, walking/exercising, eating habits, concerns with weight, "cited" friends/sorority sisters/fiancé, wedding troubles, and the like). This is a consequence, it would appear, of G's displayed surety in first building a case that S was in fact bulimic (a correct set of assertions as it turned out), then moving to rely on her nursing background as a resource for substantiating her claims and soliciting S's commitment to seek professional assistance.

Needless to say, such professional background will not always be available to family members or friends as they attempt to lay reasonable grounds toward "healing" actions: confidence and definitiveness in lay diagnosis and "prescribed" treatment will vary considerably across persons relying on more or less incomplete residual knowledge about illnesses observed (although perhaps not recognized) and what, if anything, might be done to prevent and promote healthy alternatives. In the case of G and S, however, as a family caregiver G clearly relies on both resources apparent in S's talk-in-interaction and by invoking her own professional nursing background to define the "problem" and attempt to negotiate a set of solutions.

Third, although "bulimia" is the illness addressed in this single G–S conversation, the implications extend beyond this particular set of "problems" toward understanding how family members and friends confront and address other purportedly difficult situations (e.g., chronic or terminal illness, alcoholism, drug/spousal/child abuse) and, in turn, how those actually or allegedly "in trouble" routinely deal with such circumstances. The analysis of G and S provides a foundation for developing understandings of the interactional organization of these types of family involvements, as well as a basis for comparing such talk with related institutional discourse (see later). In so doing, researchers treat casual and institutional interactions as interwoven rather than dichotomous. Everyday conversation is foundational for institutional conduct and, as shown, institutional asymmetries and constraints may be evident in family members' actions qualifying them as primordial institutions. It thus becomes possible to generalize beyond "bulimic" concerns toward recurrent patterns inherent to addressing and seeking resolution for a multiplicity of social problems.

Fourth, although inherent problems arising from offering unasked for advice or assistance have been addressed, especially how recipients of unsolicited help display resistance—passively and more indirectly, as with firsttime mothers responding to health visitors, or at times by discounting and in more rejection-implicative fashion as with G and S (but also by accounting, withholding, seeking to close troubling topics, and humorous replies)—considerably more attention needs to be given to interactional activities involving the formulation and receipt of "advice." Aside from the work by Heritage and Sefi (1992) and the present G–S analysis, relatively little is known about how "illness" or "problems with caregiving" are actually coconstructed in more informal/home environments. For example, comparatively little has been said about specific discussions involving "seeking professional help," which are interesting in their own right as "behind the scenes" displays of struggles involved in getting family members to the doctor or counselor. Thus, generalizeable features of devices for raising and responding to "problems" of different configurations, and their practical consequences for health care, do not currently appear to exist. Toward these ends examinations are needed of how speakers in everyday conversations give and receive advice, yet not addressing concerns with illness and caregiving, as essential foundations for understanding cross-situational features of these social actions.

Routine Predicaments

Similarly, more diverse institutional involvements (e.g., legal, medical, therapeutic, classroom) require exploration so that basic asymmetries in interactions might be shown to consist of the "authoritative" work achieved in part when "advice" is what is actually offered and received (compared, e.g., with suggestions, orders, commands, and sanctions initiated by bureaucratic representatives). It is useful to compare G's explicit reliance on and claiming of firsthand knowledge (as grandmother and nurse), replete with authoritative and explicit assertions of truth, with techniques employed in more formal and thus institutionalized health care settings. From these comparisons the role and task-specific nature of "casual" (e.g., family) and "institutional" (e.g., as with psychiatric interviews or AIDS counseling discussed later) interactions become better understood. The tendency to treat each as a distinct involvement and thus to artifically separate one from the other (see Drew & Heritage, 1992; Morris & Cheneil, 1995), must give way to comparative casual/institutional data in order to more fully appreciate the general diversity and complexity involved in attempting to get others to talk about their "problems."

For example, in clinical rather than home/family environments, a variety of studies focus directly on matters of direct relevance for an enhanced understanding of G and S and, in turn, how the G–S interaction is both similar to yet different from clinical interactions.

Bergmann's (1992) analysis of psychiatric intake interviews makes clear how information from patients is routinely and indirectly, even mildly, elicited. Unlike G's overwhelmingly direct and persistent orientation to S's "problems," psychiatrists (and, clearly, differing types of therapists as well, see Jones & Beach, 1995) often discretely explore and solicit patients' concerns and troubles without directly asking for or seemingly obliging disclosure—at times telling things about themselves (and what others told them) so as to prompt patients to talk out their feelings on their own terms. Although patients may respond positively to and thus affiliate with such discretion in offering information (the *medical* version of trouble), they may also treat psychiatrists' discretion as improperly raising, reporting on, and thus topicalizing an event regarding some deviant behavior(s) (the *moral* version of questionable behaviors). Similar to S's responses to G's initiation and pursuit of the "problem," when heard by patients in moral terms, psychiatrists are treated as having insinuated wrongdoing and attributed blame; so doing may "trigger uncontrollable, interactionally disastrous social situations" (Bergmann, 1992, p. 157). Clearly then, and perhaps despite the degree of directness employed in pursuing response, the key to understanding these interactional moments is whether recipients hear their behaviors as being morally questioned, and if so, not just whether but what disaffiliative techniques they might employ in avoiding, discounting, or otherwise reciprocally challenging the speaker raising such issues in the first instance.

Another clinical and thus institutional example can be drawn from Peräkylä's (1993; see also Peräkylä & Silverman, 1991) examination of how AIDS counselors work with those diagnosed as HIV-positive, particularly how they get patients to talk about uncomfortable future events surrounding illness and death. One sensitive set of concerns with possible and hostile future situations leads counselors *not* to claim what they say is true (and unequivocally so, as with G); rather, they delicately raise *hypothetical* descriptions of some possible trouble prior to asking patients (and/or their family/significant others) about their fears, as well as inquiring about their coping strategies. And these hypothetical descriptions emerge only when some future set of troubles has been raised but not fully addressed. Key to these actions is how counselors achieve continuity between prior and current talk, now focusing on the future because patients themselves initiated (however vaguely) the topic-at-hand, creating a situation in which it is unlikely the patients will fail to address questions regarding a future they are concerned about. Of interest here, especially when contrasting the G–S data, are ways counselors solicit patients' talk yet simultaneously avoid blaming or otherwise attributing lack of responsibility for their HIV-positive status. Here it is seen that the very purpose of AIDS counseling sessions is to deal with potentially distressing aftershocks of a positive (not alleged) diagnosis, not (at least in most cases) to get those with a health problem (as S's) to acknowledge or "own" a problem and its consequences. Therefore, decided differences will exist between family members attempting to motivate another to seek professional assistance, as we have learned from the G–S interaction, compared with how counselors themselves actually organize sessions and interviews.

Beginnings

As a case study, G and S represent a social/interactional approach that potentially compliments and provides substantive alternatives to biomedical and traditional psychosocial approaches to medical problems. From the foundation laid in this analysis of how family members work through bulimic problems, a wide variety of possibilities exist for examining the interactional organization of diverse conversations about illness. We bring this analysis to a close by briefly considering only a few of the following family, friendship, and medical predicaments—long-term family caregiving, Alzheimer's disease, and cancer—exceedingly common in everyday life affairs yet minimally understood as interactional achievements comprising routine social and medical problems.

First, long-term family caregiving may involve anything from seemingly omnipresent parental discussions about children's health to ongoing and frequently burdensome tasks inherent to chronic and terminal illnesses (often, but not exclusively, with elderly persons). Across these interactions little is known about how caregivers talk, not only with those experiencing health problems, but also with other family members and friends about the "problem" and their caregiving efforts over the progressive course of an illness. In the case of terminal (or potentially terminal) illness, for example, family members often report feeling uncomfortable talking about death with those dying (who not infrequently avoid elaborating on their experiences, including fears), just as they report difficulties in describing their caregiving activities (e.g., not wanting to complain about caregiving burden and solicit others' assistance) to other family members and friends aware of and variously informed about the illness predicament (see D. Beach, 1995).

Second, little is known regarding the interactional impacts memory problems, uniquely but not exclusively associated with Alzheimer's disease, might have on family functioning. Throughout ordinary conversations, competent interactants use and rely on shared knowledge of people, places, and events as key resources for making sense of removed (extra-situational) experiences, and these competencies are particularly evident when "memory" and "remembering" are recognizably done—for example, when a story gets "triggered," touched off, or otherwise occasioned by words and/or actions evident in prior speaker's turn-at-talk (see M. H. Goodwin, 1990; Jefferson, 1978). Similarly, "not remembering" is altogether common, as are interactants' attempts to assist others as they "search" (e.g., for a person's name, movie seen, details of a family gathering); moments of "forgetfulness" represent interactionally organized troubles requiring remedy (see C. Goodwin, 1987). However, with those diagnosed with Alzheimer's disease and thus assumed to have problems with "memory," a series of questions arise: In what precise ways are "memory/forgetfulness" *interactionally* problematic? How might the onset of Alzheimer's disease be interactionally identified in terms of variations in coauthored stories (e.g., initiation of stories in topically incoherent fashion)? In what ways are storytelling activities impacted due to chronic and thus clinically problematic "memory" resources? In what ways do family members attend to and/or ignore stories initiated by those with Alzheimer's? How might family members invite and/or overlook those with Alzheimer's as attentive and interested story *recipients*? Might there be a "self-fulfilling prophecy" built into interactions with Alzheimer patients, such that they are systematically heard as producing "incompetent stories" and repeatedly eliminated from storytelling activities? If so, how, and with what interactional consequences for the development and maintenance of social/family relationships? These and related questions only begin to address the socially organized consequences of diseases like Alzheimer's. Each question addresses the ability to compare and contrast "normal" conversational storytelling with interaction problems unique to individuals diagnosed with some "disease" (and why, for instance, not "Alzheimer's *illness*")?[2]

Finally, the relevance of conversational materials to understanding the composition and progression of disease and illness, i.e. over time and across multiple interactions, requires special consideration. Analysis has begun of a corpus of 56 phone calls (the "SDCL: Malignancy" corpus) occurring between family members whose wife/mother/sister was diagnosed with cancer—essentially, a natural case history of one family's reliance on interaction in dealing with the course and progression of a terminal illness. From diagnosis to death, over a 13-month period, these interactions among family members, friends (often including the wife/mother/sister), and community services (e.g., with airlines representatives when making reservations for travel, or with the kennel when making reservations for a pet), allow systematic attention to be drawn toward the routine nature of making sense of, and dealing with "problems" associated with, terminal cancer. Certain kinds of "problems" have arisen, including: how the original malignancy diagnosis was delivered by the father and receipted as "news" by the son; how this "news" was both passed on to others and continually updated and revised; and how "bad news" gave rise to a preference for "good news" as the illness progressed (see Maynard, 1995). And there are other emergent features to consider when conversations about illness are examined across discreet problems, including: inherent difficulties with describing and understanding complex medical terminology, and in so doing constructing versions of what doctors have told participants about the illness and, relatedly, lay versions of how and why doctors and medical staff are proceeding with treatments; the curious interplay between biomedical descriptions of an illness (e.g., talking about body parts such as "adrenal gland" and "tumors") and emotions displayed about the illness process (e.g., frustrations in having to wait for "results" or "tests," having little or no control over processes you don't really understand); and ways in which commiseration, comfort, confusion, or anger are initially worked through and are, in these ways, made available for repeated inspection as sequentially organized achievements.

From materials such as the "Malignancy" corpus it is of considerable significance that understandings be generated of how families and friends make sense not just of the illness per se, as with G and S regarding bulimia. It is also of central importance, for researchers and medical practitioners

---

[2]By means of contrast, consider the implications of C. Goodwin's (1995) understandings of the interactional organization of "aphasia." Analysis focused on a man who, as a result of a massive stroke impacting the left hemisphere of his brain, was aphasic and thus could interact with others with limited language resources. Although this aphasic man could utter only three words—"yes," "no," "and"—he could nevertheless, and meaningfully so, participate within and thus co-create sequences of action in a multiparty family system.

alike, to understand how the "medical industrial complex" is interactionally constructed and typified by families. Conversation is vehicular for achieving a wide variety of activities, from local and thus social constructions of medical institutions, to the often technical yet potentially emotional activities involved in what is roughly depicted as "the grieving process."

As much as is known about an illness such as cancer, in all its abominable and as yet uncured biomedical manifestations, there exists only a myopic grasp of how persons talk about the aftershocks of cancer diagnosis and treatment in family environments. And such appears to be the case with all illnesses. The examples raised above regarding medical predicaments and the conversations about illness comprising them—for example, psychiatric interviews, HIV/AIDS counseling, long-term caregiving, Alzheimer's disease, a diagnosis of cancer—can be added to the G–S interaction as a complex set of instances drawn from a literal host of everyday interactions involving health "problems." In all cases, however, whether speakers are initiating and pursuing affirmation of wrongdoing by recipients, seeking to avoid ownership for alleged problematic actions, or simply attempting to cope with a wide array of illness burdens, persons have at their disposal a complex range of possible resources for shaping and organizing interaction. And in all social occasions involving disaffiliative and asynchronous environments, or their more aligned counterparts, participants can be found to manage their actions delicately and in ways designed to specifically create and alter contingencies of talk-in-interaction. As with G and S, an amazing variety of everyday occasions involve attributions of wrongdoing and lack of responsibility, and many encounters of this type are not immediately resolved. In such cases, speakers may select to pursue affirmation, just as recipients withhold specifically admitting to "problems" as constructed. Because speakers may gradually solicit information from another party rather than immediately announce it, and because recipients avoid and withhold sufficient and detailed reponses, it is evident that failed attempts to achieve desired action can and do prompt further pursuit.

The possibilities above and more speak to just how "thick" any given occasion like the G–S interaction might be for researchers and clinicians focusing on "bulimia" and "family/grandparent caregiving," as well as for analysts of language and social interaction whose interests include conversations about illness. In keeping with the notion that G–S is not necessarily more or less special than any other encounter or set of events, but yet another set of real-time moments reflecting basic human orientations to everyday circumstances, a rationale for subjecting conversations about illness to close inspection becomes available—in just the ways interactants organize daily affairs of importance to them, activities as these are altogether routine and, perhaps, unavoidable. Analyses of a wider variety of occasions may reveal recurrent features as those identified herein, speaking to the universality of interactants' methods for engaging in such actions as attributing and negotiating such global concerns as "right from wrong" and "responsibility" in terms of illness, and by implication other matters of significance to those conversationally involved. Clearly, the communication of alternative and at times contradictory orientations to family medical predicaments is in all cases problematic. This becomes self-evident on noticing participants' solutions to evolving courses of action, embedded within interactional patterns having practical consequences for managing illness. Through the study of everyday conversations, illness becomes situated not only in bodies and individuals' perceptions, but in the meaningfully coordinated world of participants.

Appendix:
Transcription Notation
Symbols and G/S Transcript

The transcription notation system employed for data segments is an adaptation of Jefferson's work (see Atkinson & Heritage, 1984, pp. ix–xvi; W. Beach, 1989, pp. 89–90. For copies of the G/S audiorecording, send $5 for duplicating and mailing costs to: Wayne A. Beach, School of Communication, San Diego State University, San Diego, CA 92182-4516; internet: wbeach@mail.sdsu.edu). The symbols may be described as follows:

:	Colon(s):	Extended or stretched sound, syllable, or word.
___	Underlining:	Vocalic emphasis.
(.)	Micropause:	Brief pause of less than (0.2).
(1.2)	Timed pause:	Intervals occur within and between same or different speaker's utterance.
(( ))	Double parentheses:	Scenic details.
( )	Single parentheses:	Transcriptionist doubt.
.	Period:	Falling vocal pitch.
?	Question marks:	Rising vocal pitch.
↑ ↓	Arrows:	Marked rising and falling shifts in intonation.
° °	Degree signs:	A passage of talk noticeably softer than surrounding talk.
=	Equal signs:	Latching of contiguous utterances, with no interval or overlap.
[ ]	Brackets:	Speech overlap.
[[	Double brackets:	Simultaneous speech orientations to prior turn.
!	Exclamation points:	Animated speech tone.
-	Hyphens:	Halting, abrupt cut off of sound or word.
> <	Less than/greater than signs:	Portions of an utterance delivered at a pace noticeably quicker than surrounding talk.

SDCL: GRAMMA/SISSY
LENGTH: 12:51

1	G:	Si:ssy what? > time. do you have
2		to work in the morning. <
3		(1.0)
4	S:	I have ta be there at ni::ne.
5		> so I think I'll pro(bl)y get up
6		a li(tt)le bit < e:arlier. (0.5)
7		and maybe > i:f I get up e:arly enough <
8		you gon(na) go for a ↑ wa:lk with me
9		(0.6)
10	G:	A wa:lk? (0.5) my goodness (.)
11		you're on your feet e:ight hours a d:ay?
12		(0.2)
13		> you don't even have a place to sit do(wn)?
14		whadda you wanna go for a walk
15		that's like the postman goin for a walk
16		on (his) day off? <
17		(0.2)
18	S:	↑We[: : : (11)!]
19	G:	[That's stu]pid
20	S:	.hh > Ya but gramma you gotta realize
21		I work all day out < (.) in the s:tore
22		i-it's nice to get outside .hh ((clears throat))
23	S:	Where it's (.) ↑ you know fresh air and stuff.
24		.hh come on > j(us)t get up and go for a walk
25		we'll have a cup o(f) coffee before we go::? <
26		(1.0)
27	G:	Well honey you're so thin: no:w:
28		(0.6)
29	G:	I don'(t) know (.) I think you're just (0.2)
30		° (well you're) ° just wearin yourself out with
31		all your activity > I think if you slo:w down a
32		li(tt)le bit and rest a little bit more <
33		(0.4)
34	S:	GRA:[M M A] YOU'RE SO WEIRD!
35	G:	[Maybe]
36	S:	> I don't even know why you say that I- <
37		.hh I am f:i::ve thr:ee:: and I still weigh
38		a hundred an' te[n- fif]teen po:unds?
39		[((noise))]
40		(0.6)
41	G:	O:h ↓ you don't weigh a ° hundred an' °
42		fifteen ↑ pounds .hh all your clothes are
43		fallin off of ya everybody tells you ya look thi::n?
44	S:	Ya:: but fin[ally I]
45	G:	[You're b]o:ny look at acrossed
46		your chest an yer .hh your co:llar bo:nes
47		stickin o::ut > ↑ why d'ya wanna be so thi:n! <
48	S:	Gra:mma:. ↑ it's not: .hh if I could lo::se

```
49            more weight an git it off my thi::ghs?
50            I wouldn't. .hhh I wouldn't wanna lose
51            any more weight > but I ↑ can't help it if
52            my shoulders look. ba:re! < =
53     G:     = > Well dear < (.) You do that with exercise.
54            no:t di::eting (an le) an not getting the
55            right foods? =
56     S:     =Gra:mma. (.) I a:te good the other night.
57            didn't I you an(d) I both went out for a big
58            salad an:(d) s:oup. (.) why are you: sittin
59            here sayi:n my: - ( ) (0.4) > should be with
60            exerci:se. <
61                   (0.7)
62     G:     Well now Sissy with your ↑ foo:d. (1.2)
63            uh:: you don't always get the benefit of what
64            ch'u eat? > now I happen to know that <
65            (.) that's true
66                   (0.8)
67     S:     ↑ We:ll: ((high pitched voice)) (0.6)
68            ↑ I know it's hard. right no:w
69            > I mean I'm tryin to look good for my wedding? <
70            and ↑ I might not e[ at (as) ]
71     G:                         [Well Sis]sy do you? think
72            you're gonna look good < (.) when you're so: thin:
73                   (1.6)
74     G:     that chu'll be > pretty in your wedding on
75            that beautiful wedding gown when you tried
76            it on an it fit you an(d) you look so pretty <
77            .hh you weighed about (.) mm: hunerd and twelve
78            pounds
79                   (1.0)
80     G:     for your height ° five two? ° =
81     S:     = Fiv[e three:?]
82     G:          [ My gra ]cious
83                   (0.7)
84     G:     uh (.) > this is ridiculous if you wanna
85            look thinner? ↑ why [(do) yo]u wanta do that
86     S:                         [↑ We:ll]
87            .hh well [ oka:y? I'm- (.) no-                    ]
88     G:             [What does ↓ Bill think about you getting]
89            so thin =
90     S:     = He thinks I look great.
91                   (0.2)
92     S:     he doesn't wa[ (nt) ]
93     G:                  [He do] es no:t I heard him say
94            Sissy? ↓ don't you lose another POUND! ((staccato
95            delivery))
96     S:     We:ll I'm ↑ not plannin on losing anymore
97            (gra-) weight Gramma .hhh you? watch. me
98            I'll eat just fi:ne.
99     G:     Well you al:ways eat just fine?
100    G:     it's amazing that you don't weigh? more.
```

```
101            .hh so what happens to the food that you eat?
102                 (1.1)
103     G:     you- > you're not getting any bigger? but. <
104                 (1.0)
105     S:     What do you mean by tha:t?
106     G:     We:ll Sissy. (0.8) let's ↓ face it no:w (.)
107            yo:u kno:w .hh that ch'u are so: e::ager:. (.)
108            to be thin:. (0.2) that you sometimes. go
109            in the bathroom. (0.2) and throw up your food?
110            I kno:w it's tr[ ue! ]
111     S:                   [GR ]AMMA YOU ARE SO:: FULL O(F)
112            SHIT! I am so: su:r[e.]
113     G:                       [(S]i::ssy stop) ↑ sa:ying
114            such a thing as tha[ t. ]
115     S:                       [↑W]E:LL: I can't believe
116            > that ch'u would even say something like tha:t. <
117     G:     Well it's true isn't it?
118                 (0.4)
119     G:     You know I:? know more about this than you
120            think? I know.
121                 (0.5)
122     S:     Gra:mma. you (a)re so we::ird (.hh aghhh)
123                 (1.0)
124     G:     °Sissy I wanna tell you something°
125                 (0.8)
126     G:     I:? know:. (0.8) that ch'u are throwing up
127            your food purposely. (.) .h > and do you realize
128            that this is a (.) ill:ness <
129                 (0.4)
130     G:     and the m:ore > you do it (up) <
131            [(if) you don't stop right now          ]
132     S:     [ ↑ You'r::e so: FUNNY GRAMMA!]
133            .hh this is an ill:ness I can't believe
134            you're throwing up your food. ((mimmick voice))
135     G:     Well you ar:e?
136                 (1.2)
137     G:     and ↑ you know something (0.4) it's gonna
138            gro:w and gro:w > and you know what it can
139            ↑ do (t[o) you ]
140     S:            [ Gram ] ma I'm
141            no[t even gonna (s:t-)      ]
142     G:       [ it could ruin your wh]ole life
143            > ↑ Don't tell me that now.
144            you just better stop < (.) [ denyin(g)]
145     S:                              [ Gra:mma]
146            I've ↓ o:nly done that a couple a ti:m:es
147     G:     ↓ ° A couple[ of times.° ]
148     S:                 [It's not? th]at big of a deal.
149            my friends used to do it in the sorority $ all
150            the t(h)i:me.$ <
151                 (1.0)
152     G:     °Well listen?° your friends used to do a lot
```

153   of things in the sorority that you didn't
154   have to pattern after I'm quite sure?
155   (0.6)
156   G: and tha:t is probl'y the ↑ wor:st thing
157   that you could- (.) could ↑ ha:ppen.
158   to you Sissy
159   (0.6)
160   G: don't you realize what it can do to you:
161   (0.5)
162   G: it can ruin your wh:o::le life.
163   (0.6)
164   G: your h:e:alth (0.2) your teeth
165   > d'you do you (av) you ever? s:een. <
166   .hh have you (h)aven't ch'u been
167   keepin up with the news?
168   a:l[l: the things that's written and]published?
169   S: [But GRA::mma. I don't   ]
170   fee:l: ba::d:!
171   (1.5)
172   G: Well why? are ya so tir:ed
173   an can- [(canky)]
174   S: [Beca:u]se? I have to
175   ↓ work such [long hours] (.) [Gra]mma
176   [((tape noise))]   [((tn))]
177   (0.2)
178   S: you look at me. I do no:t look skinny
179   and withdra::wn from soci:ety? ((staccato))
180   .hh fi:n:e I eat a little bit (0.4) too much
181   I- I feel stuffed .hhh ↑ and I'll jis:-
182   G: ↓ O:h:: > come off it <
183   (0.2) (eh-) look at everybody else. they eat
184   [and they o:vereat and they don't run in the]
185   S: [Gra:mma I got plenty? of friends. that do-]
186   G: bathroom and [throw it up]
187   S: [Yeah and yu-] oh you don't
188   think? they do:.
189   (0.4)
190   S: H:o:ney > I got so many friends that do it
191   you don't even[know. <]
192   G: [Do you thi]nk
193   you're [(   )]
194   S: >[How do] you think I lear:ned?
195   it Gramma? <
196   (0.6)
197   G: Well listen? (.) we- how do you think
198   you learn anything. .hh you could-
199   get on do:pe? > I'm su:re there (a)re
200   quite a few of your friends that prob'ly
201   smoke a lotta po:::t .hhh and maybe (.)
202   do a little coke snorting and all that
203   kinda stuff ya read about. <
204   G: but I do:? happen to know this.

```
205          (1.0) I: (1.2) am a nur:se? (0.2)
206          I kn:ow? > what I'm talkin about <
207          I have r:ead a great deal?
208          (.) [ I have (known personally)     ]
209    S:        [ Oka:y gramma it's not:? ↓ go] nna
210          happen ag[a:in   ]
211    G:                  [Now ] you? be quiet for a moment
212              (0.4)
213    G:    I have kno:wn .hhh three people personally
214          (1.0) that have the same problem
215    G:          (0.5)
216          You know (.)[ you know (wa) ]Ju:lie hh an
217    S:              [> Well wait < I: ]
218          know who you're talkin about and
219          those are people that let it get so::
220          bad .hh that that's why it hurt em
221          .hh Grandma look at me I'm not
222          gonna let it get any worse =
223    G:    = They all said the same thing
224          when they started dear
225              (.)
226    G:    Don't 'cha realize this sorta thing
227          just grows on ya an' grows on ya an' grows on ya
228              (1.0)
229    G:    An you could just ruin your whole life (.)
230          I'm tellin ya (0.2) hh pritty soon (0.4)
231          > Yu-you don't realize it but yur personality's
232          even changin You're gettin' so: < .hhh picke:: and
233          (0.6) you're not (.) you don't seem to be ↑ ha:ppy
234          with anything Sissy anymore
235              (0.2)
236    G:    You know what I would like to do:.
237          (.) I would like to take you. (0.8)
238          to a doctor. and we'll talk it over and
239          you can tell em:
240              (0.8)
241    G:    You know they have [ways of]
242    S:                  [Wha::-!] Oh
243          Ga! .hh Gramma you are s:o weird
244          I can't believe that you'd even think that .hh
245          You wanta go to a doctor you take
246          yourself to a doctor
247              (1.9)
248    G:    Sissy (.) I'm tell:n ya
249          (.) .hhh You need HELP
250          .hhh and I mean big help
251          (.)[     You need ↑ ther:apy =     ]
252    S:    > [I need help fer my grandmother] <
253    G:    = and you need uh- some advice
254          from-uh (.) .hh rea::l uh- per
255    G:    you won't listen ta me I know because
256          peop- people have a tendancy not ta
```

257		listen to their (1.0) their <u>lo</u>ved ones.
258		(1.0)
259	G:	They'll listen to a stranger more than
260		they wi[ll:]
261	S:	[Gra]:mma: I don' wanna
262		do: [th a:t. =]
263	G:	[Somebody else]
264	S:	= I won't do it anymo::re
265	G:	Oh they ↑ always say
266		I won't do it anymore
267		> <u>you do it</u> all the time
268		I know you do <
269		(1.0)
270	G:	An' d 'you know what < (0.5) this might-
271		(0.5) y'know you <u>lo</u>:ve perfum (1.0)
272		and you spend a <u>lo</u>tta > money on it <
273		do you know that you have a
274		certain o:der abou'chu
275		(2.0)
276	G:	From this
277		(1.0)
278	G:	When I'm around you every so often
279		I get this (0.5) this jus' little
280		aroma: of (.) uh vomitis (1.5)
281	G:	I hones<u>t</u> to god do Sissy
282		(2.0)
283	G:	And I, uh an' i(t) jus, it just kills me.
284		because you know how dear you are to me
285		And I just can't sta:nd to see you
286		destroy your <u>life</u> like this
287		(1.0)
288	G:	Now you're either gunna do it (.) willingly (0.5)
289		or I, I'<u>m</u> gunna do somethin' desperate about it
290		I'm > <u>gonna talk ta Bill < if Bill</u> would know this .hh
291		I think he would brea- I think- <u>really</u> believe that he
292		would break off this engagement with you he
293		<u>w</u>ouldn't <u>w</u>ant ta' marry a girl like that?
294		(1.3)
295	G:	> I'm sure he wouldn't. <
296		(0.4)
297	G:	Now if <u>you</u>'re h<u>on</u>est about it and you say
298		this isn't <u>true</u>? (0.3) okay you'll <u>come</u> with
299		me to a doctor .hh and we'll <u>tal:k</u> about it. (.)
300		a:nd (.) we'll jus(t) do some blood tests.
301		I bet ch'ur anemic from this.
302	S:	.hh Gr<u>amma</u> > I'm anemic any<u>way</u>. <
303	G:	Su::re you are. su::re you are. .hh
304		everything that I sa:y (0.2) <u>you</u> y<u>ou</u>: (.) you den<u>y</u>:,
305		(0.5) just because of this <u>very</u> reason that ch'u
306		(eh) are <u>not</u>? (0.5) <u>willing.</u> (0.4) to b<u>e</u>:: (0.3)
307		honest with your<u>self. first</u> you have > it's just like
308		an <u>al</u>coholic Sissy, < the <u>v</u>ury first step they have to

```
309              do is say (.) look (0.2) I kno:w I'm an alco(holic)
310              (0.3). if- if anything is gonna be done about
311              (.) I: have to do it. nobody else can do it . < hh now
312              you: have to take that sa:me ste:p (0.8) with your
313              problem
314                     (0.3)
315   G:         [ It's ( )   ]
316   S:         [ Well why ] (.) > well why do we have to go to
317              a doctor let's < hh le(t)'s jus(t) try to
318              handle it here.
319   G:         You have to have professional help. hh
320              you have to go to a co:unselor (0.2)
321              > Sissy you really do: hh < it's- (.) you
322              can't bele:ve- .hh you know just the other
323              day I we- I just went- happen ta go .hh
324              in the office with little eh (.) Dorinda? (0.5)
325              when she had- when she had this ra:sh (0.2)
326              > down to the dermata(lghs) < and (.)
327              they have the whol:e table filled
328              with > everything <. .hh they've got all these
329              pamphlets.
330                     (0.4)
331   G:         One was on a:::ids (0.2) one was on buli:mia
332                     (1.0)
333   G:         And there was quite a big article there on that (.)
334              so it's a well known and recognized thing (.) and they
335              r:eally believe that people need help
336                     (0.5)
337   G:         Now I can't stand idly by: and see you destroy
338              yourself?
339                     (1.2)
340   G:         > There isn't any way <
341                     (0.4)
342   G:         Now: will you do that for me::
343                     (2.5)
344   G:         ( ° Honey ° )
345   S:         Wh- what,
346                     (1.2)
347   G:         Will you do that
348                     (1.6)
349   S:         ↑ Well:
350                     (2.0)
351   S:         Gra:mma it's gonna be so: expensive to go talk to
352              some dumb [ doctor ]
353   G:                   [.pt Well] I'll tell ya I: am I'm
354              well prepared to take care of the expense
355              [.hhh I'm taking ya to the doctor.]
356   S:         [ > Yeah but Grandma I don't want <] anybody
357              to kno::w I'm so: su:re
358   G:         Your > doctor certainly isn't gonna publish it in the
359   G:         paper yuh kno:w. < (.) > h(e) isn't gonna tell
360              anybody <
```

361 S: Yea:[:h but I can just] see you tellin my Mo::m
362 G: [An(d) if you go:]
363   (0.3)
364 G: I [will not tell anyone (0.8) b-belie:ve me. (0.8)]
365   [((clock chimes))   ]
366 G: I- I would not (.) betray your conf(idence)
367   [in any respect]
368 S: [I will go   ] o:ne time an(d) I'm not going after
369   that
370   (0.2)
371 G: Well le(t)'s take it o::ne step at a time
372   (1.4)
373 G: O:ne > step at a time Sissy <
374   (0.5)
375 G: We'll go the one ti:me (0.7) that ch'u (0.9) > promise
376   me < [that I'LL make the appointment ( )]
377 S: [OKA::::Y ALright (.) > OKAY <]
378   I'LL GO n'le(t)'s just drop it for t'night okay? (.)
379   I don't wanta talk about it anymo:re.
380   (1.5)
381 S: .hh hhhh I'm exhausted I hafta work tomorrow are you
382   still gonna go walk with me tomorrow:?
383   (0.2)
384 S: .hh And it's not because I'm a buli:mic
385 S: I just like to get out with some fresh air:.
386   (.)
387 G: We:ll I'll tell you what.
388   (0.6)
389 G: U:h (0.2) why don't we uhm:
390   (1.2)
391 S: .pt You can get up and fix the fru:it
392   drink for me:, .hh you know that health
393   f- fit for he(alth) diet or whatever
394   .hh it's not even a diet I've been
395   eating good on that:?
396 G: =Now look see there you are
397   (0.6)
398 G: Your- you're on this diet.
399   (.)
400 G: > Fit fer life that's taken from the diamonds <
401   (.) book (.) fi- fit for life(s) diet?
402   (0.4)
403 G: Okay ↑ whada'ya get. the fru::it in the morning.
404   (0.6)
405 G: There ↑ aren't any > ca:lories in that believe me. <
406   (.) it's to cle::an your system out (.) so they say.
407   (.)
408 G: Okay (.) wher- where are you getting any nourishment
409   to do all these [(   )]
410 S: [Grandma I thought] we weren't
411   gonna [talk   about   it   anymor:::e]
412 G: [You go out there and lift twenty five]pound

413   weights of
414   (0.4)
415   G: Of
416   S: Grandma I don't wanna ta- ↑look do you wa-
417   > do you want me to go: < see that <u>doctor</u>? fine.
418   (0.4)
419   S: Now let's just drop it for tonite.
420   G: Okay
421   S: > You don't wanna go on a walk tomorrow <
422   I'm not goin [on a walk with you.]
423   G: [Oka:y I'll <u>go</u>   ] for a
424   walk with you
425   (1.0)
426   G: I'll <u>go</u> for a walk. with you
427   S: Okay? fine.
428   G: And we'll wa:lk down to the corner:.
429   (0.4) you know where that little restaurant is
430   down [there on the corner]
431   S: [I know where we-]
432   G: We'll stop in there
433   S: We'll just go:: ( ) =
434   G: = and we'll have a <u>couple</u> a scrambled eggs.
435   whada'ya say.
436   S: ↑ <u>Fine</u> I don't car- .hhh I =
437   G: = Would you <u>eat</u> em?
438   S: Ya
439   G: Would you?
440   (0.6)
441   S: Why are you <u>acting</u> so amazed
442   Grand[ma. you're actin' s:<u>tupid</u>]
443   G: [Well <u>you</u>: just never] eat
444   any breakfast.
445   (1.2)
446   G: And then for <u>lunch</u> whad'ya want.
447   (.)
448   G: Some (good)
449   S: I dunno
450   G: Som:e .pt [(about) what.]
451   S: [↑ Oka::y   ] Grandma I'm <u>tired</u>
452   I just wanna go to bed (.) whatever?
453   (1.2)
454   G: Well n'I can understand that you do.
455   I'm sure that you're very tired from all::
456   that you've been through
457   (0.6)
458   G: And you haven't (been eaten)
459   (1.6)
460   G: Sissy? (.) what are you ↑ saying
461   (0.8)
462   G: Now ad<u>mit</u> just a little bit to me
463   G: .hhh thet'll (.) you do go in and -
464   have you noticed that your <u>teeth</u>

465   (.) I noticed your toothbrush has
466   a lot of ↑ p<u>in</u>k like your (I'ke) you're
467   kinda <u>bl</u>eeding?
468   <u>(2.2)</u>
469 G: Uh: (.) Do you[think that maybe this]
470 S: [Grandma I thought]
471   you said we were gonna change the subject.
472   (0.6)
473 S: Oka:y? =
474 G: = Allr<u>igh</u>t well (wh'ya) talk about.
475 S: Well <u>I</u> dunno but I'm not gonna stay up here
476   if you keep t<u>alk</u>in about that.
477   (0.6)
478 G: ↑ Well =
479 S: = Well let's[turn (.) let's turn the t-] =
480 G: [Okay you've ↑ <u>made</u> a promise.]
481 S: ↑ O<u>ka::</u>y (le-) forget it let's <u>drop</u> that
482   .hhh let's (.) let's turn the TV on:.
483   (2.0)
484 S: ↑ Oka:y just turn- go ahead and turn the TV on.
485 G: Well <u>tell</u> me Sissy (.) now how much longer
486   is it before (.) uh the w<u>edd</u>ing?
487 S: Well (we)ve got four months (long:) ((TV in
488   background)) > lemme turn this on < =
489 G: = Well don't ta- > how can I talk to you
490   when you turn the TV on so lo ud. <
491 S: ↑ Well: just a ↑ minute Grandma I wanna (.) just turn
492   it on.
493   (0.6)
494 S: Wait a second I thought the (0.4) C<u>os</u>by's were
495   gonna be on (.) hold ↑ on
496 G: No (.) they're not
497   (.)
498 S: Okay
499 G: Well (th-) eh h- ha- have you really de<u>cid</u>ed
500   on on the. bridesmaid's s- dresses [(   )]
501 S: [Well] (.) [I-]
502 G: [Did]
503   you <u>f</u>ind anything?
504 S: I don't know: to tell ya the t<u>r</u>uth::
505   I kinda wanted a black n' white wedding
506   but everybody else has been saying
507   (.) .hh D<u>o:n</u>'t have a black 'n white wedding.
508   (.) maybe I'll have a fuc:ia or real pr<u>ett</u>y p<u>in</u>k:.
509   (1.2)
510 G: °(Uh huh)°
511   [[
512 S: G<u>od</u>:: it's hard fittin everyone in my wedding?
513   .hh Grandma there's so many people different sizes?
514 G: Well of ↑ c<u>our</u>se (.) there's the n<u>ic:</u>e plump (.)
515 G: > normal l<u>ook</u>ing people < and then there are the
516   sk<u>inn</u>y people?

```
517                     (0.8)
518     S:      Grandma?
519     G:      that look $like$ they're undernourished?
520                     (1.0)
521     G:      Then (.) now [ I ]
522     S:                   [Uh] huh [  huh huh  ]
523     G:                           [But (at) first] (.)
524             [ if the  ] bride's
525     S:      [uh huh.] there's always? a clown:.
526                     (0.4)
527     S:      there's always a c:lown in the party
528             er: in the [ cro::wd ]
529     G:                 [You kn ]ow what?
530                     (0.6)
531     G:      If the bride looks pretty no::body else
532             cares about how the rest of em look (.)
533             Bride is the star::: =
534     S:      = You know I'll look prettier than
535             anybody else so we don't havta
536             [worry about that]
537     G:      [   Well I sure  ]ly do ↑ hope you ↑ will:
538                     (1.0)
539     G:      If we havta pad ya up a bit
540             here and [( t h e r e )]
541     S:               [ Hah hah hah::] (.) such a comedian:.
542                     (1.2)
543     G:      When's Bill comin (home) =
544     S:      = ((Yawning)) Not too soon man he's um
545             (0.4) he'll be uh- > or not soon enough
546             I should say < .hh he'll be here tomorrow
547             night .hh I don't get off work until
548             six o'clock so:
549                     (1.0)
550     G:      You gon [ na   go   to   work? ]
551     S:              [He's- > you gonna hav-] ta entertain
552             him for a little while before I get home. <
553                     (1.4)
554     G:      Well what (.) he's
555     S:      What's for dinner he- oh
556             you know ↑ what let's have beef stroganoff
557             he loves that.
558                     (.)
559     G:      Does he-
560     S:      We haven't had that for awhile?
561             .hh and that's very good for me ((cute voice))
562             ↑ let's have some beef stroganoff
563     G:      Oka:y, do ya I don't know how to cook (do you?)
564     S:      You're so weird
565     G:      I'll call up Ms. Mulligan and I'll ask her.
566                     (1.0)
567     G:      Doesn't she have a real good recipe for that?
568     S:      Mrs. Mulligan? (.) ya she taught me how to do that
```

569		chicken [that was go:od]
570	G:	[I was thin] king that she'd (.) gave
571		you some recipes
572	S:	Ya =
573	G:	= Why don't you do the chicken thing.
574		(it's very good)
575	S:	Well Grandma I don't have time
576		you're gonna have to do it on your ↑ own:
577	G:	And then you're so tir::ed aren't ya
578	S:	.hhh You're so weird
579		((yawning)) well I dunno but I'm
580		exhausted I think I'm goin'[to bed]
581		[((cough))]
582		(1.0)
583	S:	↑ Well
584	G:	Look at (Cosby) =
585	S:	= Grandma I'll tell you what
586		if I'm not ↑ up (0.8) okay wait
587		a second nine o'clock?
588		I have to leave by eight thirty
589		seven thirty (0.4) seven's okay (that's)
590		((end of tape))

References

Alexander, J., Giesen, B., Münch, R., & Smelser, N. J. (Eds.). (1987). *The micro–macro link* (pp. 207–234). Los Angeles: The University of California Press.

American Psychiatric Association. (1987). *Diagnostic and statistical manual of mental disorders* (3rd ed., rev.). Washington, DC: Author.

American Psychiatric Association. (1993). *Practice guidelines for eating disorders.* Washington DC: Author.

Atkinson, J. M. (1978). *Discovering suicide: Studies in the social organization of sudden death.* London: Macmillan.

Atkinson, J. M., & Drew, P. (1979). *Order in court: The organisation of verbal interaction in judicial settings.* London: Macmillan.

Atkinson, J. M., & Heritage, J. (Eds.). (1984). *Structures of social action: Studies in conversation analysis.* Cambridge, UK: Cambridge University Press.

Baker, S. (1993). Anesthesia considerations for anorexia nervosa and bulimia nervosa. *Nurse Anesthesia, 4,* 172–180.

Beach, D. L. (1993). Gerentological caregiving: Analysis of family experience. *Journal of Gerontological Nursing, 19,* 35–41.

Beach, D. L. (1994, January–February). Family care of Alzheimer victims: An analysis of the adolescent experience. *The American Journal of Alzheimer's Care and Related Disorders & Research,* 12–19.

Beach, D. L. (1995). Caregiver discourse: Perceptions of illness related dialogue. *The Hospice Journal, 10,* 13–25.

Beach, W. A. (Ed.). (1989). Sequential organization of conversational activities. *Western Journal of Speech Communication, 53,* 85–246.

Beach, W. A. (1990a). Language as and in technology: Facilitating topic organization in a Videotex focus group meeting. In M. J. Medhurst, A. Gonzalez, & T. R. Peterson (Eds.), *Communication and the culture of technology* (pp. 197–220). Pullman: Washington State University Press.

Beach, W. A. (1990b). On (not) observing behavior interactionally. *Western Journal of Speech Communication, 54,* 603–612.

Beach, W. A. (1990c). Orienting to the phenomenon. In J. Anderson (Ed.), *Communication yearbook 13* (pp. 216–244). Beverly Hills, CA: Sage. (Reprinted in *Building communication theories: A socio-cultural approach*, pp. 133–163, by F. L. Casmir, Ed., 1994, Hillsdale, NJ: Lawrence Erlbaum Associates)

Beach, W. A. (1991a). Avoiding ownership for alleged wrongdoings. *Research on Language and Social Interaction, 24*, 1–36.

Beach, W. A. (1991b). *"Okay" as projection device for fuller turn: Displaying 'state of readiness' for movements to next-positioned matters.* Unpublished manuscript.

Beach, W. A. (1991c). Searching for universal features of conversation. *Research on Language and Social Interaction, 24*, 349–366.

Beach, W. A. (1993a). The delicacy of preoccupation. *Text and Performance Quarterly, 13*, 299–312.

Beach, W. A. (1993b). Transitional regularities for 'casual' "okay" usages. *Journal of Pragmatics, 19*, 325–352. (Revised and reprinted in *The consequentiality of communication*, pp. 121–161, by S. Sigman, Ed., 1993, Hillsdale, NJ: Lawrence Erlbaum Associates)

Beach, W. A. (1995a). *Judges' sanctions.* Unpublished manuscript.

Beach, W. A. (1995b). Preserving and constraining options: "Okays" and 'official' priorities in medical interviews. In G. H. Morris & R. Chenail (Eds.), *Talk of the clinic* (pp. 259–289). Hillsdale, NJ: Lawrence Erlbaum Associates.

Beach, W. A., & Dunning, D. G. (1982). Pre-indexing and conversational organization. *Quarterly Journal of Speech, 68*, 170–185.

Beach, W. A., & Lindstrom, A. K. (1992). Conversational universals and comparative theory: Turning to Swedish and American acknowledgment tokens-in-interaction. *Communication Theory, 2*, 24–49.

Bemporad, J. R., Bereson, E., Ratey, J. J., O'Driscoll, G., Lindem, K., & Herzog, D. B. (1992). A psychoanalytic study of eating disorders: I. A developmental profile of 67 index cases. *Journal of the American Academy of Psychoanalysis, 20*, 509–531.

Bengston, V. L., & Robertson, J. F. (Eds.). (1985). *Grandparenthood: Research & policy.* Beverly Hills, CA: Sage.

Benoist, J., & Cathebras, P. (1993). The body: From an immateriality to another. *Social Science Medicine, 36*, 867–865.

Bergmann, J. R. (1992). Veiled morality: Notes on discretion in psychiatry. In P. Drew & J. Heritage (Eds.), *Talk at work: Interaction in institutional settings* (pp. 137–162). Cambridge, UK: Cambridge University Press.

Biegel, D. E., & Blum, A. (Eds.). (1990). *Aging and caregiving: Theory, research, and policy.* Newbury Park, CA: Sage.

Blouin, J. H., Carter, J., Blouin, A. G., Tener, L., Schnare-Hayes, K., Zuro, C., Barlow, J., & Perez, E. (1994). Prognostic inidicators in bulimia nervosa treated with cognitive-behavioral group therapy. *International Journal of Eating Disorders, 15*, 113–123.

Boden, D., & Zimmerman, D. (1991). *Talk and social structure.* Cambridge, UK: Polity Press.

Boskind-Lodahl, M. (1976). Cinderella's step-sisters: A feminist perspective on anorexia nervosa and bulimia. *Signs, 2*, 342–356.

Brisman, J., & Siegel, M. (1985). The bulimia workshop: A unique integration of group treatment approaches. *International Journal of Group Psychotherapy, 35*, 585–601.

Brody, E. M. (1985). Parent care as a normative family stress. *The Gerontologist, 25*, 19–28.

Brody, E. M., Johnsen, P. T., & Fulcomer, M. C. (1983). Women's changing roles and help to the elderly: Attitudes of three generations of women. *Journal of Gerontology, 38*, 597–607.

Bulich, M. A. (1988–1989). Demographic factors associated with bulimia in college students: Clinical and research implications. *Journal of College Student Psychotherapy, 3*, 13–25.

Bulik, C. M., Carter, F. A., & Sullivan, P. F. (1994). Self-induced abortion in a bulimic woman. *International Journal of Eating Disorders, 15*, 297–299.

Butler, N., & Newton, T. (1989). The psychometric analysis of bulimia and anorexia nervosa: A personal appraisal. *British Review of Bulimia & Anorexia Nervosa, 3*, 73–78.

Buttny, R. (1994). *Social accountability in communication.* London: Sage.

Button, G. (1987). Moving out of closings. In G. Button & J. R. E. Lee (Eds.), *Talk and social organization* (pp. 101–151). Clevedon, UK: Multilingual Matters.

Button, G. (1990). On varieties of closings. In G. Psathas (Ed.), *Interaction competence* (pp. 93–148). Lanham, MD: University Press of America.

Button, G., & Casey, N. (1984). Generating topic: The use of topic initial elicitors. In J. M. Atkinson & J. Heritage (Eds.), *Structures of social action: Studies in conversation analysis* (pp. 167–190). Cambridge, UK: Cambridge University Press.

Button, G., & Casey, N. (1985). Topic nomination and pursuit. *Human Studies, 8,* 3–55.

Button, G., & Casey, N. (1988–1989). Topic initiation: Business-at-hand. *Research on Language and Social Interaction, 22,* 61–91.

Byrne, P. S., & Long, B. E. L. (1976). *Doctors talking to patients: A study of the verbal behaviors of doctors in the consultation.* London: HMSO.

Cantor, M. (1983). Strain among caregivers. *The Gerentologist, 23,* 597–604.

Carter, J. A., & Eason, J. (1983). The binge-ing and purging syndrom within a college environment: Bulimarexia. *College Student Journal, 17,* 107–115.

Cassell, E. J. (1985). *Talking with patients: Vol. I & II.* Cambridge, MA: MIT Press.

Cerami, R. (1993). Anesthetic considerations with anorexia nervosa. *Aana Journal, 61,* 165–169.

Chenail, R. J. (1991). *Medical discourse and systematic frames of comprehension.* Norwood, NJ: Ablex.

Cherlin, A., & Furstenberg, F. F. (1985). Styles and strategies of grandparenting. In V. L. Bengston & J. F. Robertson (Eds.), *Grandparenthood: Research & policy* (pp. 97–116). Beverly Hills, CA: Sage.

Chomsky, N. (1965). *Aspects of the theory of syntax.* Cambridge, MA: MIT Press.

Cicirelli, V. G. (1992). *Family caregiving: Autonomous and paternalistic decision making.* Newbury Park, CA: Sage.

Cicourel, A. V. (1964). *Method and measurement in sociology.* New York: The Free Press.

Clayman, S., & Maynard, D. (1994). Ethnomethodology and conversation analysis. In P. ten Have & G. Psathas (Ed.), *Situated order* (pp. 1–29). Washington, DC: University Press of America.

Clipp, E. C., & George, L. K. (1990). Caregiver needs and patterns of social support. *Journal of Gerontology, 45,* S102–111.

Coker, S., & Roger, D. (1990). The construction and preliminary validation of a scale for measuring eating disorders. *Journal of Psychosomatic Research, 34,* 223–231.

Collings, S., & King, M. (1994). Ten-year follow-up of 50 patients with bulimia nervosa. *British Journal of Psychiatry, 164,* 80–87.

Collins, J. (1975). Send in the clowns. *Judith.* Los Angeles: Elektra/Asylum/Nonesuch Records, Warner Communications, Inc. (Adapted from Stephen Sondheim in the Broadway show *A Little Night Music*).

Cooper, M. J., Clark, D. M., & Fairburn, C. G. (1993). An experimental study of the relationship between thoughts and eating behaviour in bulimia nervosa. *Behaviour Research and Therapy, 31,* 749–757.

Coulter, J. (1973). *Approaches to insanity.* London: Martin Robertson & Co.

Coulter, J. (1979). *The social construction of mind: Studies in ethnomethodology and linguistic philosphy.* Totowa, NJ: Rowman & Littlefield.

Creasy, G., & Jarvis, P. A. (1994). Grandparents with Alzheimers disease: Effects of parental burden on children. *Family Therapy, 16,* 79–85.

Davidson, J. (1984). Subsequent versions of invitations, offers, requests, and proposals dealing with potential or actual rejection. In J. M. Atkinson & J. Heritage (Eds.), *Structures of social action: Studies in conversation analysis* (pp. 102–128). London: Cambridge University Press.

Davis, R., Freeman, R., & Solyom, L. (1985). Mood and food: An analysis of bulimic episodes. *Journal of Psychiatric Research, 19,* 331–335.

Descutner, C., & Thelan, M. H. (1991). Development and validation of Fear of Intimacy Scale. *Psychological Assessment: A Journal of Consulting and Clinical Psychology, 3*, 218–225.

de Zwann, M., Mitchell, J. E., Specker, S. M., Pyle, R. L., Mussell, M. P., & Seim, H. C. (1993). Diagnosing binge eating disorder: Level of agreement between self-report and expert-rating. *International Journal of Eating Disorders, 14*, 289–295.

Downs, V. C. (1988). Grandparents and grandchildren: The relationship between self-disclosure and solidarity in an intergenerational relationship. *Communication Research Reports, 5*, 173–179.

Drenowski, A., Yee, D. K., & Krahn, D. D. (1988). Bulimia in college women: Incidence and recovery rates. *American Journal of Psychiatry, 145*, 753–755.

Drew, P. (1978). Accusations: The use of religous geography in describing events. *Sociology, 12*, 1–22.

Drew, P. (1984). Speakers' reportings in invitation sequences. In J. M. Atkinson & J. Heritage (Eds.), *Structures of social action: Studies in conversation analysis* (pp. 129–151). Cambridge, UK: Cambridge University Press.

Drew, P. (1985). Analyzing the use of language in courtroom interaction. In T. van Dijk (Ed.), *Handbook of discourse analysis* (Vol. 3). London: Academic Press.

Drew, P. (1987). Po-faced receipts of teases. *Linguistics, 25*, 219–253.

Drew, P. (1992). Contested evidence in courtroom cross-examination: The case of a trial for rape. In P. Drew & J. Heritage (Eds.), *Talk at work: Interaction in institutional settings* (pp. 418–469). Cambridge, England: Cambridge University Press.

Drew, P., & Heritage, J. (Eds.). (1992). *Talk at work: Interaction in institutional settings.* Cambridge, UK: Cambridge University Press.

Drew, P., & Holt, E. (1988). Complainable matters: The use of idiomatic expressions in making complaints. *Social Problems, 35*, 398–417.

Drummond, K., & Hopper, R. (1993). Back channels revisited: Acknowledgment tokens and speaker incipiency. *Research on Language and Social Interaction, 26*, 179–194.

Duranti, A., & Goodwin, C. (Eds.). (1992). *Rethinking context: Language as an interactive phenomenon.* Cambridge, UK: Cambridge University Press.

Emerson, R. M., & Messinger, L. M. (1977). The micro-politics of trouble. *Social Problems, 25*, 121–134.

Engel, G. L. (1977). The need for a new medical model: A challenge for biomedicine. *Science, 196*, 129–135.

Erickson, F., & Schultz, J. (1982). *The counselor as gatekeeper.* New York: Academic Press.

Farrow, J. A. (1992). The adolescent male with an eating disorder. *Pediatric Annals, 21*, 769–774.

Frankel, R. (1984). From sentence to sequence: Understanding the medical encounter through microinteractional analysis. *Discourse Processes, 7*, 135–170.

Frankel, R. (1990). Talking in interviews: A dispreference for patient-initiated questions in physician-patient encounters. In G. Psathas (Ed.), *Interaction competence* (pp. 231–262). Lanham MD: University Press of America.

Franks, P., Campbell, T. L., & Shields, C. G. (1992). Social relationships and health: The relative roles of family functioning and social support. *Social Science Medicine, 34*, 779–788.

Freud, S. (1963). *Jokes and their relation to the unconscious.* New York: Norton.

Garfinkel, H. (1956). Conditions for successful degradation ceremonies. *American Journal of Sociology, 61*, 420–424.

Garfinkel, H. (1967). *Studies in ethnomethodology.* Englewood Cliffs, NJ: Prentice-Hall.

George, L. K. (1979). Subjective well-being: Conceptual and methodological issues in the study of psychological well-being in adulthood. *The Gerontologist, 19*, 210–216.

George, L., & Gwyther, L. P. (1986). Caregiver well-being: A multidimensional examination of family caregivers of demented adults. *Gerontologist, 26*, 253–259.

Glenn, P. J. (1989). Initiating shared laughter in multi-party conversations. *Western Journal of Speech Communication, 53*, 127–149.

Goffman, E. (1955). On face work. *Psychiatry, 18,* 219–253.

Goffman, E. (1963). *Stigma: Notes on the management of spoiled identify.* Englewood Cliffs, NJ: Prentice-Hall.

Goffman, E. (1967). *Interaction ritual: Essays on face-to-face behavior.* Garden City, NY: Doubleday.

Goffman, E. (1981). *Footing. Forms of talk.* Oxford: Basil Blackwell.

Goffman, E. (1983). The interaction order. *American Sociological Review, 48,* 1–17.

Goldbloom, D. S., Naranjo, C. A., Bremner, K. E., & Hicks, L. K. (1992). Eating disorders and alcohol abuse in women. *British Journal of Addiction, 87,* 913–919.

Goodwin, C. (1981). *Conversational organization: Interaction between speakers and hearers.* New York: Academic Press.

Goodwin, C. (1987). Forgetfulness as an interactive resource. *Social Psychology Quarterly, 50,* 115–130.

Goodwin, C. (1995). Co-constructing meaning in conversations with an aphasic man. *Research on Language and Social Interaction, 28,* 233–260.

Goodwin, C., & Duranti, A. (1992). Rethinking context: An introduction. In A. Duranti & C. Goodwin (Eds.), *Rethinking context: Language as an interactive phenomenon* (pp. 1–42). Cambridge, England: Cambridge University Press.

Goodwin, C., & Goodwin, M. H. (1990). Interstitial argument. In A. Grimshaw (Ed.), *Conflict talk* (pp. 85–117). Cambridge, UK: Cambridge University Press.

Goodwin, M. H. (1980). He-said-she-said: Cultural procedures for the construction of a gossip dispute activity. *American Ethnologist, 7,* 674–695.

Goodwin, M. H. (1982). Process of dispute management among urban black children. *American Ethnologist, 9,* 799–819.

Goodwin, M. H. (1983). Aggravated correction and disagreement in children's conversations. *Journal of Pragmatics, 7,* 657–677.

Goodwin, M. H. (1990). *He said she said: Talk as social organization among black children.* Bloomington: Indiana University Press.

Gordon, R. A. (1988–1989). Bulimia: A sociocultural interpretation. *Journal of College Student Psychotherapy, 3,* 41–55.

Gordon, R. A. (1990). *Anorexia and bulimia: Anatomy of a social epidemic.* Cambridge, MA: Basil Blackwell.

Greatbach, D. (1992). On the management of disagreement between news interviewees. In P. Drew & J. Heritage (Eds.), *Talk at work: Interaction in institutional settings* (pp. 268–301). Cambridge, England: Cambridge University Press.

Grissett, N. I., & Norvell, N. K. (1992). Perceived social support, social skills, and quality of relationships in bulimic women. *Journal of Consulting and Clinical Psychology, 60,* 293–299.

Hagestad, G. O. (1985). Continuity and connectedness. In V. L. Bengston & J. F. Robertson (Eds.), *Grandparenthood: Research and policy* (pp. 31–48). Beverly Hills, CA: Sage.

Hagestad, G. O., & Burton, L. M. (1986). Grandparenthood, life context, and family development. *American Behavioral Sciences, 29,* 471–484.

Haller, E. (1992). Eating disorders: A review and update. *Western Journal of Medicine, 157,* 658–662.

Halmi, K. A. (1985). Classification of the eating disorders. *Journal of Psychiatric Research, 19,* 113–119.

Harper, K. V., & Shillito, L. S. (1991). Group work with bulimic adolescent females in suburbia. *Social Work With Groups, 14,* 43–56.

Heath, C. (1986). *Body movement and speech in medical interaction.* Cambridge, UK: Cambridge University Press.

Heath, C. (1992). The delivery and reception of diagnosis in the general practice consultation. In P. Drew & J. Heritage (Eds.), *Talk at work: Interaction in institutional settings* (pp. 235–267). Cambridge, UK: Cambridge University Press.

Heatherington, M., & Rolls, B. J. (1989). Sensory-specific satiety in anorexia and bulimic nervosa. In L. H. Schneider, S. J. Cooper, K. A. Halmi (Eds.), *The psychobiology of human eating disorders: Preclinical and clinical perspectives* (Vol. 575, pp. 387–398). New York: Annals of the New York Academy of Sciences.

Hepworth, J. (1993). Qualitative analysis and eating disorders: Discourse analytic research on anorexia nervosa. *International Journal of Eating Disorders, 15*, 179–185.

Heritage, J. (1983). Accounts in action. In G. N. Gilbert & P. Abell (Eds.), *Accounts and action.* Aldershot, UK: Gower.

Heritage, J. (1984). A change-of-state token and aspects of its sequential placement. In J. M. Atkinson & J. Heritage (Eds.), *Structures of social action: Studies in conversation analysis* (pp. 299–345). Cambridge, UK: Cambridge University Press.

Heritage, J. (1989). Conversational accountability. In C. Antaki (Ed.), *Analyzing everyday explanation* (pp. 131–146). Beverly Hills, CA: Sage.

Heritage, J. (1990). *Oh-prefaced responses to inquiry.* Paper presented to the International Pragmatics Conference, Barcelona, Spain.

Heritage, J., & Greatbatch, D. (1991). On the institutional character of institutional talk: the case of news interviews. In D. Boden & D. Zimmerman (Eds.), *Talk and social structure* (pp. 93–137). Cambridge: Polity Press.

Heritage, J., & Roth, A. L. (1995). Grammar and institution: Questions and questioning in the broadcast news interview. *Research on Language and Social Interaction, 28*, 1–60.

Heritage, J., & Sefi, S. (1992). Dilemmas of advice: Aspects of the delivery and reception of advice in interactions between health visitors and first time mothers. In P. Drew & J. Heritage (Eds.), *Talk at work: Interaction in institutional settings* (pp. 331–358). Cambridge, England: Cambridge University Press.

Heritage, J., & Sorjonen, M. L. (1994). Constituting and maintaining activities across sequences: *And*-prefacing as a feature of question design. *Language in society, 23*, 1–29.

Herzog, D. B. (1982). Bulimia: The secretive syndrome. *Psychosomatics, 23*, 491–487.

Homolova, V. G., Hoerning, E. M., & Schaeffer, D. (Eds.). (1984). *Intergenerational relationships.* Lewiston, NY: C. J. Hogrefe.

Hopper, R. (1989). Conversation analysis and social psychology as description of interpersonal communication. In D. Roger & P. Bull (Eds.), *Conversation: An interdisciplinary perspective* (pp. 48–65). Clevedon, England: Multilingual Matters.

Hopper, R. (1992). Speech errors and the poetics of conversation. *Text and Performance Quarterly, 12*, 113–124.

Hopper, R., & Drummond, K. (1993). Some uses of *yeah. Research on Language and Social Interaction, 26*, 203–212.

Humphrey, L. L., Apple, R. F., & Kirschenbaum, D. S. (1986). Differentiating bulimic-anorexic from normal families using interpersonal and behavioral observational systems. *Journal of Consulting & Clinical Psychology, 54*, 190–195.

Hyde, M. J. (1990). Experts, rhetoric, and the dilemmas of medical technology: Investigating a problem of progressive ideology. In M. J. Medhurst, A. Gonzalez, & T. R. Peterson (Eds.), *Communication and the culture of technology* (pp. 115–136). Pullman: Washington State University Press.

Hyde, M. J. (1993). Medicine, rhetoric, and euthanasia: A case study in the workings of a postmodern discourse. *Quarterly Journal of Speech, 79*, 201–224.

Igoin-Apfelbaum, L. (1992). Body constraints. *Psychanalyse a l'Universite, 17*, 105–115.

Jefferson, G. (1977). *On the poetics of ordinary talk.* Boston: International Conference on Ethnomethodology and Conversation Analysis.

Jefferson, G. (1978). Sequential aspects of storytelling in conversation. In J. N. Schenkein (Ed.), *Studies in the organization of conversational interaction* (pp. 219–248). New York: Academic Press.

Jefferson, G. (1979). A technique for inviting laughter and aspects of its subsequent acceptance/declination. In G. Psathas (Ed.), *Everyday language: Studies in ethnomethodology* (pp. 79–96). New York: Irvington.

Jefferson, G. (1980a). *End of grant report on conversations in which "troubles" or "anxieties" are expressed* (HR 4805/2). London: Social Science Research Council (mimeo).

Jefferson, G. (1980b). On 'trouble-premonitory' response to inquiry. *Sociological Inquiry, 50,* 153–185.

Jefferson, G. (1981). *Caveat speaker: A preliminary exploration of shift implicative recipiency in the articulation of topic.* Final Report, Social Science Research Council, The Netherlands (mimeo).

Jefferson, G. (1984a). On the organization of laughter in talk about troubles. In J. M. Atkinson & J. Heritage (Eds.), *Structures of social action: Studies in conversation analysis* (pp. 347–369). London: Cambridge University Press.

Jefferson, G. (1984b). On stepwise transition from talk about a trouble to innappropriately next-positioned matters. In J. M. Atkinson & J. Heritage (Eds.), *Structures of social action: Studies in conversation analysis* (pp. 191–222). London: Cambridge University Press.

Jefferson, G. (1988). On the sequential organization of troubles talk in ordinary conversation. *Social Problems, 35,* 418–441.

Jefferson, G. (1990). List construction as a task and resource. In G. Psathas (Ed.), *Interaction competence* (pp. 63–92). Lanham MD: University Press of America.

Jefferson, G. (1993). Caveat speaker: Preliminary notes on recipient topic-shift implicature. *Research on Language and Social Interaction, 26,* 1–30.

Jefferson, G. (1996). On the poetics of ordinary talk. *Text and Performance Quarterly, 16,* 1–61.

Jefferson, G., & Lee, J. R. E. (1981). The rejection of advice: Managing the problematic convergence of a "troubles-telling" and a "service encounter." *Journal of Pragmatics, 5,* 399–422. (Reprinted in *Talk at work,* pp. 521–548, by P. Drew & J. Heritage, Eds., 1992, Cambridge: Cambridge University Press)

Jones, C., & Beach, W. A. (1995). Therapists' techniques for responding to unsolicited contributions by family members. In B. Morris & R. Cheneil (Eds.), *Talk of the clinic* (pp. 49–69). Hillsdale, NJ: Lawrence Erlbaum Associates.

Kane, R., & Kane, R. (1981). The extent and nature of public responsibility for long term care. In J. Melker, F. Farrow, & H. Richman (Eds.), *Policy options for long-term care* (pp. 78–114). Chicago: University of Chicago Press.

Kent, J. S., & Clopton, J. R. (1992). Bulimic women's perceptions of their family relationships. *Journal of Clinical Psychology, 48,* 281–292.

Kog, E., & Vandereycken, W. (1989). Family interaction in eating disorder patients and normal controls. *International Journal of Eating Disorders, 8,* 11–23.

Kornhaber, A., & Woodword, K. L. (1981). *Grandparents/grandchild: The vital connection.* Garden City, NY: Anchor Books.

Kurtzman, F. D., Yager, J., Landsverk, J., Wiesmeier, F., & Bodurka, D. C. (1989). Eating disorders among selected female student populations at UCLA. *Journal of the American Dietetic Association, 89,* 45–53.

Labov, W., & Fanshel, D. (1977). *Therapeutic discourse: Psychotherapy as conversation.* New York: Academic Press.

Lacey, J. H., Gowers, S. G., & Bhat, A. V. (1991). Bulimia nervosa: Family size, sibling sex, and birth order. A catchment-area study. *British Journal of Psychiatry, 158,* 491–494.

Lambley, P., & Scott, D. (1988). An overview of bulimia nervosa. In D. Scott (Ed.), *Anorexia and bulimia nervosa: Practical approaches* (pp. 24–36). New York: New York University Press.

Leon, G. R. (1990). *Case histories of psychopathology* (4th ed.). Boston, MA: Allyn & Bacon.

Lerner, G. H. (1989). Notes on overlap management in conversation: The case of delayed completions. *Western Journal of Speech Communication, 53,* 167–177.

Levinson, S. (1980). Speech act theory: The state of the art. *Language and linguistics teaching: Abstracts, 13*, 5–24.

Levinson, S. (1981). The essential inadequacies of speech act models of dialogue. In H. Parret, M. Sbisà, & J. Verschueren (Eds.), *Possibilities and limitations of pragmatics* (pp. 473–492). Amsterdam: Benjamins.

Levinson, S. (1983). *Pragmatics.* Cambridge, UK: Cambridge University Press.

Levinson, S. (1992). Activity types and language. In P. Drew & J. Heritage (Eds.), *Talk at work* (pp. 66–100). Cambridge, UK: Cambridge University Press.

Linnell, P., Allemyr, L., & Jonsson, L. (1993). Admission of guilt as a communicative project in judicial settings. *Journal of Pragmatics, 19*, 153–176.

Lohr, J. M., & Parkinson, D. L. (1989). Irrational beliefs and bulimia symptoms. *Journal of Rational-Emotive & Cognitive Behavior Therapy, 7*, 253–262.

Lundholm, J. K., & Waters, J. E. (1991). Dysfunctional family systems: Relationships to disordered eating behaviors among university women. *Journal of Substance Abuse, 3*, 97–106.

Mandelbaum, J. (1989). Interpersonal activities in conversational storytelling. *Western Journal of Speech Communication, 53*, 114–126.

Mandelbaum, J. (1991). Conversational noncooperation: An exploration of disattended complaints. *Research on Language and Social Interaction, 25*, 97–138.

Mandelbaum, J. (1993). Assigning responsibility in conversational storytelling: The interactional construction of reality. *Text, 13*, 247–266.

Markova, I., & Foppa, K. (Eds.). (1991). *Asymmetries in dialogue.* Hemel Hempstead, UK: Harvester Wheatsheaf.

Marx, R. (1991). *It's not your fault: Overcoming anorexia and bulimia through biopsychiatry.* New York: Villard Books.

Maynard, D. W. (1980). Placement of topic changes in conversation. *Semiotica, 49*, 263–290.

Maynard, D. W. (1985). How children start arguments. *Language in Society, 14*, 1–30.

Maynard, D. W. (1988). Language, interaction, and social problems. *Social Problems, 35*, 311–334.

Maynard, D. W. (1989). Perspective-display sequences in conversation. *Western Journal of Speech Communication, 53*, 91–113.

Maynard, D. W. (1991). Perspective-display sequences and the delivery and receipt of diagnostic news. In D. Boden & D. Zimmerman (Eds.), *Talk and social structure.* Cambridge, UK: Polity Press.

Maynard, D. W. (1992). On co-implicating recipients in the delivery of diagnostic news. In P. Drew & J. Heritage (Eds.), *Talk at work: Interaction in institutional settings* (pp. 331–358). Cambridge, UK: Cambridge University Press.

Maynard, D. W. (1995). *The benign order of everyday life: The preference for good over bad news in conversation.* Unpublished manuscript.

McLorg, P. A., & Taub, D. E. (1987). Anorexia nervosa and bulimia: The development of deviant identities. *Deviant Behavior, 8*, 177–189.

McNamara, K., & Loveman, C. (1990). Differences in family functioning among bulimics, repeat dieters, and nondieters. *Journal of Clinical Psychology, 46*, 518–523.

Meades, S. (1993). Suggested community psychiatric nursing interventions with clients suffering from anorexia nervosa and bulimia nervosa. *Journal of Advanced Nursing, 18*, 364–370.

Mehan, H. (1991). The school's work of sorting students. In D. Boden & D. Zimmerman (Eds.), *Talk and social structure* (pp. 71–92). Cambridge, England: Polity Press.

Mills, C. W. (1940). Situated actions and vocabularies of motive. *American Sociological Review, 5*, 904–913.

Minkler, M., & Roe, K. M. (1993). *Grandmothers as caregivers: Raising children of the crack cocaine epidemic.* Newbury Park, CA: Sage.

Mishler, E. (1979). Meaning in context? Is there any other kind? *Harvard Educational Review, 49*, 1–19.

Mishler, E. (1984). *The discourse of medicine: dialectics of medical interviews.* Norwood NJ: Ablex.

Montgomery, R. J. V., Gonyea, J. G., & Hooyman, N. R. (1985). Caregiving and the experience of subjective and objective burden. *Family Relations, 34,* 19–26.

Morse, J. M., & Johnson, J. L. (1991). *The illness experience: Dimensions of suffering.* Newbury Park, CA: Sage.

Morris, G. H. (1988). Finding fault. *Journal of Language and Social Psychology, 7,* 1–25.

Morris, G. H., & Cheneil, R. (Eds.). (1995). *The talk of the clinic: Explorations in medical and therapeutic discourse.* Hillsdale, NJ: Lawrence Erlbaum Associates.

Motley, M. T. (1985). The production of verbal slips and double entrendres as clues to the efficiency of normal speech production. *Journal of Language and Social Psychology, 4,* 275–293.

Nasser, M. (1988). Culture and weight consciousness. *Journal of Psychosomatic Research, 32,* 573–577.

Newton, T., Butler, N., & Slade, P. D. (1988). Denial of symptoms and self-report in eating disorders. *British Review of Bulimia & Anorexia Nervosa, 2,* 55–59.

Parsons, T. (1951). *The social system.* New York: The Free Press.

Parsons, T. (1975). The sick role and the role of the physician reconsidered. *Milbank and Memorial Fund Quarterly, 53,* 257–278.

Peräkylä, A. (1993). Invoking a hostile world: Discussing the patient's future in AIDS counseling. *Text, 13,* 302–338.

Peräkylä, A., & Silverman, D. (1991). Reinterpreting speech exchange systems: Communication formats in AIDS counseling. *Sociology, 25,* 627–651.

Phillipson, M. (1972). Theory, methodology, and conceptualization. In P. Filmer, M. Phillipson, D. Silverman, & D. Walsh (Eds.), *New directions in sociological theory* (pp. 77–116). London: Collier-Macmillan.

Pomerantz, A. (1978a). Attributions of responsibility: Blamings. *Sociology, 12,* 115–121.

Pomerantz, A. M. (1978b). Compliment responses: Notes on the co-operation of multiple constraints. In J. N. Schenkein (Ed.), *Studies in the organization of conversational interaction* (pp. 79–112). New York: Academic Press.

Pomerantz, A. (1980). Telling my side: 'Limited access' as a 'fishing' device. *Sociological Inquiry, 50,* 186–198.

Pomerantz, A. (1984a). Agreeing and disagreeing with assessments: Some features of preferred/dispreferred turn-shapes. In J. M. Atkinson & J. Heritage (Eds.), *Structures of social action: Studies in conversation analysis* (pp. 57–101). Cambridge, UK: Cambridge University Press.

Pomerantz, A. (1984b). Giving a source or basis: The practice in conversation of telling "how I know." *Journal of Pragmatics, 8,* 607–625.

Pomerantz, A. (1984c). Pursuing a response. In J. Atkinson & J. Heritage (Eds.), *Structures of social action: Studies in conversation analysis* (pp. 152–163). Cambridge, UK: Cambridge University Press.

Pomerantz, A. (1986). Extreme case formulations: A way of legitimizing claims. *Human Studies, 9,* 219–229.

Pomerantz, A. (1988). Offering a candidate answer: An information seeking strategy. *Communication Monographs, 55,* 360–373.

Pomerantz, A. M. (Ed.). (1989). Special section on the Dan Rather/George Bush episode on CBS news, in *Research on Language and Social Interaction, 22,* 213–326.

Pruitt, J. A., Kappius, R. E., & Gorman, P. W. (1992). Bulimia and fear of intimacy. *Journal of Clinical Psychology, 48,* 472–476.

Rebert, W. M., Stanton, A. L., & Schwartz, R. M. (1991). Influence of personality attributes and daily moods on bulimic eating patterns. *Addictive Behaviors, 16,* 497–505.

Richards, B. (Ed.). (1989). *Crises of the self: Further essays on psychoanalysis and politics.* London: Free Association Books.

Roger, D., & Bull, P. (1989). *Conversation: An interdisciplinary perspective.* Clevedon, England: Polity Press.

Rosen, J. C., Srebnik, D., Saltzberg, E., & Wendt, S. (1991). Development of a body image avoidance questionnaire. *Psychological Assessment, 3,* 32–37.

Sacks, H. (1963). Sociological description. *Berkley Journal of Sociology, 8,* 1–16.

Sacks, H. (1965–1971). Lectures (transcribed and indexed by G. Jefferson): Fall, 1965, lecture 7; Winter, 1969, lecture 8; Winter, 1971, February 19; Winter, 1971, March 4). University of California, Irvine.

Sacks, H. (1984a). Notes on methodology. In J. M. Atkinson & J. Heritage (Eds.), *Structures of social action: Studies in conversation analysis* (pp. 21–27). Cambridge, UK: Cambridge University Press.

Sacks, H. (1984b). On doing "being ordinary". In J. M. Atkinson & J. Heritage (Eds.), *Structures of social action: Studies in conversation analysis* (pp. 413–429). Cambridge, UK: Cambridge University Press.

Sacks, H. (1985). The inference-making machine. In T. van Dijk (Ed.), *Handbook of discourse analysis* (Vol. 3, pp. 13–23). London: Academic Press.

Sacks, H. (1992). *Lectures on conversation: Vol. I & II* (G. Jefferson, Ed.). Oxford, UK: Blackwell.

Sacks, H., Schegloff, E. A., & Jefferson, G. (1974). A simplest systematics for the organization of turn-taking for conversation. *Language, 50,* 696–735.

Schegloff, E. A. (1968). Sequencing in conversational openings. *American Anthropologist, 70,* 1075–1095.

Schegloff, E. A. (1980). Preliminaries to preliminaries: 'Can I ask you a question? *Sociological Inquiry, 50,* 104–152.

Schegloff, E. A. (1984). On some questions and ambiguities in conversation. In J. M. Atkinson & J. Heritage (Eds.), *Structures of social action: Studies in conversation analysis* (pp. 28–52). Cambridge, UK: Cambridge University Press.

Schegloff, E. (1987a). Analyzing single episodes of interaction: An exercise in conversation analysis. *Social Psychology Quarterly, 50,* 101–114.

Schegloff, E. A. (1987b). Between macro and micro: Contexts and other connections. In J. Alexander, B. Giesen, R. Munch, & N. J. Smelser (Eds.), *The macro–micro link* (pp. 207–234). Los Angeles: The University of California Press.

Schegloff, E. (1987c). Recycled turn-beginnings: A precise repair mechanism in conversation's turn-taking organisation. In G. Button & J. Lee (Eds.), *Talk and social organisation* (pp. 70–85). Avon, UK: Multilingual Matters.

Schegloff, E. A. (1986). The routine as achievement. *Human Studies, 9,* 111–152.

Schegloff, E. A. (1992). Reflections on quantification in the study of conversation. *Research on Language and Social Interaction, 26,* 99–128.

Schegloff, E. A. (1988). Presequences and indirection: Applying speech act theory to ordinary conversation. *Journal of Pragmatics, 12,* 55–62.

Schegloff, E. A. (1990). On the organization of sequences as a source of "coherence" in talk-in-interaction. In B. Dorval (Ed.), *Conversational organization and its development* (pp. 51–77). Norwood, NJ: Ablex.

Schegloff, E. A. (1991a). Reflections on talk and social structure. In D. Boden & D. H. Zimmerman (Eds.), *Talk and social structure* (pp. 44–70). Cambridge, UK: Polity Press.

Schegloff, E. A. (1992). To Searle on conversation: A note in return. In J. Searle et. al (Eds.), *(On) Searle on conversation* (pp. 113–128). Philadelphia: John Benjamin.

Schegloff, E. A. (1996a). *Confirming allusions.* Unpublished manuscript.

Schegloff, E. A. (1996b). *Some practices for referring to persons in talk-in-interaction: A partial sketch of a systematics.* Unpublished manuscript.

Schegloff, E., & Sacks, H. (1973). Opening up closings. *American Anthropologist, 7,* 289–327.

Schenkein, J. N. (Ed.). (1978). *Studies in the organization of conversational interaction.* New York: Academic Press.

Schiefflen, B. B., & Ochs, E. (Eds.). (1986). *Language socialization across cultures.* New York: Cambridge University Press.

Schisslak, C. M., McKeon, R. T., & Crago, M. (1990). Family dysfunction in normal weight bulimic and bulimic anorexic families. *Journal of Clinical Psychology, 46,* 185–189.

Schmidt, A. (1982). Grandparent–grandchild interaction in a Mexican American Group (Occasional paper #16). Berkeley, CA: Spanish Speaking Mental Health Research Center.

Schrag, C. O. (1980). *Radical reflection and the origin of the human sciences.* West Lafayette, IN: Purdue University Press.

Schwartz, D. M., Thompson, M. G., & Johnson, C. L. (1982). Anorexia nervosa and bulimia: The socio-cultural context. *International Journal of Eating Disorders, 1,* 20–36.

Searle, J. (1969). *Speech acts.* Cambridge, UK: Cambridge University Press.

Searle, J. (1987). Notes on conversation. In D. G. Ellis & W. A. Donahue (Eds.), *Contemporary issues in language and discourse processes* (pp. 7–19). Hillsdale, NJ: Lawrence Erlbaum Associates.

Siegel, M., Brisman, J., & Weinshel, M. (1988). *Surviving an eating disorder: New perspectives and strategies for family and friends.* New York: Harper & Row.

Sigman, S. J. (Ed.). (1995). *The consequentiality of communication.* Hillsdale, NJ: Lawrence Erlbaum Associates.

Silverman, D. (1987). *Communication and medical practice.* London: Sage.

Simpson, W. S., & Ramberg, J. A. (1992). Sexual dysfunction in married female patients with anorexia and bulimia nervosa. *Journal of Sex and Marital Therapy, 18,* 44–54.

Smaldino, A. (Ed.). (1991). *Psychoanalytic approaches to addiction.* New York: Brunner/Mazel.

Spear, M. (1973). *How to observe face-to-face communication: A sociological introduction.* Pacific Palisades, CA: Goodyear.

Spitzack, C. (1993). The spectacle of anorexia nervosa. *Text and Performance Quarterly, 13,* 1–20.

Steiger, H., Puentes-Neuman, G., & Leung, F. Y. (1991). Personality and family features of adolescent girls with eating symptoms: Evidence for restricter/binger differences in a nonclinical population. *Addictive Behaviors, 16,* 303–314.

Steiner-Adair, C. (1991). New maps of development, new models of therapy: The psychology of women and the treatment of eating disorders. In C. L. Johnson (Ed.), *Psychodynamic treatment of anorexia nervosa and bulimia* (pp. 225–244). New York: Guilford Press.

Streek, J. (1980). Speech acts in interaction: A critique of Searle. *Discourse Processes, 3,* 133–154.

Strober, M., & Humphrey, L. L. (1987). Familial contributions to the etiology and course of anorexia nervosa and bulimia. *Journal of Consulting & Clinical Psychology, 55,* 654–659.

Strober, M., & Yager, J. (1988–1989). Some perspectives on the diagnosis of bulimia nervosa. *Journal of College Student Psychotherapy, 3,* 3–12.

Sudnow, D. (1967). *Passing on: The social organization of dying.* Englewood Cliffs, NJ: Prentice-Hall.

Terasaki, A. K. (1976). *Pre-announcement sequences in conversation* (Social Science Working Paper 99). Irvine: University of California.

Thelan, M. H., Kanakis, D. M., Farmer, J., & Pruitt, J. (1993). Bulimia and interpersonal relationships: An extension of a longitudinal study. *Addictive Behaviors, 18,* 145–150.

Thienemann, M., & Steiner, H. (1993). Family environment of eating disordered and depressed adolescents. *International Journal of Eating Disorders, 14,* 43–48.

Troll, L. E. (1985). The contingencies of grandparenting. In V. L. Bengston & J. F. Robertson (Eds.), *Grandparenthood: Research & policy* (pp. 135–149). Beverly Hills, CA: Sage.

Vitousek, K. B., Daly, J., & Heiser, C. (1991). Reconstructing the internal world of the eating-disordered individual: Overcoming denial and distortion in self-report. *International Journal of Eating Disorders, 10,* 647–666.

Vitousek, K., & Manke, F. (1994). Personality variables and disorders in anorexia nervosa and bulimia nervosa. *Journal of Abnormal Psychology, 103,* 137–147.

Wagner, J. (1980). Strategies of dismissal: Ways and means of avoiding personal abuse. *Human Relations, 33,* 603–622.

Waller, G. (1994). Bulimic women's perceptions of interaction within their families. *Psychological Reports, 74,* 27–32.

Waller, G., Slade, P., & Calam, R. (1990). Who knows best?: Family interaction and eating disorders. *British Journal of Psychiatry, 156,* 546–550.

Whalen, J., Zimmerman, D. H., & Whalen, M. R. (1988). When words fail: A single case analysis. *Social Problems, 35,* 335–362.

Williamson, D. A., Davis, C. J., & Duchmann, E. G. (1992). Anorexia and bulimia nervosa. In V. B. Van Hasselt & D. J. Kolko (Eds.), *Inpatient behavior therapy for children and adolescents* (pp. 341–364). New York: Plenum Press.

Woodside, D. B. (1993). Anorexia nervosa and bulimia nervosa in children and adolescents. *Current Opinion in Pediatrics, 5,* 415–418.

Wootton, A. J. (1988). Remarks on the methodology of conversation analysis. In D. Roger & P. Bull (Eds.), *Conversation: An interdisciplinary perspective* (pp. 238–258). Clevedon, England: Multilingual Matters.

Wurman, V. (1988–1989). A feminist interpretation of college student bulimia. *Journal of College Student Psychotherapy, 3,* 167–180.

Yager, J. (1988). The treatment of eating disorders. *Journal of Clinical Psychiatry, 49,* 18–25.

Yager, J. (1992). Has our 'healthy' life-style generated eating disorders? *Western Journal of Medicine, 157,* 679–680.

Yager, J., Gwirtsman, H. F., & Edelstein, C. W. (Eds.). (1991). *Special problems in managing eating disorders.* Washington, DC: American Psychiatric Press.

Yanovski, S. Z. (1991). Bulimia nervosa: The role of the family physician. *American Family Physician, 44,* 1231–1238.

Yanovski, S. Z., Nelson, J. E., Dubbert, B. K., & Spitzer, R. L. (1993). Association of binge eating disorder and psychiatric comorbidity in obese subjects. *American Journal of Psychiatry, 150,* 1472–1479.

Yates, A. (1990). Current perspectives on the eating disorders: II. Treatment, outcome, and research directions. *Journal of the American Academy of Child and Adolescent Psychiatry, 29,* 1–9.

Zaner, R. M. (1981). *The context of self: A phenomenological inquiry using medicine as a clue.* Athens: Ohio University Press.

Zimmerman, D. H. (1988). On conversation: The conversation analytic perspective. In J. A. Anderson (Ed.), *Communication yearbook 11* (pp. 406–432). Newbury Park, CA: Sage.

Zimmerman, D. H. (1992). The interactional organization of calls for emergency assistance. In P. Drew & J. Heritage (Eds.), *Talk at work: Interactions in institutional settings* (pp. 359–417). Cambridge, England: Cambridge University Press.

Zimmerman, D. H., & Boden, D. (1991). Structure-in-action: An introduction. In D. Boden & D. H. Zimmerman (Eds.), *Talk and social structure: Studies in ethnomethodology and conversation analysis* (pp. 3–21). Cambridge, England: Polity Press.

Author Index

A

Alexander, J., 15, 126
Allemyr, L., 42, 133
Apple, R. F., 8, 131
Atkinson, J. M., 7, 12–14, 17, 22, 23, 28,
    40, 67, 126

B

Baker, S., 62, 126
Barlow, J., 7, 127
Beach, D. L., 9, 109, 126
Beach, W. A., 8, 12, 13, 15, 17, 18, 49, 56,
    57, 73, 74, 76, 84, 107, 126, 127, 132
Bemporad, J. R., 1, 3, 6, 127
Bengston, V. L., 9, 10, 127
Benoist, J., 4, 5, 127
Bereson, E., 1, 3, 6, 127
Bergmann, J. R., 18, 107, 127
Bhat, A. V., 6, 132
Biegel, D. E., 9, 127
Blouin, A. G., 7, 127
Blouin, J. H., 7, 127
Blum, A., 9, 127
Boden, D., 8, 12, 15, 127
Bodurka, D. C., 5, 132
Boskind-Lodahl, M., 4, 127
Bremner, K. E., 3, 130

Brisman, J., 6, 39, 127, 136
Brody, E. M., 9, 127
Bulich, M. A., 4, 127
Bulik, C. M., 62, 127
Bull, P., 15, 135
Burton, L. M., 9, 130
Butler, N., 62, 127, 134
Buttny, R., 28, 127
Button, G., 24, 63, 73, 128
Byrne, P. S., 4, 17, 128

C

Calam, R., 7, 137
Campbell, T. L., 6, 129
Cantor, M., 9, 128
Carter, F. A., 62, 127
Carter, J., 7, 127
Carter, J. A., 5, 128
Casey, N., 24, 63, 128
Cassell, E. J., 4, 128
Cathebras, P., 4, 5, 127
Cerami, R., 4, 128
Chenail, R. J., 4, 107, 128, 134
Cherlin, A., 10, 128
Chomsky, N., 14, 128
Cicirelli, V. G., 9–11, 128
Cicourel, A. V., 7, 103, 128
Clark, D. M., 8, 128

Clayman, S., 15, 128
Clipp, E. C., 9, 128
Clopton, J. R., 6, 132
Coker, S., 8, 128
Collings, S., 8, 128
Cooper, M. J., 8, 128
Coulter, J., 7, 128
Crago, M., 7, 136
Creasy, G., 9, 128

D

Daly, J., 39, 136
Davidson, J., 25, 36, 70, 128
Davis, C. J., 62, 137
Davis, R., 3, 128
de Zwann, M., 8, 129
Descutner, C., 7, 129
Downs, V. C., 10, 129
Drenowski, A., 1, 5, 129
Drew, P., 8, 12–18, 22, 23, 25, 28, 31, 40,
    67, 77, 83, 84, 86, 88, 89, 92, 95, 96,
    100, 103, 107, 129
Drummond, K., 73, 129, 131
Dubbert, B. K., 3, 137
Duchmann, E. G., 62, 137
Duranti, A., 13, 103, 104, 129

E

Eason, J., 5, 128
Edelstein, C. W., 6, 137
Emerson, R. M., 88, 129
Engel, G. L., 4, 129
Erickson, F., 17, 129

F

Fairburn, C. G., 8, 128
Fanshel, D., 4, 18, 132
Farmer, J., 7, 136
Farrow, J. A., 1, 3, 129
Foppa, K., 16, 133
Frankel, R., 4, 129
Franks, P., 6, 129
Freeman, R., 3, 128
Freud, S., 83, 129
Fulcomer, M. C., 9, 127
Furstenberg, F. F., 10, 128

G

Garfinkel, H., 8, 43, 53, 129
George, L. K., 9, 10, 128, 129
Giesen, B., 15, 126
Glenn, P. J., 77, 129
Goffman, E., 14, 43, 66, 93, 130
Goldbloom, D. S., 3, 130
Gonyea, J. G., 10, 134
Goodwin, C., 12, 13, 23, 103, 104, 110, 129,
    130
Goodwin, M. H., 14, 21, 23, 65, 109, 130
Gordon, R. A., 1, 5, 130
Gorman, P. W., 7, 134
Gowers, S. G., 6, 132
Greatbach, D., 16, 130
Grissett, N. I., 7, 8, 130
Gwirtzman, H. F., 6, 137
Gwyther, L. P., 10

H

Hagestad, G. O., 9, 10, 130
Haller, E., 1, 3, 4, 39, 130
Halmi, K. A., 3, 130
Harper, K. V., 6, 130
Heath, C., 4, 17, 45, 130
Heatherington, M., 62, 130
Heiser, C., 39, 136
Hepworth, J., 8, 130
Heritage, J., 8, 12–18, 23, 25, 26, 28, 30,
    32–34, 40, 55, 67, 70, 72, 73, 103,
    106, 107, 126, 129, 131
Herzog, D. B., 1, 3, 6, 127, 131
Hicks, L. K., 3, 130
Hoerning, E. M., 9–11, 131
Holt, E., 31, 83, 84, 86, 88, 89, 95, 96, 100,
    129
Homolova, V. G., 9–11, 131
Hooyman, N. R., 10, 134
Hopper, R., 15, 57, 73, 83, 129, 131
Humphrey, L. L., 6, 8, 131, 136
Hyde, M. J., 105, 131

I

Igoin-Apfelbaum, L., 4, 131

J

Jarvis, P. A., 9, 128
Jefferson, G., 12–14, 17, 21, 30–32, 34, 36,
    57, 67, 73, 76, 77, 80, 82, 83, 91,
    93–95, 98, 99, 109, 131, 132, 135
Johnsen, P. T., 127
Johnson, C. L., 5, 136
Johnson, J. L., 10, 134
Jones, C., 107, 132
Jonsson, L., 42, 133

K

Kanakis, D. M., 7, 136
Kane, R., 9, 132
Kappius, R. E., 7, 134
Kent, J. S., 6, 132
King, M., 8, 128
Kirschenbaum, D. S., 8, 131
Kog, E., 7, 132
Kornhaber, A., 9, 132
Krahn, D. D., 1, 5, 129
Kurtzman, F. D., 5, 132

L

Labov, W., 4, 18, 132
Lacey, J. H., 6, 132
Lambley, P., 3, 132
Landsverk, J., 5, 132
Lee, J. R. E., 17, 30–32, 34, 36, 132
Leon, G. R., 4, 132
Lerner, G. H., 72, 132
Leung, F. Y., 3, 7, 136
Levinson, S., 18, 133
Lindem, K., 1, 3, 6, 127
Lindstrom, A. K., 8, 15
Linnell, P., 42, 133
Lohr, J. M., 3, 133
Long, B. E. L., 4, 17, 128
Loveman, C., 6, 133
Lundholm, J. K., 7, 133

M

Mandelbaum, J., 13, 14, 21–23, 31, 133
Manke, F., 3, 62, 133, 137
Markova, I., 16

Marx, R., 1, 133
Maynard, D. W., 15, 16, 22, 26, 30, 58, 59,
    73, 110, 128, 133
McKeon, R. T., 7, 136
McLorg, P. A., 5, 133
McNamara, K., 6, 133
Meades, S., 3, 7, 133
Mehan, H., 15, 133
Messinger, L. M., 88, 129
Mills, C. W., 67, 133
Minkler, M., 8, 9, 133
Mishler, E., 4, 103, 133, 134
Mitchell, J. E., 129
Montgomery, R. J. V., 10, 134
Morris, G. H., 40, 107, 134
Morse, J. M., 10, 134
Motley, M. T., 83, 134
Munch, R., 15, 126
Mussell, M. P., 129

N

Naranjo, C. A., 3, 130
Nasser, M., 5, 134
Nelson, J. E., 3, 137
Newton, T., 62, 127, 134
Norvell, N. K., 7, 8, 130

O

O'Driscoll, G., 1, 3, 127
Ochs, E., 103, 136

P

Parkinson, D. L., 3, 133
Parsons, T., 45, 134
Peräkylä, A., 18, 108, 134
Perez, E., 7, 127
Phillipson, M., 103, 134
Pomerantz, A., 21, 23, 25, 26, 28, 40–44,
    51, 53, 70, 87–89, 98, 134
Pruitt, J. A., 7, 134, 136
Puentes-Neuman, G., 3, 7, 136
Pyle, R. L., 129

R

Ramberg, J. A., 3, 136
Ratey, J. J., 1, 3, 6, 127
Rebert, W. M., 3, 134
Richards, B., 62, 135
Robertson, J. F., 9, 10, 127
Roe, K. M., 8, 9, 133
Roger, D., 8, 15, 128, 135
Rolls, B. J., 62, 130
Rosen, J. C., 8, 135
Roth, A. L., 8, 130

S

Sacks, H., 13–16, 20, 21, 23, 24, 30, 39, 57,
    73, 80, 82, 89–91, 135
Saltzberg, E., 8, 135
Schaeffer, D., 9–11, 131
Schegloff, E. A., 12–15, 21, 28, 31, 48, 49,
    67, 94, 97, 135
Schenkein, J. N., 136
Schiefflen, B., 103, 136
Schisslak, C. M., 7, 136
Schmidt, A., 10, 136
Schnare-Hayes, K., 7, 127
Schrag, C. O., 103, 136
Schultz, J., 17, 129
Schwartz, D. M., 5, 136
Schwartz, R. M., 3, 134
Scott, D., 3, 132
Searle, J., 18, 136
Sefi, S., 18, 25, 30, 32–34, 40, 106, 131
Seim, H. C., 129
Shields, C. G., 6, 129
Shillito, L. S., 6, 130
Siegel, M., 6, 39, 127, 136
Sigman, S. J., 12, 13, 136
Silverman, D., 4, 108, 134, 136
Simpson, W. S., 3, 136
Slade, P. D., 7, 62, 134, 137
Smaldino, A., 62, 63, 136
Smelser, N. J., 15, 126
Solyom, L., 3, 128
Sorjonen, M. L., 26, 131
Spear, M., 16, 136
Specker, S. M., 129
Spitzack, C., 8, 136
Spitzer, R. L., 3, 137
Srebnik, D., 8, 135
Stanton, A. L., 3, 134

Steiger, H., 3, 6, 7, 136
Steiner, H., 6, 136
Steiner-Adair, C., 3, 136
Streek, J., 18, 136
Strober, M., 1, 6, 136
Sudnow, D., 7, 17, 136
Sullivan, P. F., 62, 127

T

Taub, D. E., 5, 133
Tener, L., 7, 127
Terasaki, A. K., 49, 66, 71, 136
Thelan, M. H., 7, 129, 136
Thienemann, M., 6, 136
Thompson, M. G., 5, 136
Troll, L. E., 10, 136

V

Vandereycken, W., 7, 132
Vitousek, K. B., 3, 39, 62, 136, 137

W

Wagner, J., 40, 137
Waller, G., 6, 7, 137
Waters, J. E., 7, 133
Weinshel, M., 6, 39, 136
Wendt, S., 8, 135
Whalen, J., 14, 17, 137
Whalen, M. R., 14, 17,
Wiesmeier, F., 5, 132, 137
Williamson, D. A., 62, 137
Woodside, D. B., 3, 137
Woodword, K. L., 9, 132
Wootton, A. J., 12, 137
Wurman, V., 4, 5, 137

Y

Yager, J., 1, 5, 6, 132, 136, 137
Yanovski, S. Z., 3, 62, 137
Yates, A., 4, 137
Yee D. K., 1, 5, 129

Z

Zaner, R. M., 7, 137
Zimmerman, D. H., 8, 12–15, 17, 127, 137
Zuro, C., 7, 127

Subject Index

A

Advice giving, 17, 24, 59, 106, 107
  advice-giving sequence, 32–34
  problems with unsolicited assistance,
    32–35, 62, 106, 107
  and seeking professional help, 106
  offering unsolicited advice, 17, 106
  troubles offering and receiving
    diagnosis and advice, 18, 106 (*see
    also* Avoiding ownership, Troubles
    and problems)
Anorexia, 1, 8, 18
Avoiding ownership, 17, 19, 35–38, 60–79
  accounting, 28, 30, 67–70
    as moves-in-a-series, 68, 69
    as provisional acceptance, 67
    explanations, excuses, and
      justifications, 50, 67, 68, 70, 72
    treating actions as normal, 67, 68
  counterevidence, 42, 72
  discounting, 17, 30, 45, 49, 51, 52, 55, 56,
    64–68
    challenging viability of assertions, 21,
      65–67
    discrediting, 21
    forestalling, 67
    self–other shifts, 66
      void of self-evaluation, 66

statements of disbelief, 30, 50, 65, 68
  humor and laughter, 76–78
    as displays of trouble, 76 (*see also*
      Troubles and problems)
    downgrading seriousness of
      attributions, 76–78
    taking troubles lightly, 76, 77
  mimicking, 78
  "po-faced" responses to, 77
  minimizing responsibility, 21–24, 69
    "don't know," 30, 67
    offering "no problem" response, 47
    "safety in numbers," 72, 73, 77
    unwillingness to "own" the problem,
      int, 39, 40, 42
  topic closure, *see* Troubles and prob-
    lems
  withholding, 21, 29, 43, 44, 47, 48, 61,
    70–73, 105 (*see also* Families, tough
    love; Overcoming resistance; Pursuit)
    admission, 50
      indirect admissions, 61, 70
    as disaffiliation/disagreement, 21–24,
      27–32, 46, 70, 78
    delaying explanation, 21, 50
    displays of agreement/affiliation/
      alignment, 21–24, 49, 50, 53–59
    neither admitting nor denying, 21,
      50

Avoiding ownership *(cont.)*
  withholding *(cont.)*
    of commitment to seek medical advice,
      24
      through no-talk or silence, 70–73
        as embedded in three-part
          sequence, 71
          noticeably absent responses, 70–72
        via "oh-prefaced" responses, 54–56
        (see also Families, tough love)

B

Bulimia, 1–11, 15, 18–19, 34, 38–40, 42–46,
    50–51, 53, 60–64, 101–107
  contrasted with other social problems,
    106–112 *(see also* Social problems)
  diagnosis and symptoms, 1–3, 61–64
    developmental problems, 4
    medical complications, 4
    personality attributes, 3, 5
      low self-esteem, 3, 5–7, 102
      desire to please others, 3, 6, 102
      fear of intimate relationships, 7
      less socially effective, 8
      moody, 7
      need for external approval, 3, 6, 102
    preoccupations, *see* Troubles and
      problems/throwing up
    psychiatric disorders, 3
    strategy for coping and managing
      stress, 5–7
  overview of research, 3, 4
  self-report measurements of, 2–7, 19,
    62–64, 80, 81, 102–104
    individuals as units of analysis, 2, 7, 8
    interviews, 8
    overreliance on, 2, 7, 8, 80, 102–104
    ratings and coding, 8
  and social interaction, 2, 6–8, 102
    in dysfunctional family environments,
      2, 6–8, 102
      high pressure, 6, 102
      low affective involvement and
        responsiveness, 6, 102
      low cohesiveness and increased
        conflict, 6, 7, 102
      overly critical and protective parents,
        6
      poor family communication, 6, 102
  sociocultural influences, 5, 6

press and media, 5
  expectations and demands for thinness,
    5
    body image, 5–7
  impacts of "healthy lifestyles," 5
  social acceptance and avoidance of
    stigma, 5
theories of, 2–9, 19, 61–64, 103, 104
  causes and consequences, 1–8
  "saying" vs. "doing," 102 *(see also*
    Denial)

C

Conversations, 7–10
  about illness, 104–112
  aggregate cases, 13, 14
    generalized action types, 14
  context, 11–14, 101, 103, 104
    adjacent ordering of actions and
      utterances, 14, 21–24
      "chaining" of paired actions, 46
      reciprocal counters, 22
      rejection-implicative responses, 21–27
    context-shaping and renewing, 13
    collaborative actions, 11
    participant orientations, 11, 12
    projected relevance of, 14
    practically achieved character, 12
    continuous and negotiated, 12
    locally occasioned, 13
      culture/institution/illness as, 15
    moment-by-moment contingencies, 11
      impossibility of capturing through
        self-reports, 11
      "real time" details, 13
    interactionally produced social order, 14
      order at all points, 14
    sequentially implicative, 14
    recipient design, 14
  conversation analysis, 2, 11–18
    macro–micro debates, 15
      underspecification of a priori theory,
        15
      premature theory construction, 15
    naturally occurring interactions, 12, 13
      nonreliance on intuited or idealized
        data, 15
      recordings and transcriptions, 13
    unmotivated analysis, 15

conversational "poetics," *see*
    Preoccupations
personality attributes embodied in social
    actions, 13, 15,
single cases, 13
    contrastive data brought to bear on, 16
talk and action, 12
    projected consequences, 12

D

Denial, 19, 42–44, 46, 61–67, 71, 78–80

F

Families, 6, 7, 15–18, 101–112
    compared with formal institutional
        interactions, 16, 30–32, 105
    asking and answering questions, 16, 17
    contrasts with legal and medical
        interactions, 16, 17, 28, 107–111
        AIDS counseling, 108
        Alzheimer's disease, 108–111
        cancer, 108–111
        community nurses and first-time
            mothers, 32–35, 106
        cross-examinations, 28
        long-term family caregiving, 108–111
        psychiatric interviews, 107, 108
        suicide prevention centers, 30–32
    initiating and restricting elaboration of
        topics, 17
    imposing sanctions, 17
    interrogation-like character, 17
    restrictive turn taking, 16
    specialized knowledge and vocabulary,
        17
    "taking control" of interaction, 17
    tough love
        withholding commiseration and
            sympathy, 29–31 (*see also*
            Avoiding ownership)
    troubles in, *see* Troubles and problems
    family caregiving, 9, 27,
        essential problematics of, int, 35
        making another's business your own,
            see Pursuit
    institutionally relevant "constraint
        systems" in, 15–18, 32
    site for the exercise of authority, 16, 32

aysymmetries, 16
agendas and tasks, 16, 32
normalized responsibilities, 17
roles and professional identities, 16,
    34, 56
nursing background, 54–56
work-related interactions at home,
    16, 17
as primordial societal institutions, 16

G

Grandparent caregiving, 2, 9–11, 15, 18–19,
    101–107
    by African-American grandmothers, 9–10
    participant observation of and
        interviews with, 9
    grandparenthood in isolation, 9
    intergenerational relationships, 11
        problems with theoretical constructs, 11
    interventions by caregivers, 11, 27
        decisions about health-related actions,
            11
    omnipresence of interaction in
        accomplishing, 10, 11, 32
    selective investment, 10
    self-report measurements of, 9, 10, 19,
        102, 103
        individuals as units of analysis, 9, 10
        overreliance on, 10, 11, 102, 103
        paradoxes in data and theory, 10, 104
        what grandparents "do," 10, 11, 32,
            102
    the wider family context, 10, 11
    perceptually rooted "empirical
        context," 11

I

Invitations, 24–27, 30, 35–38, 40, 63
    re-do, 28, 29, 35–38, 63, 74
    rejection-implicative reponses to, 25, 26,
        29, 35–38
    delaying, 25
    repair initiator as challenge to, 25

L

Laying grounds for the reasonableness of
    assertions, *see* Overcoming
    resistance, Pursuit

O

Overcoming resistance, 34, 39–60, 62
  attributing incompetence to make health
    decisions, 45 (*see also* Sick role)
  attributing knowledge, 21, 41, 42, 48–50
  attributing lack of responsibility, 40
  attributing motive, 21, 25–27, 29, 40, 41,
    48–50, 73
  chiding, 50
  citing sources and offering evidence, 21,
    25, 29, 40, 42, 53–59, 73
    behavioral observations, 53–59
    establishing credibility, 53–59
    others' written and spoken assessments,
      53–59
    others struggling with bulimia, 53–59,
      73
  claiming and imputing knowledge, 47–50,
    66
    claiming knowledge and "truth," 21,
      24, 47, 48
    common/shared knowledge, 42–46
    confidence in asserting, 49
    declarative assertions, 41
    extreme case formulations, 41
  getting another to "own" the problem,
    39, 44–46 (*see also* Avoiding
    ownership)
    getting another to treat you seriously,
      24, 41, 50–53
  laying out consequences, 42, 50–53
    portraying unpleasant outcomes, 51
    upgrading, 52, 53
  "oh-prefaced" responses, 55, 56, 66, 67, 69
    marking inappropriateness, 55, 73
    as my-world proposals, 55
    as signaling topic shift, 72, 73
  reprimands, threats, and warnings, 46,
    53, 65 (*see also* Pursuit)

P

Perspective-display sequence, 25–27, 58, 59
Preoccupations, 19, 38, 47, 52, 57, 76,
  79–100
  as conversational "poetics," 82,
    contrasted with "Freudian slips," 83, 84
  evident in dissaffiliations and their
    consequences, 85–93

complaints and idiomatic expressions,
  82, 83, 85, 86, 89, 93–100
  conflict, 81, 86
  poetic aftershocks, 96–100
    "if/then" turn construction, 97, 98
  sarcastic responses, 81, 82
    "fake" laughter, 94
    seditious witticism, 83–85
    teasing, 92 (*see also* Avoiding
      ownership, humor and laughter)
  tailored descriptions, 81, 83, 87–90
    "caught up in" and "occupied with,"
      81, 85, 91
  withholdings of commiseration and
    sympathy, 83, 86–88, 92, 93 (*see also*
    Avoiding ownership)
social predicaments, 80, 81
speech errors, 57, 81–83, 94–100
  and recycled turns, 94, 95
topical puns, 90, 91
  sound rows, 82, 91
  word selections, 83–85, 88–90, 92
    "God," 88–91
    "double trouble," 83, 93
repeated attempts to pursue topics, 76
  mobilizing help to remedy trouble, 88,
    92 (*see also* Pursuit, Troubles and
    problems)
with food and thinness, 3
  bingeing and purging, 5, 6, 47, 48, 52,
    53
  See also Troubles and problems,
    throwing up
as intentional, 84, 85
treating answers as tied to the "problem,"
  int, 26–29, 47
as unwitting and unintentional, 82,
  84–86,
with wedding plans, 80, 81, 87–100
  contradictions with "party/crowd,"
    94–98
  reported troubles planning, 81
  disaffiliative responses to, 81, 83
Psychotherapeutic interview, 18
  "speech acts" in, 18
    interpretive problems in assessing
      intentions, 18
    translations rules for identifying, 18
Pursuit, 19, 27, 28, 35–38, 40, 46–60, 88–90
  chaining of alternative methods, 40, 44, 59
  claiming intimacy, 23, 24
  confrontation, 23, 24, 39, 42

occasioning the "problem," *see*
Troubles and problems
"fishing device," 88
holding others accountable, 21, 27
information seeking, 26, 30
as purposeful and motivated, 26, 27,
29
laying grounds for reasonable assertions,
17, 38, 40, 42, 43, 46–60
initiating a course of action, 19, 26, 27
disaffiliative aftershocks, 43, 49, 50
pre-sequence/announcement, 49, 50, 66,
71, 77, 96, 97
proposing solutions, 38
reinitiating "closed" topic, 75
stepwise solicitation, 38 (*see also*
Invitations)
making another's business your own,
23,
yet not making explicit what you're
"up to," 25–27, 34–38, 47
"my side telling," 88
persistance/tenacity, 21, 50, 51, 60, 62, 87,
92
"pursuing a response" and variations,
42–44
and topic organization, *see* Troubles and
problems
resumption following silence, 71 (*see also*
Avoiding ownership)
seeking answers tied to the "problem,"
26, 27
seeking help and mobilizing assistance,
62, 63, 88
soliciting promises, 74–76
and abiding with, 92, 93 (*see also* overcoming resistance, preoccupations)

S

Sick role, 45
Social Context, 103, 104
problems with self-reports, 103
"context-stripping," 103
and theories of social action, 104 (*see
also* Bulimia, Context, Grandparent
caregiving)
Social problems, 101–112
bulimia and other troubling
circumstances, 106–112
Alzheimer's disease, 107–111

cancer, 107–111
long-term family caregiving, 107–111
psychiatric interviews, 107–111
cooperation in addressing and resolving,
105
contradictory orientations to illness
"problems," 104, 105
withholdings of commiseration and
sympathy, 105 (*see also* Avoiding
ownership; *see also* Families)
as lay diagnosis, 106
and the "medical industrial complex,"
111

T

Troubles and problems, 20–38, 44–46,
80–100
alleging and rejecting wrongdoings, 21–24
attributing knowledge and motive, *see*
Overcoming resistance
avoidance and pursuit sequence
indicating, 36, 37
contradictory and asynchronous
orientations, 20, 27, 34, 37, 38, 40,
42, 64, 69, 78, 85–90, 104, 105
facing problems together, 21, 51, 63, 64
"getting off" troubling topics, 21, 73–76,
93–100
conversation restarts, 73, 74, 93, 94
pre-closing devices and attrition, 73,
74
shifts in "footing," 93, 94
through humor, 76–78, 92–94 (*see also*
Avoiding ownership, Preoccupations)
via sequence closing assessment, 97, 98
work of "okay" in, 56, 57, 74
as soliciation devices, 75, 76 (*see also*
Avoiding ownership/
Preoccupations)
occasioning the "problem," 23–27, 29, 30,
40, 42, 47, 48
treating another's actions as motivated,
23–27
stigma and degradation, 43
talk about troubles, 20, 29–32, 73–76, 83,
86–90
alleged wrongdoings as trouble-source,
31, 34
guessing not-yet-delivered bad news,
31

Troubles and problems *(cont.)*
  "throwing up," 20, 50, 65 *(see also*
    Bulimia/binging and purging)
  topically generative, 24, 34, 42, 55, 56,
    66, 67, 73–76 *(see also* Avoiding
    ownership)
    business as usual, 24, 63
    business at hand, 24, 63

querying other about own problem, 62,
  63
unfinished business, 71
troubles-recipient, 29, 82–90
troubles reporting, 81, 83, 86–90
  "redo," 89
unarticulated "problem," 29, 30, 31, 37
  (see also Preoccupations)